DEWEY
Decimal Classification®

DEWEY

Decimal Classification
and
Relative Index

Devised by

MELVIL DEWEY

9th Abridged Edition

FOREST PRESS, INC.
OF
LAKE PLACID CLUB EDUCATION FOUNDATION

LAKE PLACID CLUB
NEW YORK 12948 U.S.A.
1965

THIS BOOK WAS COMPOSED, PRINTED AND BOUND
IN THE UNITED STATES OF AMERICA
AT KINGSPORT PRESS, INC., KINGSPORT, TENNESSEE

Contents

Publisher's Foreword

The 1st abridged edition of the Decimal Classification was publisht in 1894 "in answer to a strong demand for a short form adapted to the needs of small and slowly growing libraries." Of the 194 pages of that edition 50 were devoted to tables and 118 to index. The tables contained approximately 1,100 numbers and virtually constituted no more than a third summary: few numbers extended beyond three digits. As Melvil Dewey's "Explanation" explained, the small and slowly growing libraries "wish short class numbers, but it is a mistake to assume that they will have only works on general subjects." Even the smallest library, he went on to say, is likely to have a few books or pamphlets on the most specific topics, but "as these minor subjects will differ in each library, it is obviously impossible to make any abridged classification that will meet every want." However, he concluded, "these short (three figure) forms can be changed to the full class numbers at any time without other alteration than adding extra figures to those here given."

With successive abridged editions, the number of topics in which even "the small and slowly growing libraries" might have books increast well beyond the 1,100 numbers of the first edition. The 6th abridged edition (1945) grew to 343 pages, its tables had nearly 2,000 numbers and its index some 21,000 entries. The 8th abridged edition (1959) increast to 495 pages, with 2,097 numbers in the tables and 18,000 entries in the index. This 9th abridged edition, which was prepared under contract for Forest Press, Inc. (a not-for-profit organization) entirely by the Library of Congress with the policy advice of the Decimal Classification Editorial Policy Committee, has 2,528 numbers in its tables and well over 21,000 entries in the index.

Meanwhile the abridged edition has discovered other uses than those originally foreseen for it. Among these uses has been to serve, especially in short courses, as a substitute for the unabridged edition as an instrument for teaching the theory and application of the Decimal Classification and classification in general.

This is the 9th edition of the Abridged Decimal Classification to be

1

publisht in 71 years as compared with 17 editions of the full Classification in 89 years. Over the period the connection between the abridged and the full editions has become closer; at first it was not felt necessary to follow each full edition with an abridged edition, but this has been the case beginning with the 4th abridged edition. Also, for many years the abridged edition tended to be publisht midway between full editions with a corresponding intermediacy of content; but the chronological and substantive connection between the full and the following abridged edition has now reacht the point that this 9th abridged edition is publisht within a few months of its big brother, whose content and organization it closely reflects, but modestly, as a younger brother should.

If experience can illumine the future, it may be confidently expected that this 9th abridged edition of the Decimal Classification will be used to introduce an entire generation of librarians to an understanding of one of the principal techniques—namely, book classification—by which books are made useful and by which modern library service is made possible. To this noble mission the publishers, the trustees into whose hands Melvil Dewey placed his Classification, take much satisfaction in dedicating this volume.

21 June 1965

Preface

This ninth edition of the abridged Dewey Decimal Classification is based on the seventeenth edition of the full schedules, which was publisht in June 1965. Like the larger work it reflects the effort of the Editor and the Editorial Policy Committee to keep the classification abreast of current thought but not to impose an impossible amount of reclassification upon the libraries using it. We hope that a proper middle course between tradition and change has been attained.

One innovation which should be noted is the provision of an "area table," which can be applied to all classes requiring a geographical arrangement. It is believed that this table will be easier to use than the history schedules which in the past had to be adapted to use as a guide to the geographic arrangement of other classes.

The abridged edition is intended for the use of smaller libraries of all sorts, but particularly for public and school libraries. Suggestions have been made that special editions for school libraries or for children's literature might be useful. It has been felt, however, that the schedules as presented in this edition are suitable for limited collections of any sort, and that special editions are unnecessary.

The Editorial Policy Committee consists at present of Edwin B. Colburn, Godfrey Dewey, Virginia Drewry, Carlyle J. Frarey, Esther J. Piercy, Joseph W. Rogers, Pauline A. Seely, Mrs. Marietta Daniels Shepard, and Wyllis E. Wright.

Wyllis E. Wright

CHAIRMAN, DECIMAL CLASSIFICATION
EDITORIAL POLICY COMMITTEE

Williams College Library
Williamstown, Massachusetts
17 June 1965

Introduction

1. Book classification

A major objective of libraries is to see that optimum use is made of their collections, to bring the right reader to each book and the right book to each reader. As an aid to the achievement of this purpose, nearly all libraries find it helpful, indeed necessary, to impose upon their books and other materials one or more forms of subject control.

One such form is classification. To classify a collection of objects or concepts is to place together in "classes" those objects or concepts which have certain characteristics in common and to separate from them the objects or concepts which do not have those characteristics. For instance, one might classify a collection of postage stamps according to countries of issue, each of which would be a separate class, e.g., stamps issued by Canada, by Italy, by Japan. Or one might choose another principle as the basis of division: color, size, shape, subject pictured, or for that matter any other characteristic that has significance for the utilization and enjoyment of a specific collection. If division were by country of issue, one might then classify the stamps of each country by monetary denomination, each of which would be a subclass, e.g., one-cent, two-cent, five-cent, one-dollar stamps issued by Canada; and each of these might then be further separated into subsubclasses according to year of issue.

A system of "notation," while not an essential part of a classification system, is a major convenience, (1) in designating briefly the different classes and subclasses, especially if there are a great many of them in a complex pattern of relationships, (2) in identifying the objects that belong in the various classes, and (3) in determining, for some categories of objects, the slots, bins, envelopes, or shelves where they belong according to a desired and usually systematic sequence.

Libraries classify their "books" or "works"—in this introduction, either term is used to mean all printed and written forms, sound recordings, films, slides, pictures, prints, globes, and other mediums of information and communication collected by libraries and related institutions—according to various kinds of characteristics. For example, because of differing problems of shelving, handling, and giving service, they usually separate recordings, films, atlases, newspapers, and the like from bound volumes of more or less conventional size; in this case the characteristic of division is physical form. Libraries of rare books often classify their works according to date and place of publication. Another common characteristic upon which division is based is specific kind of use, so that reference books, children's books, books in specific languages, books for popular reading collections, books of current interest may be set aside in separate groups. But most commonly, either overall or within such categories as those named above, libraries classify books according to subject. Such an arrangement is most useful for maximum retrieval of the kind of information wanted by the majority of patrons and the librarians serving them.

Like the amateur stamp collector, the librarian may develop his own system of subject classification for the book collection for which he is responsible, catering to the special needs of its users. In the past a good many librarians did just this, and some, usually in special libraries, still do. (Some public libraries have organized their collections of current popular interest in somewhat heterogeneous groups according to a "reader-interest" arrangement, rearranging titles and developing new categories as interests of patrons shift. Practical as this has proved to be, it is not classification by *subject*.) However, the development of an integrated plan that will provide systematically for the tens and hundreds of thousands of subjects on which books are and may be written in this age of multiversity and specialization is no part-time occupation or avocation. It requires the intense efforts of specialists in librarianship, in subject classification, and in the countless disciplines of which the world of knowledge is composed, from religion to mathematics to musicology to public administration to aeronautical engineering. For this reason, librarians have generally found it advantageous to follow, with local adaptations where necessary to meet local needs, one of the commonly used book classification systems, of which the best known and most widely used is the Dewey Decimal Classification.

2. Dewey Decimal Classification

In the United States the Dewey Decimal Classification—or merely the Decimal Classification, or the DDC or the DC; we shall call it all of these in this introduction—is followed by perhaps 90% of all libraries, including nearly all public libraries, and school libraries virtually without exception;

in other English-speaking countries and countries now or formerly part of the British Commonwealth it is followed by a majority of libraries; elsewhere, it has adherents in almost every nation on the globe. It has been translated, with or without abridgment, expansion, adaptation, into scores of languages, from Spanish, Danish, and Turkish to Japanese, Sinhalese, and Portuguese.

At present the system is used, in one form or another, by such varied current services as the Library of Congress printed catalog cards, the American Library Association's *Booklist; the* H. W. Wilson Company's *Standard Catalog Series, Book Review Digest,* and catalog cards; and the R. R. Bowker Company's *Publishers' Weekly* and *American Book Publishing Record.* Titles in thousands of reading lists, book guides, and bibliographies have been arranged or their subjects identified by the Dewey Decimal Classification.

2.1 Basic plan The Dewey Decimal Classification arranges all knowledge as represented by books within ten "classes" numbered 0, 1, 2, thru 9. Class 0 is used for works like general newspapers and encyclopedias that are on many subjects from many points of view, and also for certain specialized disciplines that deal with knowledge generally, such as library science and journalism. Classes 1–9 consist each of a major discipline or group of related disciplines, and together with class 0 they embrace the whole of human knowledge and intellectual endeavor. Thus, class 1 consists of philosophy and related disciplines, class 2 of religion, class 3 of the social sciences, class 5 of the pure sciences, class 6 of the applied sciences. The notation used (or available) to designate each class consists of 100 three-digit numbers, e.g., 000–099 for generalities and 600–699 for applied sciences. Each class is divided into ten subclasses, or "divisions," with the first division being devoted to general works on the entire class. Thus, 600–609 is given over to general works on the applied sciences, 610–619 to the medical sciences, 620–629 to engineering and allied operations, 630–639 to agriculture and agricultural industries, 640–649 to domestic arts and sciences. Again, each division is separated into ten subsubclasses, or "sections," with the first section devoted to general works on the entire division. Thus, 630 is assigned to agriculture and agricultural industries in general, 631 to farming activities, 632 to plant diseases and pests and their control, 633 to production of field crops, 636 to livestock and domestic animals. The system permits further subdivision to any degree desired, with a continued decimal notation, which consists of the addition, following any set of three digits from 000 to 999, of a decimal point and as many more digits as may be required. Thus, 631 Farming is divided into 631.2 for farm structures, 631.3 for farm tools, machinery, appliances, 631.5 for crop production, and others; and each of these may be still further divided.

No notation is ever less than three digits, zero (0) being used with its normal arithmetical value to fill vacant digital positions. Hence the notation for class 6 Applied sciences is 600.

Preceding the classification "tables" or "schedules"—this introduction uses both terms—are three summaries, showing the ten classes, the 100 divisions, and the almost 1000 sections.

Every book acquired by a library may be assigned to one of the classes, divisions, sections, or sub-(to whatever degree)-sections provided by the tables of the DDC, and may be identified as belonging to its specific class by use of the appropriate notation. (From this point forward, the word "class" will be used to refer to a subdivision of any degree; the 10 major classes will be called "major" or "main" classes.) The notation, or "number," designates the book's class; when written on the book and on the cards that describe the book, it provides a shorthand identification of the book's subject, and determines its relative position within the library's entire collection and within the appropriate discipline.

This class number and the book number used by most libraries together constitute the call number, which is unique for each book and distinguishes it from all others in the library. The book number usually is based on authorship, but may, as in biography, be based on alphabetical subarrangement of individual subjects within the class notation. For the use and construction of book numbers the reader should consult Bertha R. Barden's *Book Numbers* (Chicago, American Library Association, 1937). Most libraries follow the Cutter or Cutter-Sanborn alphabetic-order tables, or the Library of Congress author numbers. Other systems frequently used for arrangement within classes are by authors' surnames spelled out, by initials of authors' surnames, and by dates of publication.

A class is not necessarily limited to a specific subject. Altho many subjects have their own numbers, e.g., representative democracy as a political entity 321.8, many other specific notations denote groups or collections of specific subjects, e.g., aristocracy, oligarchy, theocracy, plutocracy as political entities all 321.5.

2.11 DISCIPLINE   The concept of "discipline," or field of specialization, is basic to an understanding of the Dewey system. The primary basis for DDC arrangement and development is by discipline, with subject arrangement being secondary. There is no one place for any subject in itself; a subject may appear in any or all of the disciplines. No class can be said to cover the scope of marriage, or water, or tomatoes, or Brazil; in common parlance, there is no single number for any of these concepts or subjects. A work on marriage belongs in 301 if it deals with the sociological aspects of the subject, in 155 if the psychological, in 173 if the ethical, in 234 or 265, depending on the aspect, if the sacramental (Christian), in 296 if Jewish and 297 if Islamic; in 390 if it deals with marriage customs, in 613 if hygiene; in 700 or 800 if it deals with marriage as a subject of art or literature (belles-lettres). Similarly, a work on water may fall in one of many disciplines: metaphysics, religion, economics, commerce, physics, chemistry, geology, oceanography, meteorology, history, and various others. Tomatoes may fall under economics, botany, horticulture, cookery, the art of painting, and elsewhere. Brazil's geography goes in 918, its general history in 981, its social situation in 309, its political situation in 320; and Brazil may turn up as an area concept under any discipline, such as arts of Brazil, languages of Brazil, paleozoology of Brazil.

No other feature of the DDC is more basic than this: that it splits subjects by discipline. This becomes quite obvious when one consults the index. Here, under any subject, will be found the places to class it according to its "aspects," that is, the disciplines under which it may fall, e.g.:

Barbershops	
economics	338.4
management	658
public health	614
technology	646.7

2.12 HIERARCHY The system is hierarchical both as to disciplinary and subject relationships and, with certain minor exceptions, as to notation.

2.121 Hierarchy in notation means that, for the most part, each successive division of the discipline or subject corresponds to a lengthening of the significant notation by one digit, e.g.,

600	Applied sciences
630	Agriculture and agricultural industries
631	Farming
631.5	Crop production

The reader will observe that "600" is main class 6 plus two zeroes to fill out the three-digit number, and "630" is division 63 plus one such zero.

9

The digit 0 when not at the end of a number is used to indicate a different basis for division of the discipline or subject represented by the digits preceding the 0, e.g.,

600	Applied sciences
610	Medical sciences
616	Medicine
616.0	[Indicates special basis for division]
616.07	Pathology
616.08	Psychosomatic medicine
616.1	Diseases of cardiovascular system
616.2	Diseases of respiratory system

Here the reader will observe that 616.01–.08 are used for topical (or "problem") subdivisions of the subject medicine *in general,* and 616.1–.9 are used for specific diseases. 0 is never used as a terminating digit following the decimal point; 616.0 is not itself used and has no meaning.

Sometimes, it will be found, there is a step in the successive divisions of the discipline or subject for which a position in the lengthening digital notation is not available. Such steps are shown in the tables by spans of numbers; these are called "centered headings." For example, 631–632 deals with general principles of agriculture, 633–635 with production of specific crops, 636–638 with animal husbandry. Each of these major subdivisions of 630 is without the possibility of digital expression in the notation, and is shown in the tables, therefore, by a centered heading, e.g.:

▶   633–635 Production of specific crops

633   Field crops

In a few instances the indention is "irregular," that is, the notation is not hierarchically expressive. For example, in 598.3–.9 there are various orders of birds, all equal in subject value, represented usually by numbers of four digits but in the case of 598.89 by a number of five digits. The tables show the equality of subject value by printing all the headings at the same indention.

2.122   Hierarchy in disciplinary and subject relationships means, for example, that whatever applies to or is true of 600 applies to or is true of *all* its subdivisions, what applies to 630 applies to all *its* subdivisions, what applies to the span 631–632 applies to all its subdivisions, and what applies to 631 applies to all its subdivisions. Hence the note under 625, "Planning, structural analysis and design, construction methods, maintenance, repairs," applies to each subdivision: to 625.1 Railroads, to 625.2 Railroad rolling stock, to 625.7 Roads and highways, and so on. Similarly, the instruction under 631–632 General principles, "Class general principles applied to specific crops in 633–635," applies to every part of 631–632; consequently, harvesting corn should be placed not in 631.5 Crop production but in 633 Field crops, and damage to lemon trees from low temperatures not in 632 but in 634.

2.2 Memory aids and synthesis of notation We have said in section 1 that notation is not an essential part of a classification system. However, arrangement and manipulation of a system without notation would be most difficult and awkward, and it is, in fact, its notation system rather than any theoretical excellence of its arrangement and development of the world of knowledge that has been largely responsible for the wide-spread acceptance and usage of the Decimal Classification. The notation is simple, consisting only of ten digits and a decimal point, is almost universally understood, and lends itself readily to subject synthesis with the benefit of numerous memory aids, or mnemonics.

2.21 Most notable memory aid is the constant repetition of a standard pattern of areal arrangement. In nearly all areal developments, the digits 44, for instance, stand for France, 45 for Italy, 46 for Spain, 52 for Japan, 73 for United States. General history is class 9 (or 900 with two zeroes filling in the empty spaces), and it follows that 944 is general history of France, 945 of Italy, 946 of Spain, 952 of Japan, 973 of United States; general geography is division 91 (or 910 with the empty space filled), and it follows that (with a decimal point following the third digit) 914.4 is general geography of France, 914.5 of Italy, 917.3 of United States; international relations is 327, and 327.44 is international relations of France, 327.73 of United States, and even 327.440 73 international relations between France and United States, for libraries requiring such close differentiation. The **area table** appears following the general tables.

2.22 Another common repetition is that of the arrangement of languages in class 4. Instead of a more or less systematic sequence by location on the surface of the earth like the area table, this sequence emphasizes, by bringing forward and assigning short notation, those languages, races, cultures most likely, as it seemed when the DC was devised in 1876, to be emphasized in American libraries; in 1965, with many values changed, we may regret that it does less well by Russian (917) than by Provençal (49), Latin (7), and Greek (8), but the classifier will find that it is not invariably followed to the hilt, so that in some sequences Russian does manage to fare better than it does under linguistics, e.g., general periodicals in Russian 057, in Provençal 054. The reader will observe a degree of repetition and memory pattern between the language sequence and that for European countries in the areal arrangement: 2 English (and Anglo-Saxon), 3 German (and Germanic), 4 French (and related), 5 Italian (and related), 6 Spanish, 69 Portuguese, compared with 42, 43, 44, 45, 46, 469 for England (and Wales), Germany (and other central European countries), France, Italy, Spain, Portugal, respectively. In most occurrences of the language sequence 1 is used for either United States or United States and Canadian. Thus, encyclopedias are 030 (03 plus a zero to fill in), and United States and Canadian English-language encyclopedias are 031, other English-language 032, Spanish and Portuguese 036; literature (belles-lettres) is 800 (8 plus two zeroes), and American literature is 810 (81 plus one zero), other English-language 820, Portuguese 869.

2.23 Many other patterns appear in full development at one place with repetition by analogy at other places. To name but a few, the Old and New Testaments are each given the same development as the Bible as a whole ("divided like" 220.1–220.9); many languages are given the same development as English ("divided like" 421–428); the general principles of botany and zoology are given the same development as biology ("divided like" 574.1–574.9). In fact, some topics, among them bibliographies and catalogs of specific subjects in 016, are given the same development as the whole classification, e.g., bibliography of applied sciences 016.6, of agriculture and agricultural industries 016.63, of soil and soil conservation 016.631 4. (The space between the sixth and seventh digits is not a basic part of the notation, but, in this book for ease in reading, is left between each successive set of three digits after the decimal point.)

2.24 Still another patterned repetition is that of the **standard subdivisions,** the table of which appears immediately following the general tables. Virtually any subject or discipline may be presented in various forms: as a synopsis or outline, as a periodical, as a collection of writings, in tables, in illustrations. Similarly, most subjects may have certain modes of treatment in common: theory, technique, study and teaching, history. These common forms and modes are known collectively as the "standard subdivisions," and may be applied to any class to which they are appropriate. The notation consists of two or more digits, of which the first is zero, e.g., 05 Serial publications, and may be added to any DC notation taken or derived from the main tables, e.g., serials on the applied sciences

605 (class 6, without the two zeroes that fill empty spaces in 600, plus standard subdivision 05), serials on agriculture and agricultural industries 630.5 (division 63, without the zero that fills an empty space in 630, plus 05, with a decimal point following the third digit), serials on farming 631.05, on crop production 631.505.

2.3 The abridged edition A valuable feature of the DC notation is its adaptability to the needs of libraries of different sizes and natures. The DC can be used equally well for broad classification and for close. For example, a small library or a large one with only a few titles on the subject can class the production of field crops in 633 without subdivision. A somewhat larger library, using the 17th unabridged edition of the DC, can class general works in 633, works on production of cereal crops in 633.1, of forage crops in 633.2, and so on. A library with a still larger collection can divide its books into such detail as it requires. As any library's collection increases in size, it can differentiate its books to a finer and finer degree of specificity simply by adding further digits to the notation. For example, a work on damage to lemon trees from low temperatures can, according to the unabridged edition, be placed in 634, 634.3, 634.33, 634.334, 634.334 9, 634.334 91, 634.334 911 depending on the degree of closeness in classification required. The full edition of the DDC may be used by general libraries of any size, from the largest, which may follow it in full detail at least in some subjects, to the smallest, which may reduce ("cut back") any or all schedules to the degree considered desirable. This abridged edition supplies reduction on a ready-made basis and is convenient for small libraries to use on that account, but, except at its own level, it does not allow for judicious decision on what schedules to reduce and how far to reduce them to meet specific local needs.

Any user of this Abridged edition 9, which contains 2528 entries in the general tables, may, at any time, for any part of its collections, divide its classes in more detail and expand into the unabridged Edition 17, which contains 17,117 entries in the general tables and thousands of opportunities not provided here to expand further thru the use of synthetic devices; all that is necessary for such expansion is to add further digits to the ends of the appropriate notations on the books and the records that represent them.

Use of the abridged edition will be greatest for the following:
Small public, college, and junior college libraries that aim to have well-rounded book collections with no particular specialization requiring more detailed classification.

Branch collections, if they are treated as separate groups, even in those public libraries that follow the unabridged edition with little adaptation for their main collections.

School libraries of all sizes except possibly some of the very largest and those with special collections of great size, e.g., libraries in some technical high schools.

Special libraries, even tho using the unabridged edition or special detailed classification systems for their specialties, will find the abridged useful as a guide for classification of related, supporting, and general materials.

Large libraries that have relatively small collections in certain subject fields may prefer to use the abridged edition in these specific areas, rather than either to follow the unabridged or to make their own reductions from it.

Private and personal libraries may, in many cases, be arranged to advantage according to the abridged DC. And individuals (as well as libraries) will find it useful in organizing loose-leaf scrapbooks of clippings, vertical files of pamphlets, etc., and card files of information and bibliographical citations.

3. How to use DC

To the beginner, whether student or practitioner, a first view of the Dewey Decimal Classification may be somewhat intimidating; it is the purpose of this, the practical part of the introduction, to lay open DDC's fundamental simplicity by presenting advice on how to use it to class a book or classify a library. What follows is intentionally didactic in form.

3.1 **Preliminaries** Before you try to use it, acquaint yourself with the system. Study the three main summaries preceding the general tables. Learn the ten main classes, and look thru the sequence of divisions and sections. Then leaf thru the tables. Knowledge of the pattern will come rapidly with use, and especially so if the tables rather than the index are consulted first in classifying. Notice the effect of the principle of hierarchy: Each entry except the ten main classes is a part of and governed by every entry superior to it. To understand the full meaning and force of 631.5, you must view it as a part of 631, which, in turn, is a part of 631–632, which is a part of 630, which is a part of 600. (This is known colloquially in the Decimal Classification Office as the "drip" principle: the qualities of each superior entry "drip" to those below it.)

Do not fail to look thru the special tables of standard subdivisions and areas.

Be sure also to observe the special nature of main classes 8 and 0. In class 8, subject is disregarded for works of belles-lettres, e.g., a play about Julius Caesar and Roman history, whether by Shakespeare or an amateur, is a piece of imaginative literature, good, bad, or indifferent, and belongs in the appropriate part of 800 instead of under history or biography. Arrangement of belles-lettres is first by the discipline belles-lettres, then by original language, then by form (but note that literature itself may be a subject). In class 0, general encyclopedias (030), periodicals (050), newspapers (071–079), collections and anthologies (080), and general publications of general societies (060–068) have no specific subject and form part of no one discipline; the most significant thing about them, after their generality, is their respective forms. Arrangement of generalities is first by form, then by language or place as the tables provide. In all other classes (including 000–029, 069, 070.4–.9, 090) arrangement is first by most specific discipline and most specific subject under it, then by areal specification of the subject if the tables permit, then by temporal specification if the tables permit, then by form of presentation.

3.2 Analysis of a book   Before you can fit a book into the system, or "class" it, you must know exactly what its subject is, and from what point of view and in what form that subject is treated. To discover this is not always easy:

Sometimes the *title* indicates what the book is about; however, it is often misleading, and some further method should always be used as a check.

The *table of contents* is usually an excellent guide.

If there is no table of contents, *chapter headings* and *marginal notes* are likely to give a good indication of the contents. Clues may also be provided by bibliographies and lists of sources used by the author.

It is always wise to scan the *preface* for the author's point of view, even if it merely verifies a decision already based on some other aid.

If the sources named above prove unsatisfactory, a careful examination of the *text* may be necessary.

If the subject is complex or unfamiliar to you, you may have to go to external sources. Information regarding the subject of the book may be obtained from bibliographies, catalogs, biographical dictionaries, histories of literature, encyclopedias, reviews, and other *reference books*.

Subject *experts* should be consulted when all other methods fail, and sometimes for verification of a tentative decision. But do not let the subject experts who are not also book classification experts occupy your time telling you how to remake the classification tables; what you need from them is assistance in placing given books on difficult subjects within an existing scheme.

Note well that many books are on two or three or many subjects, considered separately or in their interrelationships; and that many books are on two or more aspects of one or more subjects, that is, on a subject or subjects within two or several disciplines, e.g., on both the economics and the technology of the textile manufacturing industry, or on both nuclear physics and nuclear engineering, or on both architectural design and construction principles of dwelling houses, or on the sociological, ethical, religious aspects of divorce. Note, too, the current trend toward interdisciplinary studies in depth, particularly in the social sciences. To become a good classifier, it is most important that you analyze each book carefully, not only to ascertain its subject or subjects but also to determine to what extent it crosses traditional lines of study.

3.3 Selection of class number Before becoming involved in the application of the tables to such compound and complex subjects as those just mentioned, we shall consider the procedures for classing a book on one subject in one discipline.

3.31 APPROACH Having determined the book's subject, and the point of view from which the subject is treated, you are ready to class it. There are two basic approaches to the classification tables: direct, and thru the index. Beginners will usually find the latter approach speedier, but it is not recommended because it delays the process of becoming fully acquainted with the system. Note that, whether you are beginner or expert, you must not and, in fact, you cannot class directly from the index. The index provides leads to the tables but is not exhaustive and can never be a substitute for them. In any event, if your approach in a given situation is thru the index, find first the subject and then look under it for the proper aspect. If, for example, your book is on metals, you will find under "Metals" various aspects, most with subaspects and subsubaspects. Finding the one that characterizes your book, you can then turn to the correct part of the tables and analyze the specific number that appears to fit. The better approach is to go direct to the tables, using the index if necessary to locate the proper discipline; only when you are lost in the tables is it recommended that you turn to the index for your initial subject lead-in. For more detailed information on use of the index, see section 3.6.

If your approach is direct, first determine into which of the ten major classes the book falls. If the subject is metals, is it the science of metals (class 5), the technology (class 6), the economics (class 3), artistic work in or on metals (class 7), or even metals in the Bible (class 2)? Having chosen the proper major class, then, as if there were no other, determine into which of its divisions the book falls. If the subject is metal technology, is it metals as engineering materials (division 62), mining of metals (also 62), treatment (66), fabrication (67), metals in hardware (68), in building (69)? Then in the same way determine the proper section, subsection, and subsubsection, until you have come to the most specific head (used by your library) that will encompass the subject of the book. Even if that head is less specific than the subject of the book (as is frequently the case when you use this abridged edition), you have arrived at the right place; referral to the unabridged DC, as your library grows, will probably give you a more detailed number. For example, a book on education of royalty belongs under 371.9, even tho the head encompasses other topics as well. At each stop on the way look carefully at the notes and directions, making certain that you have not followed a false trail. Do not depend solely on the summaries; they exist only to speed you to tentative decisions and lack the fine distinctions that must be considered before any decision is final.

If you know the tables well or if you come to them via the index, you may start at once with a specific number. In that case it is most important that you go up the ladder, testing at each level to see if the particular subject of your book belongs within the concept named and described. Whether you go up or down, analyze every step, including centered headings, which are readily spotted by the inch-long lines preceding them and the indicators adjacent to them. Read every heading, note, and cross reference carefully.

3.32 HEADINGS Each heading consists of a word or phrase so inclusive that it covers all subordinate topics and entries. The actual wording may be incomplete, because the heading must be read as part of the larger group that includes it, e.g., in 440 "French, Provençal, Catalan" means those languages, but in 840 the same heading means those literatures; in 012 "Of individuals" means special bibliographies and catalogs (012–016) of individuals.

3.33 DEFINITIONS AND SCOPE NOTES In some instances a heading requires, for complete understanding, the qualifications stated in the note following, e.g., 012 Of individuals: "Works by or about persons not clearly associated with a specific subject." Others are followed by definitions, e.g., 330 Economics: "The science that deals with production, distribution, consumption of wealth." (Observe that this definition, and the one at 300 The social sciences, "The sciences that deal with social activities and institutions," rule out home economics as a subdivision of 330; the latter is, in fact, an applied science, is defined as "Care of household, family, person," and belongs in 640.) When no definition is given, the term is understood to be used as delimited by its subdivisions, or as defined in Webster's *Seventh New Collegiate Dictionary*, *The American College Dictionary*, or other general collegiate-level desk dictionaries of the English language. Still other headings are followed by notes enumerating specific qualifications applicable to the subject and its subdivisions, e.g., 629: "Planning, structural analysis and design, construction methods, operations, maintenance, repairs" of air vehicles (629.13), land vehicles (629.2), space vehicles (629.4) as distinct from "activities and facilities for human intercourse thru . . . transportation" (380) by the same vehicles (387.7, 388, 387.8). Still others are followed by notes stating the "scope," that is, subordinate qualifications not obviously part of the heading, that "drip" down thru the subdivisions, e.g., 362 welfare services to special groups, "Scope: rehabilitation," a concept that applies to each subdivision of the number.

3.34 INCLUSION NOTES   Notes beginning "Including" do *not* "drip"; they are enumerations of subordinate topics not obviously part of the heading on which there is as yet insufficient literature to justify separate provision. For example, 301.45 Nondominant groups is a subject with four named subdivisions: ethnic and national groups each with its own number, socioeconomic and religious groups each given "standing room" in the general number.

3.35 INSTRUCTION NOTES   Notes of instruction are of various kinds.

3.351 *Optional provision*   If you desire for local reasons to place books in numbers other than those provided by the schedules, you will do so without official encouragement. However, a few official alternatives are provided, but with the editors' preference, which will be followed by the printed catalog card service of the Library of Congress, always clearly shown. For example, 901.9 Civilization: "If preferred, class in 909"; 909 World history: "(Optional: civilization; prefer 901.9)."

3.352 *Use of more than one 0 in standard subdivisions*   As stated in section 2.24, standard subdivisions, which consist of two or more digits, the first being 0, may be used with any number at any level whenever they are appropriate. But in some places, for various reasons, notation beginning with 0 is used in this or the unabridged edition for another purpose, in which case you are instructed (for example) to "Use 335.001– 335.009 for standard subdivisions." On occasion you are instructed to use three 0's for standard subdivisions, and sometimes, as at 350 and 351, not to use any standard subdivisions at all. This instruction does not "drip"; it applies only exactly as stated.

3.353 *Synthesis of notation* Frequently the opportunity is presented to expand a given number synthetically without enumerating its subdivisions.

3.353 1 *Area notation* When a given heading has particular geographic significance and there are numerous books dealing with the subject in a given continent, country, locality, or other area, provision is made to expand the number for that heading by area. For example, under 309.1 Historical and geographical treatment of social situation and conditions, you will find the instruction, "Add area notations 1–9 to 309.1." This means that a book on social conditions in British Isles is to be placed in 309.142, that is, 309.1 plus the number 42 for British Isles from the area table. Social conditions in London would fall in 309.142 1, in rural regions in general in 309.117 3. Observe that social conditions in rural regions of British Isles does not belong in 309.117 3 (because under area 1 appears the note, "Not limited by continent, country, locality"), but rather in 309.142. (Even where specific provision for adding area numbers is not stated, they may be added to standard subdivision 09, as shown in the table of standard subdivisions, e.g., special education in British Isles 371.909 42. For full information see section 3.37.) The instruction to add area notations does not "drip" to subdivisions of the number under which it appears; instead it is an instrument for authorizing the formation of those subdivisions without explicitly stating them.

3.353 2 *Division* The same is true of the instruction to "divide like" another number or sequence. This is another important basis for synthesis of notation, or "number building." It may appear under a single number or a sequence of numbers, and it directs you to divide that number or sequence like a single number or like a sequence. Actually, in every case, one sequence, the primary one, is to be divided like another sequence, the secondary one. Many classifiers have found the procedure confusing, but it need not be so if one works methodically. First, determine and set down the full span of the secondary sequence. Second, set down the number from that sequence that is appropriate to the work in hand.

Third, cancel the repeating digits of the secondary sequence, i.e., the digits that appear thruout its entire length without change. (There may be none.) Fourth, substitute for them the repeating digits of the primary sequence. Fifth, insert the decimal point appropriately and delete any terminal 0's. For example, class Latter-Day Saint missions under 266.1–.9, and "divide like 281–289":

1. 281–289   Full span of secondary sequence.
2. 289.3   Number in this span for Latter-Day Saints.
3. (28) 9.3   Cancel all repeating digits of secondary sequence.
4. (266) 9.3   Substitute repeating digits of primary sequence.
5. 266.93   Desired number.

Class bibliography of agriculture under 016, and "divide like 001–999," with no digits common to secondary sequence:

1. 001–999
2. 630
3. 630   Nothing to cancel.
4. (016) 630   Prefix 016.
5. 016.63

"Divide like" means to divide like the secondary sequence to the extent that is appropriate to the heading, definition, and scope governing the primary sequence. For example, 572.8 Specific races is to be divided like 420–490. In the sequence 420–490 appears 499.9 Artificial languages. Since no races normally speak artificial languages, 572.899 9 is not applicable to races, and is, in fact, an absurdity.

3.354 *Priorities of arrangement* As we saw in section 1, many subjects may be divided according to more than one principle. We also saw (in section 2.121) that the digit 0 is used to introduce a change in the basis of division. Two 0's and three 0's may be used to introduce still other bases of division. A given book may divide its subject simultaneously according to two or more principles, e.g., pathology (616.07) of diseases of the cardiovascular system (616.1). This raises a question of priority: by which characteristic should one class the book? With rare exceptions where the schedules themselves specify otherwise, subdivisions without 0 take precedence in choice over those with one 0, those with one 0 over those with two 0's, those with two 0's over those with three 0's. Consequently, the book goes in 616.1 not 616.07. But two or more principles of division may be provided for in numbers none of which have 0's (or all of which have the same number of 0's). Then the schedules themselves give instructions on priority of choice, so that the classifier may avoid the confusions of cross classification. You may have a book on labor by aged Negro women slaves; should you class it in 331.3, 331.4, 331.5, or 331.6? The instruction under centered heading 331.3–331.6 tells you, by a table of precedence, to use 331.3. Now, suppose your book is on night work by aged Negro women: 331.3 or 331.81? The first note under 331.3–331.6 specifies that work periods of special classes of workers belong there, but, if you happen to arrive first at 331.81, you will find at 331.8 an instruction to class the topics that follow in relation to special classes of workers in 331.3–331.6. Either way, the correct number is 331.3.

We have not yet come to cross references, but it is appropriate to point out here that many cross references serve the same purpose of eliminating the dangers of cross classification by indicating the preferred basis of division, e.g., the cross reference from 331.2 to 331.3–331.6 tells you that books on wages of aged Negro women are to be placed in the latter span.

In any case of cross classification where the bases of division include subject, place, form, the order of preference is as follows, regardless of the absence of instructions or cross references: (1) subject, (2) place, (3) form. Only the presence of explicit directions to the contrary and the rule that non-0 takes precedence over 0 supersede this order of precedence. Examples: (1) The general principle tells you to class taxation in the United States in 336.209 73 not in 336.73. (2) Explicit directions to the contrary at 325.3 tell you to class colonization in Australia in 325.94 not in 325.309 94. (3) The rule of non-0 preceding 0 tells you to class pathology of cardiovascular diseases in 616.1 not 616.07. (4) The general principle tells you to class a periodical on science research methodology in 501 not in 505, i.e., standard subdivisions of a substantive nature take precedence over those that are forms.

Otherwise, the editors have tried to anticipate most situations where cross classification is likely to be a problem, and to provide specific guidance. Where they have not anticipated the need for a note, the following precedence formula is a generally reasonable and helpful one to follow, altho it may require modification in certain places: Class the subject by (1) kinds, (2) parts, (3) materials, (4) properties, (5) processes within it, (6) operations upon it, (7) agents. (Observe that the classing of pathology of cardiovascular diseases in 616.1 reflects this formula by giving kinds of diseases precedence over disease processes.)

3.355 *Relocations* A relocation is an adjustment in the tables resulting in the shifting of a topic from the number provided for it in Abridged edition 8 to a number in the present edition that differs in respects other than length, e.g., the shift of astronautics from 629.138 to 629.4, whereby the original digits are not added to or cut off, but all following 629 is changed. There are 281 such adjustments in this edition. If the relocation is total, i.e., the entire number formerly used is to be vacated, the number is enclosed in square brackets, and there is an instruction showing where the subject formerly in that number is now placed, e.g., [629.138] Astronautics: Class in 629.4. If the relocation is only partial, it is indicated in a note of instruction, e.g., 243 Evangelistic writings: Class evangelistic sermons [*formerly* 243] in 252. Total relocations are not to be confused with entries and instructions showing that concepts normally belonging in standard subdivision notations are to be placed instead in other numbers, e.g., [301.209] Historical and geographical treatment: Do not use; class in 301.29. Relocation notes "drip." For example, the note under 338, "Class public administration aspects of government control and regulation of production in 350," applies to this subject thruout 338. This relocation note tells you to class all works on public administration of production, formerly in 338 and various of its subdivisions, in 350 *and its subdivisions*.

3.36 CROSS REFERENCES These direct you from the stated or implied totality of a given subject to component parts of that subject provided for elsewhere than in the number referred from or numbers subordinate to it, e.g., under 385 Railroad transportation: *For local rail transit systems, see* 388.4. Cross references are not used to lead from a subject in one discipline to the same or a related subject in another discipline. They lead only from the whole subject within its discipline to parts of the subject within the same discipline located elsewhere. However, a few subjects from a single point of view are considered parts of two separate disciplines, e.g., the scientific aspect of geomagnetism, which is equally part of physics and of earth sciences. This subject is provided for in 538 under magnetism with a cross reference from 551.1 Gross structure and properties of the earth.

Cross references "drip." For example, the reference from 338.1–338.4 to 338.6–338.8 means that any subdivision of 338.1–338.4 if applied to systems and organization belongs in 338.6–338.8, e.g., mining corporations 338.7 not 338.2.

3.37 STANDARD SUBDIVISIONS   Having analyzed thru all the steps of the ladder the number chosen for the book in hand, and decided that it is the correct and most specific number, you are now ready to consider what further specification is desirable, i.e., whether any of the standard subdivisions are applicable. If your book deals with technique and apparatus of the subject, you may add 028; if it consists of a collection of articles on the subject, you may add 08; most common of all, if the book deals with the subject in the United States only (or in Morocco), you may add 097 3 (or 096 4). The table of standard subdivisions follows the general tables.

Observe here two very important limitations in the use of standard subdivisions: do not add them where you are told not to, e.g., at 331.7, lest you interfere with later expansion; and do not add them to the number chosen for a book that deals with a subject more specific than the content of the number, i.e., if the subject of the book does not have its own specific number. For example, class a collection of writings on architecture of suburban and rural type dwellings in 728.608 but class a collection of writings on architecture of farmhouses in 728.6. The reason is that there is always the chance that later you will want to expand and will then face complications in adjustment; for example, in Edition 17 farmhouses are provided for specifically in 728.67; when or if you expand, you can then use 728.670 8 for your book.

It is their standard meanings that make these subdivisions "standard." Nevertheless, sometimes a given standard subdivision when applied to a given subject may logically be given one or more meanings that are extensions of and compatible with the basic meaning, and you will then find in the tables an entry or group of entries specifying the extension. For example, 770.282–.284 is used for a special expansion, applicable only to photography, of standard subdivision 028 Techniques, apparatus, equipment.

Frequently standard subdivisions are to be placed in 001–009 or 000 1–000 9; as we have seen in section 3.352, instruction notes tell you when.

Sometimes, most often for 09, a concept ordinarily placed in a standard subdivision number is found instead with an irregular notation; most of these date from earlier editions of the DC that were prepared before the table of standard subdivisions became so detailed. These instances are all noted under the numbers where you would normally expect to find them. Examples:

730.2 Miscellany
    Class techniques, apparatus, equipment in 731.3–731.4

[747.09] Historical and geographical treatment
    Do not use; class in 747.2

It is obvious that you should not use a standard subdivision until you have made sure from the tables that its use is not irregular as to notation or meaning. The warning not to use standard subdivisions for a book that deals with less than the whole subject covered by the number applies equally to those situations where standard subdivision concepts, including areal and temporal specification, appear in irregular notation.

When a standard subdivision or span of standard subdivisions is specifically named in the tables, it is understood that, unless there are contrary instructions, the usual subsubdivisions may be used, e.g., 332.06 Organizations is to be divided into 332.061, .062 and so on just like any standard subdivision 06.

3.38 SUBJECT NOT PROVIDED FOR In the world of today, knowledge grows so fast that any edition of the DDC is outdated before it appears. With little doubt, you will have books on subjects for which the tables and index have provided a place neither explicitly nor implicitly. Do *not* make up your own number for such a subject; as sure as you do, the next edition or the unabridged will be found to place the subject in another number and use the number you chose for something else! The guiding principle is to follow exactly the same procedure outlined above: determine the correct main class, then the correct division, then the correct section, continuing until you have arrived at the most specific head that will contain the subject of your book. It may be that you cannot go beyond three digits; stop right there and give your book standing room, and wait for the unabridged edition, the next abridged edition, or the editors to supply a more detailed number, which you may then use simply by adding digits to the number you have already chosen. Do this carefully, and you will rarely go wrong. An example for the future is a bit difficult to imagine, but two from the past may be illustrative. Abridged edition 8 provided for astronautical engineering in 629.138 (now relocated to 629.4) but for no other aspects of man in space. A classifier with a book on the physiology of man in space might have been tempted to class it in 629.138, but that would have been wrong; he should have used 612, which Edition 17 expands to 612.014 5 for the precise subject. Abridged edition 8 provided no place for transportation by overland air-cushion vehicles (hovercraft), but a classifier following the principles outlined here would have used 388.3, and found his decision confirmed by the appearance of 388.35 in the present edition.

3.4 Compound and complex subjects The foregoing rules and principles provide a basis for classing a book on one subject in one discipline. But, as we have seen, your analysis of the book may have shown that it deals with two or three or many subjects, considered separately or in their interrelationships; or with two or more aspects of one or more subjects. Assuming that you are using the DDC as a shelf classification, obviously you must choose one place and class the book there. Since most libaries employ other methods of subject control in addition to shelf classification, the chances are that the subject catalog, whether alphabetical or itself classified, will provide additional leads. Where, then, should you class the book?

3.41 MORE THAN ONE SUBJECT (1) Class a book dealing with two or more interrelated subjects with the one that receives the chief emphasis. For example, class an analytical work dealing with Shakespeare's influence on Keats with Keats. The emphasis may be a reflection of the relative amount of space devoted to each subject, or of the author's purpose, or of both. The author's purpose in the work imagined above may be said to be an exposition of Keats's work. If the treatment of Keats occupies only a small portion of the book, say less than a third, and does not permeate the portion that deals specifically with Shakespeare, then the heavy preponderance of space devoted to Shakespeare should carry more weight than the author's purpose of explaining Keats, and the book should be placed with other works on Shakespeare. But if the author's purpose is pervasive thruout the book, even tho the treatment of Shakespeare actually occupies more space, then greater weight should be given to purpose, and the book should be placed with other works on Keats. Such decisions are sometimes very difficult to make. (2) Class a book dealing with two or more subjects, not particularly interrelated, e.g., a descriptive work on the beliefs and practices of Judaism, Christianity, and Islam, with the one that preponderates. (3) If no emphasis or preponderance is apparent, (a) class a book on two subjects with the one coming first in the classification tables, or (b), optionally, class a book on two subjects that are both subdivisions of a broader subject with the broader one; and (c) class a book on three or more subjects that are all subdivisions of a broader subject with the broader one. Examples: (a) class a book dealing with equal emphasis with Judaism (296) and Islam

25

(297) in 296, or (b), optionally, in 290; (c) class a similar book dealing with Hinduism (294.5), Judaism, and Islam in 290.

3.42 MORE THAN ONE ASPECT (1) Class a book dealing with a subject from two or more points of view or aspects, i.e., within two or more disciplines, with the aspect that receives the most emphasis. For example, class a book dealing with both the scientific and engineering principles of electrodynamics in 537.6 if the engineering aspects are introduced primarily for illustrative purposes, in 621.31 if the basic scientific theories are introduced primarily as a preliminary to the author's development of an exposition of engineering principles and practices. (See also section 3.44.) (2) Class a book dealing with a subject from two or more aspects but having no apparent emphasis with the one that preponderates. (3) If no emphasis or preponderance is apparent, class a book dealing with a subject from two or more aspects with the underlying or broader discipline, e.g., science underlies technology, art is broader than belles-lettres. (4) Lacking any other principle, class in the discipline that comes first in the schedules.

To class a book on two or more interrelated subjects considered from two or more aspects, you may have to apply a combination of all the foregoing rules. Do not overlook the possibilities of class 0, e.g., 001.3–001.4, 080.

3.43 CENTERED HEADINGS As seen above in section 2.121, centered headings are steps in the successive divisions of a discipline or subject for which positions in the lengthening digital notation are not available. Since a given book can have but one class number, it is necessary to indicate how to class books dealing with concepts in centered headings. (1) If the span of entries directly subordinate to the centered heading is three or more, (a) class comprehensive works in the next higher number, e.g., classical physics (531–538) in 530, England (area 421–428) in area 42; but (b) always check to see if a general-special subdivision of the next higher number has been provided, i.e., a subdivision based on a 0-notation, e.g., transportation services (385–388) in 380.5; and (c) class elsewhere only in the rare instances where you are so instructed in a note under the centered heading, e.g., metallurgy of nonferrous metals (669.2–669.7) in 669.7; but (d) note that when the centered heading covers "specific" parts of something, general works may be in a preceding specific number without notice at the centered heading, e.g., Old Testament (specific parts 222–224) in 221. (2) If the span of entries directly subordinate to the centered heading is only two, (a) class comprehensive works in the first of the two numbers, e.g., metaphysics (110–120) in 110; but (b) class elsewhere if you are so instructed, e.g., technology of food and drink (663–664) in 664.

3.44 APPLICATIONS Class an application of a principle, concept, science, procedure, technique with the application. For example, class general principles of radio communication engineering in 621.384 1; special developments of radio engineering, e.g., the circuitry and instruments used in space communication, in 621.384 19; but the application of space communication to astronautical engineering in 629.43 and 629.45.

3.5 Reduction We have indicated in section 2.3 that a valuable feature of the DC notation is its adaptability to both close and broad classification. How close or how broad the classification of a specific library should be is a matter of administrative determination. It is not likely that any library will follow the unabridged edition to its full detail. The detail supplied herein is intended to be approximately as much as most small libraries will require, but even this edition may be too detailed in some classes for some libraries, and you will wish to cut back, either from the tables themselves or from the numbers recommended by central classification services for specific titles.

Do not cut notation to less than three digits, no matter how small your collection may be.

Do not cut a number so that it ends in a 0 to the right of the decimal point.

Cut at a reasonable spot, i.e., one that will bring about a useful grouping. This requires special care when applied to synthesized numbers. For example, you *may* find it desirable to class a book on economic conditions in Oxfordshire in 330.942 5, but most smaller and many large libraries consider geographic breakdown below country unnecessarily detailed except in 9+ for general history and 91+ for geography. Indeed, with a quite small collection you may consider 330.94 satisfactory for books on economic conditions in all parts or any part of Europe.

Be sure that when you cut you do just that; do not change digits. For example, if your collection of books on birds is so small that you do not wish to take advantage of the differentiation provided by 598.3, 598.4 . . . 598.9, do *not* use 598.2 as a general gathering place for all books on birds, even tho it is headed "Aves (Birds)"; instead cut right down to 598. (You can still use 598.1 for books on reptiles.) If you use 598.2, you will be obliged, if future growth requires that your books on birds be divided, to remove the "2" and substitute "3," "4". . ."9."

Record in the schedules all decisions for reduction. Do not try to record decisions of this nature in the index; an index entry (like a cross reference, relocation, or other note of instruction) leading to a number that is cut back will then be understood to lead only to the most detailed number that has been retained. Thus, if the schedule 301 is cut back to four figures (i.e., to 301.1, 301.2, 301.4, etc.), the index entry for discriminatory practices leading to 301.45 will be understood to lead only to 301.4, and the cross reference from 301.4 to 301.18 will be understood to lead only to 301.1.

3.6 Index In the event that your initial lead-in to the classification is thru the index, which, as we saw in section 3.31, is not recommended except when a direct approach to the tables has proved fruitless, you should know how the index is constructed and how to use it.

3.61 The index is *relative* (and is traditionally known as the "relative index"): rather than recapitulate the tables alphabetically, it reverses them, in that it brings together the various aspects of a subject to show their dispersion thruout the tables. For example, if you have a book on metals and look under that term, you will find numerous aspects and subaspects, each leading you to a number in the tables. This number may be the most specific one available in this edition, as is the case with 546 for the chemical aspects. Or, it may be a general number of which a subdivision best fits your book, as in the case with 669 for the technical metallurgical aspects; this index entry and number are set in **boldface,** which means that the topic is subdivided in the tables, either by stated subdivisions or by provision for number building.

Perhaps you have a work on some metal product, such as automobiles. Most likely you would look for this subject under its own name (and would find a lead to "Motor vehicles"), but if you should look first under "Metals," you would find under the aspect "products" the cross reference, "*see spec. subj.*," meaning, see the name of the specific subject of the work at hand.

Having read this far, you will have observed that the index entries are closely interrelated and that the index cannot be used carelessly.

3.62 The index is *limited:* only those aspects appearing most frequently in the literature are included. It is clear by now to the reader of this introduction that almost any subject can be treated within almost any discipline. Metals may turn up not only in chemistry, geology, industry, and engineering, but also in bibliography, library science, parapsychology and occultism, economics, military science, physics, nutrition, medicine, and many others. Obviously, the index cannot enumerate all these aspects; if your book deals with an unusual aspect of a subject, you must classify direct from the tables by successive narrowing of choices as suggested above in section 3.31.

Aspects are often replaced by blanket references, an example of which is the reference from "Metals products" to specific subjects.

Generally speaking, under each subject entered in the index there appear from two to five aspects or references, but in a few cases only one; remember that *in no case* does this exhaust the aspects from which the subject may be treated and under which you may class it. Entries under geographical names lead only to the area table; as we have seen in section 3.353 1, area numbers may be added, either directly or with standard subdivision 09, under any number in the general tables.

Another form of limitation is the use of individual cross references leading from one heading to another. These may be from synonyms or near-synonyms, e.g., Metalwork, industrial *see* Metals industries, or from specific topics to broader or related terms, e.g., Children's clothing *see* Garments, Cricket *see* Bat games. In the first example, the numbers for garments are used for all subdivisions, including children's clothing. But the number for Bat games general works, 796.35, is set in boldface, and cricket is, in fact, in 796.358, which may be found by surveying in the schedule the subdivisions of 796.35.

Still another form of limitation is the deliberate omission of thousands of terms, obviously parts of broader concepts, the inclusion of which would make the index look more like an unabridged dictionary. If you have a book on how to pitch in baseball, you will find no index entry for pitching. It should require little thought to send you next to Baseball, where you will find a reference to Bat games. Under the latter you will find **796.35**, a single index entry covering numerous schedule entries. Under 796.35 in the tables you will quickly find that the desired number is 796.357 2. Similarly, with a handful of exceptions, the area numbers for cities and towns can be found only by looking for the countries, states, counties in which they are located.

3.63 The index is *coordinated with the tables:* it is a guide to them but must not, indeed cannot, be used without them. Without observing all the instructions, definitions, references in the tables at the numbers to which the index has led you, you can never be sure that your work is correct; in fact, you must be guided not only by the information at the exact number and its subdivisions to which the index has led you, but also, in accordance with the suggestions made in section 3.31, you must test that number all the way up the hierarchical ladder. It is obvious that you must **never** classify from the index alone.

If the subject you want is not found in the index, look for it under a synonym, under another word of the same root, under a related term, or under a broader subject.

3.64 Index entries are arranged alphabetically by word. Explanatory words in parentheses are not considered in alphabeting. When the same word appears in both geographic and subject senses, the geographic comes first. Hyphenated words are considered to be single words. Abbreviations are filed as if spelled out; a list of those used precedes the index.

Most nouns are entered in the plural form; the singular form is more often employed for nouns used as adjectives.

Names beginning with Mc and M' are arranged as if spelled Mac. Germanic modified vowels, such as ä, ö, ü, are arranged as a, o, u.

Numbers preceded by "*s.s.–*" are to be found in the table of standard subdivisions, and may be added to class numbers as appropriate. Numbers preceded by "*area –*" are to be found in the area table, and may be added to class numbers as appropriate. Both these auxiliary tables appear between the general tables and the index.

A dagger (†) preceding a number indicates that one or more topics—not necessarily the topic named at that entry—have been relocated to the number from elsewhere in Abridged edition 8. Details of relocation appear only in the tables.

3.7 General suggestions Class translations of, reviews of, keys of, analyses of, indexes to, and other works about a specific work with that work.

Save time by seeing if one of the centralized classification services has already assigned a number; even if you do not follow the same edition of DDC or the policies of the central service, or have made local adaptations of your own, the decision of experts will be helpful. Among the more important sources for DC numbers from the latest unabridged edition are Library of Congress catalog cards, the ALA *Booklist, Publishers' Weekly,* and *American Book Publishing Record;* numbers from the latest abridged edition appear on H. W. Wilson Company catalog cards and in *Book Review Digest* and the various parts of the *Standard Catalog Series.*

To promote consistency and future efficiency, make a record of all decisions. This should consist of a shelflist or record of each book in classified order. and a record of decisions on specific problems, which may be kept separately or written in the margins of the classification tables.

4. Variations from recommended practice

4.1 Principle of usefulness Every library has its own unique clientele, and, in serving that clientele's special needs, may find it desirable to modify specific printed provisions in ways other than reduction. An important advantage of the DDC is that its notation provides a universal language that can be understood from one library to another and even from one country to another; for example, in the primary school, the metropolitan public library, and the university, in the U.S.A. and India, in Israel and Brazil, 623 always means military and naval engineering. This advantage, however, should not be permitted to outweigh a *real* and *permanent* local need. By "real" we mean that each variation should have a demonstrable reason that can be recorded and defended. By "permanent" we mean that a specific need of a temporary or short-term nature may be met by special displays and rearrangements; it should not be met by adjustment of class numbers.

Record in the schedules every decision for variation. As with reduction (section 3.5), do not try to record decisions of this nature in the index.

4.2 Officially recognized variations A number of important variations appear in the printed tables. They are officially recognized and recommended for use by libraries whose needs they will serve, but are not reflected in the practices of the Decimal Classification Office as printed on Library of Congress catalog cards. These are known as "options." Certain topics are given two specific placements. One placement is considered to be preferred by the editors, and at it, in each case, appears a note, "If preferred [i.e., if you prefer], class [this subject at another location]"; the other placement is considered by the editors to be optional, and at it, in each case, appears a note, "(Optional; prefer [another location])." Several examples follow.

Most public libraries prefer to have their belles-lettres in each language divided by form, and this is the traditional DC arrangement, e.g., 820 English literature, 821 Poetry, 822 Drama, 823 Fiction, 824 Essays. This procedure separates the poetry of, say, Matthew Arnold from his prose. However, most college and many school libraries prefer to have all works of a given author together, and all authors writing in each language arranged in one alphabetical sequence. Consequently, under centered heading 821–828 Specific forms, you will find a note, "If preferred, class [single authors] regardless of form in 828," and under 828, "(Optional: class here . . . single authors regardless of form; prefer 821–828)."

Traditionally, DC has placed the various branches of geography under the specific topics that are areally considered, e.g., economic geography 330.9, biogeography 574.9. However, with a growing academic and research interest in geography, numerous libraries have in recent years come to prefer an arrangement that brings all geography together. This is supplied optionally at 910.1 Topical geography, which is divided by subject, e.g., economic geography 910.133, biogeography 910.157 4.

Treatment of biography varies greatly from one library to another. Many libraries prefer it arranged with pertinent subjects, e.g., biography of engineers with engineering, of statesmen with general history, of artists with art, but many others prefer all or most biography together, either subarranged by subject or (for individual biography) in one alphabet by biographee. Accordingly, while standard subdivision 092 with each subject is the editors' preferred treatment of biography, there appears a note under standard subdivision 092, "If preferred, class biography in 920.1–928," and under standard subdivision 092 4 Individual, "If preferred, class in 92 or B," the latter being traditional notations used widely for individual biography in one alphabetical span.

General geography of specific continents, countries, localities is placed by editors' preference in 913–919, but, optionally, may be placed in 930–990 with general history of these areas.

4.3 Unofficial variations Other variations may prove to be useful in specific situations even tho not recognized in the tables.

4.31 ATTRACTION Because of special local interest or special collections of books, it may on occasion be desirable to class a given subject in the wrong discipline, e.g., all works on Jews, not just their religion, in 296, all works on automobiles, not just their engineering, in 629:2.

An extension of this practice is the complete reversal of DC order. For example, a library devoted to travel and area study might make an administrative decision to arrange its collections by place; if so, it could use the area notations for the basic classes, and divide each after 0 by subject. Then everything on Japan would be placed in class 52: religion in 520 2, economic situation in 520 33, art in 520 7. In such a system works not areally specified could be placed in notation 0 followed by the regular DC notation, e.g., economic conditions of the whole world 033. Needless to say, this kind of use of DC, while thoroly practical, would also be purely local.

4.32 ALPHABETICAL ARRANGEMENT As an alternative to systematic arrangement, alphabetical arrangement (using the Cutter, Cutter-Sanborn, or Library of Congress tables) may serve specific local purposes. It is most useful when there is a very large number of specifics. When names of specifics are not precise and generally accepted, it should be used with great caution lest the same concept turn up under two or more terms, e.g., the use of names of specific occupations might call welders metalworkers and shoemakers cobblers.

Sometimes the editors are asked why a given subject should not be given alphabetical geographical arrangement, e.g., by U.S. states alphabetically instead of by area notations 74–79 and 969. It is true that the sequence Alabama, Alaska, Arizona, Arkansas, California . . . Wyoming is quite familiar and easy to understand. It is true also that under many subjects, e.g., statistics, such an arrangement is entirely satisfactory. But under others, e.g., fauna and flora, it is more satisfactory to find Virginia and West Virginia side by side rather than separated by Washington state. And a separate arrangement for cities, distinct from that for states, will bring close together treatment of churches (or any other subject you choose) in Baltimore and Boston, but only separate churches in Boston from those in Quincy, Newton, and Lynn. On the whole, it is best to follow the area table.

4.33 RELOCATIONS Libraries that have followed the recommendations of earlier editions may find it inconvenient to adopt the relocations in the present edition. If you find that you must ignore any or all relocations, you will do so in full awareness that you may be blocking yourself from taking advantage of future editorial improvements.

5. Acknowledgments

It is my pleasant duty to give public thanks to those who have contributed materially to such success as this 9th abridged edition may merit.

Thanks, first, to DDC's users. To the scores of librarians who studied and criticized or reviewed Editions 16 and Abridged 8, some in print, some in correspondence, some face to face, and to the reviewers and critics of draft schedules of Edition 17, both at home and abroad. To the hundreds of individuals who took time to answer questions. To interested groups in formal organizations, notably the Classification Committee and the Policy and Research Committee of the Cataloging and Classification Section of the Resources and Technical Services Division of the American

Library Association, and the Dewey Decimal Classification Revision Sub-Committee of the Research Committee of the (United Kingdom) Library Association.

Thanks, second, to all those officially connected with the Dewey Decimal Classification. To the directors of Forest Press, Inc.: Verner W. Clapp, Deo B. Colburn, Jack Dalton, Walter A. Hafner, and Howard Haycraft. To the members of the Decimal Classification Editorial Policy Committee: Edwin B. Colburn, Godfrey Dewey, Virginia Drewry, Carlyle J. Frarey, Esther J. Piercy, Joseph W. Rogers, Pauline A. Seely, Mrs. Marietta Daniels Shepard, and Wyllis E. Wright; to their statesmanship, foresight, and imaginative understanding of libraries' needs may be credited the basic principles which underlie this edition. To my superiors in the Library of Congress for support and encouragement at all times: L. Quincy Mumford, John W. Cronin, William J. Welsh.

Thanks, third, to the staff of the Decimal Classification Office, who really did the grubbing: Harriet Helliwell, Elaine Hicks, Mrs. Peggy C. Kans, Mrs. Emily K. Spears, and Edna E. Van Syoc. To the Assistant Chief, Decimal Classification Office, Elva L. Krogh, for numerous profitable suggestions based on her daily use of the DC to class books. To the Assistant Editor, Dewey Decimal Classification, Mrs. Marie M. Henshaw, for her uncompromising insistence that the editorial operations hew to the line of consistency, and for her brilliant development of many original editorial ideas. Mrs. Henshaw prepared most of the text of the present edition.

6. Conclusion

The foreword to the 15th edition "earnestly" requested "all users to give us the benefit of their criticism in order that sometime our successors may actually bring out 'the perfect book.'" It appears unlikely that this or any other general classification will ever be "perfect"; nevertheless, improvement is always possible and devoutly to be pursued. So, once again, we urge all who use the DC, whether students, teachers, or appliers, to continue to give us the "benefit of their criticism."

Benjamin A. Custer
EDITOR

Decimal Classification Office
Processing Department
The Library of Congress
Washington, D.C. 20540
31 March 1965

Summaries

First Summary
The 10 Classes

000 **Generalities**

100 **Philosophy & related disciplines**

200 **Religion**

300 **The social sciences**

400 **Language**

500 **Pure sciences**

600 **Technology (Applied sciences)**

700 **The arts**

800 **Literature & rhetoric**

900 **General geography, history, etc.**

Second Summary
The 100 Divisions

000	**Generalities**		**500**	**Pure sciences**
010	Bibliographies & catalogs		510	Mathematics
020	Library science		520	Astronomy & allied sciences
030	General encyclopedic works		530	Physics
040			540	Chemistry & allied sciences
050	General periodicals		550	Earth sciences
060	General organizations		560	Paleontology
070	Newspapers & journalism		570	Anthropolog. & biol. sciences
080	General collections		580	Botanical sciences
090	Manuscripts & book rarities		590	Zoological sciences
100	**Philosophy & related**		**600**	**Technology (Applied sci.)**
110	Ontology & methodology		610	Medical sciences
120	Knowledge, cause, purpose, man		620	Engineering & allied operations
130	Pseudo- & parapsychology		630	Agriculture & agric. industries
140	Specific philosophic viewpoints		640	Domestic arts & sciences
150	Psychology		650	Business & related enterprises
160	Logic		660	Chemical technology etc.
170	Ethics (Moral philosophy)		670	Manufactures processible
180	Ancient, med., Oriental philos.		680	Assembled & final products
190	Modern Western philosophy		690	Buildings
200	**Religion**		**700**	**The arts**
210	Natural religion		710	Civic & landscape art
220	Bible		720	Architecture
230	Christian doctrinal theology		730	Sculpture & the plastic arts
240	Christ. moral & devotional theol.		740	Drawing & decorative arts
250	Christ. pastoral, parochial, etc.		750	Painting & paintings
260	Christ. social & eccles. theol.		760	Graphic arts
270	Hist. & geog. of Chr. church		770	Photography & photographs
280	Christ. denominations & sects		780	Music
290	Other religions & compar. rel.		790	Recreation (Recreational arts)
300	**The social sciences**		**800**	**Literature & rhetoric**
310	Statistical method & statistics		810	American literature in English
320	Political science		820	Engl. & Anglo-Saxon literature
330	Economics		830	Germanic languages literature
340	Law		840	French, Provençal, Catalan lit.
350	Public administration		850	Italian, Romanian etc. literature
360	Welfare & association		860	Spanish & Portuguese literature
370	Education		870	Italic languages literature
380	Commerce		880	Classical & Greek literature
390	Customs & folklore		890	Lits. of other languages
400	**Language**		**900**	**General geog. & history etc.**
410	Linguistics & nonverbal lang.		910	General geography
420	English & Anglo-Saxon		920	General biog., geneal., etc.
430	Germanic languages		930	Gen. hist. of ancient world
440	French, Provençal, Catalan		940	Gen. hist. of modern Europe
450	Italian, Romanian, etc.		950	Gen. hist. of modern Asia
460	Spanish & Portuguese		960	Gen. hist. of modern Africa
470	Italic languages		970	Gen. hist. of North America
480	Classical & Greek		980	Gen. hist. of South America
490	Other languages		990	Gen. hist. of rest of world

Third Summary
The 1000 Sections
Generalities

000	**Generalities**		**050**	**General periodicals**
001	Knowledge		051	American
002			052	Other English-language
003			053	Other Germanic languages
004			054	French, Provençal, Catalan
005			055	Italian, Romanian, etc.
006			056	Spanish & Portuguese
007			057	Slavic languages
008			058	Scandinavian languages
009			059	Other languages
010	**Bibliographies & catalogs**		**060**	**General organizations**
011	General bibliographies		061	In North America
012	Of individuals		062	In England & Wales
013	Of specific classes of writers		063	In central Europe
014	Of anonymous & pseudon. works		064	In France
015	Of works from specific places		065	In Italy & adjacent territories
016	Of specific subjects		066	In Iberian Peninsula etc.
017	General subject catalogs		067	In eastern Europe
018	General author catalogs		068	In other countries
019	General dictionary catalogs		069	Museums
020	**Library science**		**070**	**Newspapers & journalism**
021	The library		071	In North America
022	Physical plant of libraries		072	In England & Wales
023	Library personnel & positions		073	In central Europe
024	Regulations for use of libraries		074	In France
025	Library economy		075	In Italy & adjacent territories
026	Special libraries		076	In Iberian Peninsula etc.
027	General libraries		077	In eastern Europe
028	Reading & reading aids		078	In Scandinavia
029	Indexing & documentation		079	In other countries
030	**General encyclopedic works**		**080**	**General collections**
031	American		081	American
032	Other English-language		082	Other English-language
033	Other Germanic languages		083	Other Germanic languages
034	French, Provençal, Catalan		084	French, Provençal, Catalan
035	Italian, Romanian, etc.		085	Italian, Romanian, etc.
036	Spanish & Portuguese		086	Spanish & Portuguese
037	Slavic languages		087	Slavic languages
038	Scandinavian languages		088	Scandinavian languages
039	Other languages		089	Other languages
040			**090**	**Mss. & book rarities**
041			091	Manuscripts
042			092	Block books
043			093	Incunabula
044			094	Notable printing
045			095	Notable binding
046			096	Notable illustrations & materials
047			097	Notable ownership & origin
048			098	Notable content
049			099	Notable format

Philosophy and related disciplines

100 Philosophy & related

101 Theory
102 Miscellany
103 Dictionaries, encyclopedias, etc.
104
105 Serial publications
106 Organizations
107 Study & teaching
108 Collections & anthologies
109 Historical treatment

110 Ontology & methodology

111 Ontology
112 Classification of knowledge
113 Origin of universe
114 Space
115 Time, duration, eternity
116 Motion & change
117 Matter & form
118 Force & energy
119 Number & quantity

120 Other metaphysical topics

121 Epistemology
122 Cause & effect
123 Freedom & necessity
124 Teleology
125 Finite & infinite
126 Consciousness & personality
127 Unconscious & subconscious
128 Man
129 Origin & destiny of soul

130 Pseudo- & parapsychology

131 Pseudopsychology
132
133 Parapsychology & occultism
134
135 Dreams & the mystic traditions
136
137 Personality anal. & improvement
138 Physiognomy
139 Phrenology

140 Specific viewpoints

141 Idealism & related systems
142 Critical philosophy
143 Intuitionism & Bergsonism
144 Humanism & related systems
145 Sensationalism & ideology
146 Naturalism & related systems
147 Pantheism & related systems
148 Liberalism & other systems
149 Other systems & doctrines

150 Psychology

151
152 Physiological & experimental
153 Intelligence & intellect
154 Subconscious states & processes
155 Differential & genetic psychology
156 Comparative psychology
157 Abnormal & clinical psychologies
158 Applied psychology
159 Other aspects

160 Logic

161 Induction
162 Deduction
163
164 Symbolic & mathematical logic
165 Fallacies & sources of error
166 Syllogism
167 Hypothesis
168 Argument & persuasion
169 Analogy

170 Ethics (Moral philosophy)

171 Systems & doctrines
172 Ethics of political relationships
173 Ethics of family relationships
174 Profes. & occupational ethics
175 Ethics of recreation
176 Sexual ethics
177 Ethics of social relations
178 Ethics of temperance etc.
179 Other applications of ethics

180 Anc., med., Oriental

181 Oriental
182 Pre-Socratic
183 Sophistic, Socratic & related
184 Platonic
185 Aristotelian
186 Skeptic & Neoplatonic
187 Epicurean
188 Stoic
189 Medieval Western

190 Modern Western philosophy

191 United States & Canada
192 British Isles
193 Germany & Austria
194 France
195 Italy
196 Spain & Portugal
197 Russia & Finland
198 Scandinavia
199 Other

Religion

200	**Religion**	**250**	**Christ. pastoral & parochial**
201	Philosophy of Christianity	251	Preaching (Homiletics)
202	Miscellany of Christianity	252	Sermons
203	Dictionaries of Christianity	253	Pastor
204		254	Parish govt. & administration
205	Serial publs. on Christianity	255	Religious congregations & orders
206	Organizations on Christianity	256	
207	Study of Christianity	257	
208	Collections on Christianity	258	Parochial welfare work
209	Hist. & geography of Christianity	259	Other parochial activities
210	**Natural religion**	**260**	**Chr. social & eccles. theol.**
211	Knowledge of God	261	Social theology
212	Nature of God	262	Church govt., org., nature
213	Creation	263	Times of religious observance
214	Theodicy	264	Public worship
215	Science & religion	265	Other rites & ceremonies
216	Good & evil	266	Missions
217	Worship & prayer	267	Associations for religious work
218	Immortality & eternity	268	Religious training & instruction
219	Analogy	269	Organized spiritual renewal
220	**Bible**	**270**	**Hist. & geog. of Chr. church**
221	Old Testament	271	Religious congregations & orders
222	Historical books	272	Persecutions
223	Poetic books	273	Heresies
224	Prophetic books	274	Christian church in Europe
225	New Testament	275	Christian church in Asia
226	Gospels & Acts	276	Christian church in Africa
227	Epistles	277	Christian church in No. America
228	Revelation (Apocalypse)	278	Christian church in So. America
229	Apocrypha, pseudepigrapha, etc.	279	Christian church elsewhere
230	**Christian doctrinal theology**	**280**	**Christ. denominations & sects**
231	God, Trinity, Godhead	281	Primitive & Oriental churches
232	Jesus Christ & his family	282	Roman Catholic Church
233	Man	283	Anglican churches
234	Salvation (Soteriology)	284	Protestants of Continental origin
235	Invisible world	285	Presb., Amer. Ref., Congr. chs.
236	Eschatology	286	Bapt., Disc. of Christ, Adventists
237		287	Methodist churches
238	Creeds & confessions of faith	288	Unitarianism
239	Apologetics & polemics	289	Other denominations & sects
240	**Christ. moral & devotional**	**290**	**Other religions etc.**
241	Moral theology	291	Comparative religion
242	Prayers & meditations	292	Classical (Gr. & Rom.) religion
243	Evangelistic writings	293	Germanic religion
244		294	Brahmanism & related religions
245	Hymns	295	Zoroastrianism
246	Symbolism etc.	296	Judaism
247	Sacred furniture etc.	297	Islam & its derivatives
248	Personal religion	298	
249	Worship in family life	299	Other religions

The social sciences

300	**The social sciences**	**350**	**Public administration**
301	Sociology	351	Central governments
302		352	Local units of government
303		353	United States federal & states
304		354	Other central governments
305		355	General military administration
306		356	Foot forces
307		357	Mounted forces
308		358	Armored, technical, air, space
309	Social situation & conditions	359	Sea (Naval) forces
310	**Statistical method & statistics**	**360**	**Welfare & association**
311	Statistical method	361	Organization of social welfare
312	Statistics of populations	362	Welfare services to spec. groups
313		363	Other services
314	General statistics of Europe	364	Criminology
315	General statistics of Asia	365	Penology
316	General statistics of Africa	366	Association
317	Gen. statistics of North America	367	Social clubs
318	Gen. statistics of South America	368	Insurance
319	Gen. statistics of rest of world	369	Other kinds of associations
320	**Political science**	**370**	**Education**
321	Types & forms of states	371	The school
322	Relation of state to org. groups	372	Elementary education
323	Rel. of state to individuals etc.	373	Secondary education
324	Suffrage	374	Adult education
325	International migration	375	Curriculums
326	Slavery & emancipation	376	Education of women
327	International relations	377	Schools & religion
328	Legislation	378	Higher education
329	Practical politics	379	Govt. supervision & support
330	**Economics**	**380**	**Commerce**
331	Labor	381	Internal commerce
332	Lucrative capital	382	International commerce
333	Land (Natural resources)	383	Postal communication
334	Cooperative systems	384	Other systems of communication
335	Collectivist systems & schools	385	Railroad transportation
336	Public finance	386	Inland waterway transportation
337		387	Water, air, space transportation
338	Production	388	Ground transportation
339	Distribution & consumption	389	Metrology & standardization
340	**Law**	**390**	**Customs & folklore**
341	Internat. law (Law of nations)	391	Costume
342	Constitutional law	392	Customs of life cycle
343	Criminal law	393	Death customs
344	Martial law	394	Public & social customs
345	United States statutes & cases	395	Etiquette
346	British statutes & cases	396	
347	Private law & judicial system	397	
348		398	Folklore
349	Statutes & cases not U.S.-Brit.	399	Customs of war

Language

400	**Language**	**450**	**Italian, Romanian, etc.**	
401	Philosophy & theory	451	Written & spoken Italian	
402	Miscellany	452	Italian etymology	
403	Dictionaries, encyclopedias, etc.	453	Italian dictionaries	
404		454		
405	Serial publications	455	Italian structural system	
406	Organizations	456	Italian prosody	
407	Study & teaching	457	Nonstandard Italian	
408	Collections & anthologies	458	Standard Italian usage	
409	Hist. & geographical treatment	459	Romanian & Rhaeto-Romanic	
410	**Linguistics & nonverbal**	**460**	**Spanish & Portuguese**	
411	Notations	461	Written & spoken Spanish	
412	Etymology	462	Spanish etymology	
413	Polyglot dictionaries	463	Spanish dictionaries	
414	Phonology	464		
415	Structural systems	465	Spanish structural system	
416	Prosody	466	Spanish prosody	
417	Dialectology & paleography	467	Nonstandard Spanish	
418	Usage (Applied linguistics)	468	Standard Spanish usage	
419	Nonverbal language	469	Portuguese	
420	**English & Anglo-Saxon**	**470**	**Italic languages**	
421	Written & spoken English	471	Written & spoken Latin	
422	English etymology	472	Latin etymology	
423	English dictionaries	473	Latin dictionaries	
424		474		
425	English structural system	475	Latin structural system	
426	English prosody	476	Latin prosody	
427	Nonstandard English	477	Old, Postclassical, Vulgar Latin	
428	Standard English usage	478	Standard Latin usage	
429	Anglo-Saxon (Old English)	479	Romance & other Italic langs.	
430	**Germanic languages**	**480**	**Classical & Greek**	
431	Written & spoken German	481	Written & spoken classical Greek	
432	German etymology	482	Classical Greek etymology	
433	German dictionaries	483	Classical Greek dictionaries	
434		484		
435	German structural system	485	Class. Greek structural system	
436	German prosody	486	Classical Greek prosody	
437	Nonstandard German	487	Postclassical Greek	
438	Standard German usage	488	Standard classical Greek usage	
439	Other Germanic languages	489	Other Greek languages	
440	**French, Provençal, Catalan**	**490**	**Other languages**	
441	Written & spoken French	491	East Indo-European & Celtic	
442	French etymology	492	Semitic languages	
443	French dictionaries	493	Hamitic & other languages	
444		494	Ural-Altaic, Dravidian, etc.	
445	French structural system	495	East & Southeast Asian langs.	
446	French prosody	496	African languages	
447	Nonstandard French	497	North American Indian langs.	
448	Standard French usage	498	South American Indian langs.	
449	Provençal & Catalan	499	Austronesian & other languages	

Pure sciences

500	**Pure sciences**		**550**	**Earth sciences**
501	Philosophy & theory		551	Physical & dynamic geology
502	Miscellany		552	Petrology
503	Dictionaries, encyclopedias, etc.		553	Economic geology
504			554	Geology of Europe
505	Serial publications		555	Geology of Asia
506	Organizations		556	Geology of Africa
507	Study & teaching		557	Geology of North America
508	Collections, travels, surveys		558	Geology of South America
509	Hist. & geographical treatment		559	Geology of other parts of world
510	**Mathematics**		**560**	**Paleontology**
511	Arithmetic		561	Paleobotany
512	Algebra		562	Invertebrate paleozoology
513	Synthetic geometry		563	Protozoa, Parazoa, Metazoa
514	Trigonometry		564	Mollusca & molluscoidea
515	Descriptive geometry		565	Other invertebrates
516	Analytic (Coordinate) geometry		566	Vertebrate paleozoology
517	Calculus		567	Anamnia (Fishes etc.)
518			568	Sauropsida (Reptiles & birds)
519	Probabilities & statistical math.		569	Mammalia (Mammals)
520	**Astronomy & allied sci.**		**570**	**Anthropol. & biological sci.**
521	Theoretical astronomy		571	
522	Practical & spherical astronomy		572	Human races (Ethnology)
523	Descriptive astronomy		573	Somatology (Phys. anthropol.)
524			574	Biology
525	Earth (Astronomical geography)		575	Organic evolution
526	Mathematical geography		576	Microbiology
527	Celestial navigation		577	Gen. properties of living matter
528	Ephemerides (Naut. almanacs)		578	Microscopes & microscopy
529	Chronology		579	Coll. & preservation of specimens
530	**Physics**		**580**	**Botanical sciences**
531	Mechanics		581	Botany
532	Mechanics of fluids		582	Spermatophyta
533	Mechanics of gases		583	Dicotyledones
534	Sound & related vibrations		584	Monocotyledones
535	Visible light etc.		585	Gymnospermae
536	Heat		586	Cryptogamia
537	Electricity & electronics		587	Pteridophyta
538	Magnetism		588	Bryophyta
539	Modern physics		589	Thallophyta
540	**Chemistry & allied sciences**		**590**	**Zoological sciences**
541	Physical & theoret. chemistry		591	Zoology
542	Laboratories & equipment		592	Invertebrates
543	General analytical chemistry		593	Protozoa, Parazoa, Metazoa
544	Qualitative analytical chemistry		594	Mollusca & molluscoidea
545	Quantitative analytical chemistry		595	Other invertebrates
546	Inorganic chemistry		596	Chordata (Vertebrates)
547	Organic chemistry		597	Anamnia (Fishes etc.)
548	Crystallography		598	Reptiles & birds
549	Mineralogy		599	Mammalia (Mammals)

Technology (Applied sciences)

600	**Technology (Applied sci.)**	**650**	**Business & related**
601	Philosophy & theory	651	Office services
602	Miscellany	652	Writing
603	Dictionaries, encyclopedias, etc.	653	Shorthand
604		654	
605	Serial publications	655	Printing & related activities
606	Organizations	656	
607	Study & teaching	657	Accounting
608	Collections, patents, etc.	658	Management
609	Hist. & geographical treatment	659	Other activities & techniques
610	**Medical sciences**	**660**	**Chemical technology etc.**
611	Human anatomy	661	Industrial chemicals
612	Human physiology	662	Explosives, fuels, etc.
613	General & personal hygiene	663	Drinks, stimulants, etc.
614	Public health	664	Food technology
615	Therapeutics & pharmacology	665	Industrial oils, fats, gases
616	Medicine	666	Ceramic & allied industries
617	Surgery	667	Cleaning, color & related
618	Other specialized medicine	668	Other organic products
619	Compar. & experim. medicine	669	Metallurgy
620	**Engineering & allied**	**670**	**Manufactures processible**
621	Applied physics	671	Metal manufactures
622	Mining engineering & operations	672	Ferrous metals manufactures
623	Military & naval engineering	673	Nonferrous metals manufactures
624	Civil engineering	674	Lumber, cork, wood-using indus.
625	Railroads & highways	675	Leather & fur industries
626		676	Pulp & paper industries
627	Hydraulic engineering etc.	677	Textiles
628	Sanitary & municipal engineering	678	Elastomers & their products
629	Other branches	679	Other products
630	**Agriculture & agr. indus.**	**680**	**Assembled etc. products**
631	Farming	681	Precision mechanisms etc.
632	Plant pathology & its control	682	Small forge work
633	Field crops	683	Hardware
634	Orchards, small fruit, forestry	684	Furnishings & wheeled supports
635	Garden crops (Horticulture)	685	Leather goods & substitutes
636	Livestock & domestic animals	686	
637	Dairy & related industries	687	Clothing
638	Insect culture	688	Other final products
639	Nondomesticated animals	689	
640	**Domestic arts & sciences**	**690**	**Buildings**
641	Food & drink	691	Materials
642	Food & meal service	692	Construction practices
643	The home & its equipment	693	Systems of construction
644	Household utilities	694	Wood construction
645	Household furnishings	695	Roofing & auxiliary structures
646	Clothing & care of body	696	Plumbing, heating, ventilating
647	Housekeeping	697	Heating, ventilating, etc.
648	Household sanitation	698	Detail finishing
649	Child rearing & home nursing	699	

The arts

700	**The arts**		**750**	**Painting & paintings**
701	Philosophy & theory		751	Processes & forms
702	Miscellany		752	Color theory & practice
703	Dictionaries, encyclopedias, etc.		753	Abstractions, mythology, etc.
704	Collections, iconography, etc.		754	Subjects of everyday life
705	Serial publications		755	Religion & religious symbolism
706	Organizations		756	Historical events
707	Study & teaching		757	Human figures & their parts
708	Galleries, museums, etc.		758	Other subjects
709	Hist. & geographical treatment		759	Hist. & geographical treatment
710	**Civic & landscape art**		**760**	**Graphic arts**
711	Area planning (Civic art)		761	Relief processes for prints
712	Landscape design		762	
713	Landscape design of trafficways		763	Lithographic processes
714	Water in landscape design		764	Chromolithography & serigraphy
715	Woody plants in landscape design		765	Metal intaglio processes
716	Herbaceous plants in design		766	Mezzotinting etc. processes
717	Structures in landscape design		767	Etching & drypoint processes
718	Landscape design of cemeteries		768	
719	Natural landscapes		769	Prints
720	**Architecture**		**770**	**Photography & photographs**
721	Architectural construction		771	Equipment, supplies, chemistry
722	Ancient period		772	Metallic salt processes
723	Medieval period		773	Pigment processes of printing
724	Modern period		774	
725	Public structures		775	
726	Buildings for religious purposes		776	
727	Bldgs. for educational purposes		777	
728	Residential buildings		778	Specific fields of photography
729	Design & decoration		779	Collections of photographs
730	**Sculpture & plastic arts**		**780**	**Music**
731	Processes etc. of sculpture		781	General principles & techniques
732	Ancient nonclassical sculpture		782	Dramatic music
733	Ancient classical sculpture		783	Sacred music
734	Medieval sculpture		784	Voice & vocal music
735	Modern sculpture		785	Instrumental ensembles & music
736	Carving & carvings		786	Keyboard instruments & music
737	Numismatics		787	String instruments & music
738	Ceramic arts		788	Wind instruments & their music
739	Art metalwork		789	Percussion, mechan., electr. inst.
740	**Drawing & decorative arts**		**790**	**Recreation (Recr. arts)**
741	Freehand drawing & drawings		791	Public entertainment
742	Perspective		792	Theater (Stage presentations)
743	Freehand drawing by subject		793	Indoor games & amusements
744	Technical drawing		794	Indoor games of skill
745	Design & crafts		795	Games of chance
746	Textile handicrafts		796	Athletic & outdoor sports
747	Interior decoration		797	Aquatic & air sports
748	Glass		798	Equestrian & animal sports
749	Furniture & accessories		799	Fishing, hunting, shooting

Literature (Belles-lettres) and rhetoric

800	**Literature & rhetoric**	**850**	**Italian etc. literature**
801	Philosophy & theory of literature	851	Italian poetry
802	Miscellany about literature	852	Italian drama
803	Dictionaries etc. of literature	853	Italian fiction
804		854	Italian essays
805	Serials of & about literature	855	Italian speeches
806	Organizations on literature	856	Italian letters
807	Study & teaching of literature	857	Italian satire & humor
808	Rhetoric & collections of lit.	858	Italian miscellany
809	History & criticism of literature	859	Romanian & Rhaeto-Romanic
810	**American lit. in English**	**860**	**Spanish & Portuguese lit.**
811	Poetry	861	Spanish poetry
812	Drama	862	Spanish drama
813	Fiction	863	Spanish fiction
814	Essays	864	Spanish essays
815	Speeches	865	Spanish speeches
816	Letters	866	Spanish letters
817	Satire & humor	867	Spanish satire & humor
818	Miscellany	868	Spanish miscellany
819		869	Portuguese
820	**English & Anglo-Saxon lit.**	**870**	**Italic languages literature**
821	English poetry	871	Latin poetry
822	English drama	872	Latin dramatic poetry & drama
823	English fiction	873	Latin epic poetry & fiction
824	English essays	874	Latin lyric poetry
825	English speeches	875	Latin speeches
826	English letters	876	Latin letters
827	English satire & humor	877	Latin satire & humor
828	English miscellany	878	Latin miscellany
829	Anglo-Saxon (Old English)	879	Other Italic languages
830	**Germanic languages lit.**	**880**	**Classical, modern Greek lit.**
831	German poetry	881	Classical Greek poetry
832	German drama	882	Classical dramatic poetry
833	German fiction	883	Classical epic poetry & fiction
834	German essays	884	Classical Greek lyric poetry
835	German speeches	885	Classical Greek speeches
836	German letters	886	Classical Greek letters
837	German satire & humor	887	Classical Greek satire & humor
838	German miscellany	888	Classical Greek miscellany
839	Other Germanic languages	889	Modern Greek
840	**French etc. literature**	**890**	**Lits. of other languages**
841	French poetry	891	East Indo-European & Celtic
842	French drama	892	Semitic languages
843	French fiction	893	Hamitic & other languages
844	French essays	894	Ural-Altaic, Dravidian, etc.
845	French speeches	895	East & Southeast Asian langs.
846	French letters	896	African languages
847	French satire & humor	897	North American Indian langs.
848	French miscellany	898	South American Indian langs.
849	Provençal & Catalan	899	Austronesian & other languages

General geography and history and related disciplines

900	**Gen. geog. & history etc.**	950	**Gen. hist. of modern Asia**
901	Philos. & theory of gen. hist.	951	China & adjacent areas
902	Miscellany of general history	952	Japan & adjacent islands
903	Dictionaries etc. of gen. hist.	953	Arabian Peninsula & adj. areas
904	Collected accounts of events	954	South Asia
905	Serial publications of gen. hist.	955	Iran (Persia)
906	Organizations on gen. hist.	956	Middle East
907	Study & teaching of gen. hist.	957	Siberia (Asiatic Russia)
908	Collections of general history	958	Central Asia
909	World history	959	Southeast Asia
910	**General geography**	**960**	**Gen. hist. of modern Africa**
911	Historical geography	961	North Africa
912	Atlases, maps, charts, etc.	962	Egypt & Sudan
913	Geography of ancient world	963	Ethiopia
914	Geography of modern Europe	964	Northwest coast & offshore isls.
915	Geography of modern Asia	965	Algeria
916	Geography of modern Africa	966	West Africa & offshore islands
917	Geography of North America	967	Central Africa & offshore islands
918	Geography of South America	968	South Africa
919	Geography of rest of world	969	South Indian Ocean islands
920	**Gen. biography, geneal., etc.**	**970**	**Gen. hist. of North America**
921		971	Canada
922		972	Middle America
923		973	United States
924		974	Northeastern states of U.S.
925		975	Southeastern states of U.S.
926		976	South central states of U.S.
927		977	North central states of U.S.
928		978	Western states of U.S.
929	Genealogy, names, insignia	979	Great Basin & Pacific Slope
930	**Gen. hist. of ancient world**	**980**	**Gen. hist. of South America**
931	China	981	Brazil
932	Egypt	982	Argentina
933	Palestine	983	Chile
934	India	984	Bolivia
935	Mesopotamia & Iranian Plateau	985	Peru
936	Northern & western Europe	986	Northwestern South America
937	Italian peninsula & adjacent	987	Venezuela
938	Greece	988	Guiana
939	Other parts of ancient world	989	Other parts of South America
940	**Gen. hist. of modern Europe**	**990**	**Gen. hist. of rest of world**
941	Scotland & Ireland	991	Malay Archipelago
942	British Isles	992	Sunda Islands
943	Central Europe	993	New Zealand & Melanesia
944	France	994	Australia
945	Italy & adjacent territories	995	New Guinea (Papua)
946	Iberian Peninsula & adjacent isls.	996	Other parts of Pacific
947	Eastern Europe	997	Atlantic Ocean islands
948	Scandinavia	998	Arctic islands
949	Other parts of Europe	999	Antarctica

General Tables

Use of the General Tables

Full instructions on use appear in the introduction, section 3.

A number in square brackets is not in force or is no longer in force with the meaning indicated.

000   Generalities

001   Knowledge

.2   Intellectual life (Scholarship and learning)

.3   Humanities

.4   Research [*formerly* 007]

> Including endowment [*formerly* **378.3**], other incentives, methodology

.5   Communication [*formerly* 384]

> Communication theories, cybernetics [*both formerly* **006**], the book [*formerly* **002**], microreproductions [*formerly* **099**], other recorded knowledge

[002]   The book

> Class generalities in **001.5**, bookmaking and book arts in **655**

[006]   Communication theories and cybernetics

> Class in **001.5**

[007]   Research

> Class in **001.4**

010   Bibliographies and catalogs

> Of books, other printed and written mediums, nonmusical recordings, information films and slides
>
> Class book collecting in **020.75**, documentation in **029.7** [*both formerly* **010**]
>
> *For bibliographies and catalogs of books for children and young adults, see* **028.52**

011   General bibliographies

> Lists of works not limited to a specific kind of coverage or place of publication
>
> Including general classified bibliographies [*formerly* **016**]

▶ **012–016 Special bibliographies and catalogs**

012 **Of individuals**

Works by or about persons not clearly associated with a specific subject

013 **Of specific classes of writers**

Works whose authors have common characteristics

For bibliographies and catalogs of individuals, see 012

014 **Of anonymous and pseudonymous works**

015 **Of works from specific places**

Works issued or printed in specific continents, countries, localities, or by specific firms

Scope: national bibliographies

Add area notations 3–9 to 015

016 **Of specific subjects**

If preferred, class in standard subdivision 01

Do not use standard subdivisions

Divide like 001–999, e.g., bibliographies of newspapers in England 016.072

Class general classified bibliographies [*formerly* 016] in 011

For bibliographies and catalogs of music scores and parts, see 781.9

▶ **017–019 General catalogs**

Lists of works held in a specific collection or group of collections and not limited to a specific kind of coverage or place of publication

017 **Subject catalogs**

Alphabetically arranged [*formerly* 019] and classified

018 **Author catalogs**

019 **Dictionary catalogs**

Class alphabetically arranged subject catalogs [*formerly* 019] in 017

020 Library science

The knowledge and skill by which printed and written records are recognized, collected, organized, utilized

For bibliographies and catalogs, see **010**

.6 Organizations

Class friends-of-the-library organizations [*formerly* **020.6**] in **021.7**

.7 Study and teaching

.75 Book collecting [*formerly* 010]

021 The library

Do not use standard subdivisions

Class specific libraries and kinds of libraries in **026–027**

► 021.1–021.8 Establishment and purpose of libraries

.1 Libraries as storage centers

.2 Libraries as educational force

.3 Libraries in relation to other educational institutions

.4 Libraries as social force

.6 Library extension and cooperation

Including union catalogs [*formerly* **025.3**]

Class branches, bookmobiles [*both formerly* **021.6**] in **027.4**

For cooperation in a specific activity, see the activity. e.g., cooperative cataloging **025.3**

.7 Promotion of libraries

Including friends-of-the-library organizations [*formerly* **020.6**]

For friends of specific libraries, see **026–027**

.8 Libraries and the state

Library commissions, official exchange of publications, monetary aid and subsidies, gifts of books, copyright deposits

Including governing boards [*formerly* **023**]

Class library laws [*formerly* **021.8**] in **340**

022   Physical plant of libraries

> Location, planning, equipment, facilities
>
> Class insurance of libraries [*formerly* 022] in **368**
>
> *For maintenance of physical plant, see* **025**

023   Library personnel and positions

> Qualifications, titles, job descriptions of administrative and staff personnel
>
> Class pensions, retirement, classification and pay plans in **658.32**, governing boards in **021.8** [*all formerly* 023]

024   Regulations for use of libraries

025   Library economy

> Practical application of library science to the founding, organizing, administration of libraries
>
> Including maintenance of physical plant
>
> Use **025.001–025.009** for standard subdivisions
>
> *For indexing and documentation, see* **029**

.1   Administration

> Including finance, printing, publishing, specific duplication processes

.17   Treatment of special materials

> Arrangement, care, use of manuscripts, archival material, rarities, pamphlets, broadsides, clippings, serials, documents, maps, other audio-visual materials, books in raised characters
>
> *For a special kind of treatment, see the kind, e.g., cataloging* **025.3**

.2   Acquisition

> Selecting and acquiring books, periodicals, other materials by purchase, exchange, gift
>
> Including physical preparation for shelves

025.3	Cataloging

Including descriptive cataloging, cataloging of special materials, cooperative cataloging

Class union catalogs [*formerly* 025.3] in 021.6

.33	Subject cataloging

Do not use standard subdivisions

For classification, see 025.4

.37	Filing

.4	Classification

Principles, systems, notations, schedules

.5	Services to patrons

Reader advisory services [*formerly also* 028.8], reference services

For a specific service, see the subject, e.g., circulation services 025.6; *reference and reader advisory services to specific groups,* 027.6; *reading aids,* 028

.6	Circulation services

Lending materials, keeping records of loans

Class regulations for interlibrary loans in 024

.7	Binding and repair services

026–027 Specific kinds of libraries

Scope: specific libraries, friends of specific libraries

Class a specific library activity or service with the subject

026	Special libraries

Including libraries devoted to specific subjects

Do not use standard subdivisions

For libraries for special groups and specific organizations, see 027.6

027   General libraries

> Including private, family, proprietary, rental libraries
>
> Do not use standard subdivisions

.4   Public libraries

> Institutions that serve free all residents of a community, district, or region, usually receiving their financial support, in whole or in part, from public funds
>
> Scope: branches, bookmobiles [*both formerly* 021.6], reference, research, county, regional libraries
>
> Add area notations 3–9 to 027.4
>
> > *For libraries devoted to specific subjects, see* 026

.5   Government libraries

> National, state, provincial
>
> > *For libraries devoted to specific subjects, see* 026

.509   Historical and geographical treatment

> Do not use for specific institutions

.6   Libraries for special groups and specific organizations

> Libraries of learned societies [*formerly* 027.7], for minority groups, industrial workers, government agencies, welfare institutions, religious organizations, old-age groups
>
> Scope: reference and reader advisory services to special groups
>
> > *For libraries for educational institutions, see* 027.7–027.8; *libraries devoted to specific subjects,* 026

.62   Libraries for children and young adults

> Including storytelling in libraries
>
> Do not use standard subdivisions

───────────

▶ 027.7–027.8 Libraries for educational institutions

For libraries devoted to specific subjects, see **026**

027.7 College and university libraries

Class libraries of learned societies [*formerly* **027.7**] in **027.6**

.709 Historical and geographical treatment

Do not use for specific institutions

.8 School libraries

Libraries in public, private, church-supported elementary and secondary schools

.809 Historical and geographical treatment

Do not use for specific institutions

028 Reading and reading aids

.1 Book reviews

Class technique of book reviewing in **808.06**, critical appraisal of literature in **809**

.5 Reading of children and young adults

.52 Bibliographies and catalogs

.7 Use of books and libraries as sources of information

.8 Use of books as sources of recreation and self-development

Class reader advisory services [*formerly* **028.8**] in **025.5**

029 Indexing and documentation

Former heading: Literary methods

.5 Indexing

[.6] Authorship and editorial techniques

Class in **808.02**

029.7   Documentation [*formerly* 010]

> Assembling, coding, disseminating recorded knowledge as an integral procedure to achieve maximum accessibility and usability, utilizing semantics, psychological aids, techniques of reproduction
>
> Including information storage and retrieval

030   General encyclopedic works

───────────

►   031–032 English-language

031   **American**

> English-language encyclopedias originating in Western Hemisphere and Hawaii

032   **Other English-language**

> Encyclopedias originating outside Western Hemisphere and Hawaii

033   **Other Germanic languages**

> Class Scandinavian-language encyclopedias in **038**

034   **French, Provençal, Catalan**

035   **Italian, Romanian, Rhaeto-Romanic**

036   **Spanish and Portuguese**

037   **Slavic languages**

038   **Scandinavian languages**

039   **Other languages**

[040] General collected essays, addresses, lectures

> Class in **080**

050   **General periodicals and their indexes**

If preferred, arrange periodicals alphabetically under **050**, using **A1** for comprehensive works about them and **Z9** for general indexes to them

---

051–052 English-language

051   American

English-language periodicals of Western Hemisphere and Hawaii

052   Other English-language

Periodicals outside Western Hemisphere and Hawaii

053   Other Germanic languages

Class Scandinavian-language periodicals and their indexes in **058**

054   French, Provençal, Catalan

055   Italian, Romanian, Rhaeto-Romanic

056   Spanish and Portuguese

057   Slavic languages

058   Scandinavian languages

059   Other languages

060   **General organizations**

Societies, academies, foundations, associations, conferences, congresses whose activity is not limited to a specific field

Scope: comprehensive works on organizations

Class organizations having a specific purpose, field or subject with the subject

061   In Canada and United States

062   In England and Wales

Class organizations in Scotland and Ireland in **068**

063   In central Europe

064   In France

065   In Italy and adjacent territories

066   In Iberian Peninsula and adjacent islands

067   In eastern Europe

068   In other countries

069   Museums

> Class museums specializing in a specific subject in standard subdivision **074**

.09   Historical and geographical treatment

> Do not use for specific museum buildings

070   Newspapers and journalism

> Use **070.01–070.08** for standard subdivisions
>
> Class journals on a specific subject with the subject, general periodicals in **050**

[.3]   Business management of newspapers and periodicals

> Class in **658**

.4   Editorial management and journalistic techniques

> Of newspapers, periodicals, newsreels, radio, television
>
> Class news writing [*formerly* **070.4**] in **808.06**
>
> *For school journalism, see* **371.89**

.9   Historical and geographical treatment of newspapers and journalism

> Class treatment by country and locality in **071–079**

▶ ## 071–079 Treatment of newspapers and journalism by country and locality

Scope: specific general newspapers and works about them

If preferred, arrange newspapers alphabetically under **070**, using A1 for comprehensive works about them

071   In Canada and United States

072   In England and Wales

Class newspapers and journalism in Scotland and Ireland in **079**

073   In central Europe

074   In France

075   In Italy and adjacent territories

076   In Iberian Peninsula and adjacent islands

077   In eastern Europe

078   In Scandinavia

079   In other countries

080   **General collections and anthologies**

Scope: general collected essays, addresses, lectures [*all formerly* **040**], quotations

If preferred, arrange collections and anthologies alphabetically under **080**

▶ ## 081–082 English-language

081   American [*formerly also* 082]

English-language collections and anthologies of Western Hemisphere and Hawaii

Class other English-language collections and anthologies in **082**, collections and anthologies in other languages in **083–089** [*both formerly* **081**]

082   Other English-language [*formerly also* 081]

> Collections and anthologies outside Western Hemisphere and Hawaii
>
> Class American collections and anthologies in **081**, collections and anthologies in other languages in **083–089** [*both formerly* **082**]

─────────────

►   083–089 Other languages [*formerly* 081–082]

083   Other Germanic languages

> Class Scandinavian-language collections and anthologies in **088**

084   French, Provençal, Catalan

085   Italian, Romanian, Rhaeto-Romanic

086   Spanish and Portuguese

087   Slavic languages

088   Scandinavian languages

089   Other languages

090   **Manuscripts and book rarities**

> Description and history

091   Manuscripts

092   Block books

093   Incunabula

> Books printed before 1501
>
> Including books printed by Caxton [*formerly* **094**]

094   Books notable for printing

First editions, limited editions, special editions, typographic masterpieces

Class books printed by Caxton [*formerly* 094] in 093

For block books, see 092; *incunabula,* 093

095   Books notable for bindings

096   Books notable for illustrations and materials used

097   Books notable for ownership or origin

098   Works notable for content

Prohibited works, literary forgeries and hoaxes

099   Books notable for format

Miniature editions, unusual dimensions and shapes

Class microreproductions [*formerly* 099] in 001.5

---

100 **Philosophy and related disciplines**

Use 100.1–100.9 for standard subdivisions

Class philosophy of a specific subject with the subject, e.g., philosophy of history 901

► 101–109 Standard subdivisions of philosophy

101 Theory

102 Miscellany

103 Dictionaries, encyclopedias, concordances

105 Serial publications

106 Organizations

107 Study and teaching

108 Collections and anthologies

Class collected writings of individual philosophers in 180–190

109 Historical treatment

Not limited by period or place

Class history, description, critical appraisal, biographical treatment of philosophy of specific periods and places in 180–190

► 110–120 Metaphysics (Speculative philosophy)

110 **Ontology and methodology**

111 Ontology

Nature of relations and being

Class existentialism [*formerly* 111] in 142

For cosmology, see 113–119

.1 Existence and essence

.8 Transcendental properties of being

Unity, truth, goodness, evil, beauty (esthetics)

128   Man

His soul, mind, nature

For origin and destiny of the individual soul, see 129

129   Origin and destiny of the individual soul

Incarnation, reincarnation, immortality

130   Pseudopsychology, parapsychology, occultism

131   Pseudopsychology

Class physiological psychology [*formerly* 131] in 152

For pseudopsychology of character and mental capacity, see 137–139

.3   Personal well-being, happiness, success

Including extrascientific methods of eradicating mental disturbances

Class mental hygiene [*formerly* 131.3] in 614.58

[.34]   Psychoanalysis

Class psychoanalytic systems in 150.19, psychoanalysis as therapy in 616.89

[132]   Abnormal and clinical psychologies

Class in 157

133   Parapsychology and occultism

For esoteric and cabalistic traditions, see 135.4

.1   Apparitions (Ghosts)

.3   Divinatory arts

Crystal gazing, radiesthesia, geomancy, fortunetelling by cards, numbers, tea leaves, coffee grounds

For chiromancy, see 133.6; *dream books,* 135.3; *divinatory graphology,* 137

.4   Magic, witchcraft, demonology

133.5	**Mundane astrology**
	Zodiacal signs, horoscopes, ephemerides
.6	**Palmistry**
	Chirognomy and chiromancy
.8	**Extrasensory perception**
	Telepathy, clairvoyance, clairaudience, precognition
.9	**Spiritualism**
	Communication with discarnate spirits
[134]	**Hypnotism**
	Class in **154.7**
135	**Dreams and the mystic traditions**
	Class sleep phenomena in **154.6**, daydreams in **154.3** [*both formerly* 135]
.3	**Dream books**
.4	**Esoteric and cabalistic traditions**
	Mysteries of the ancient elements, Rosicrucian mysteries
[136]	**Differential and genetic psychology**
	Class in **155**

▶ **137–139 Pseudopsychology of character and mental capacity**

137	**Personality analysis and improvement**
	Including analytic and divinatory graphology (handwriting analysis)
	Class psychology of personality [*formerly* 137] in **155.2**
	For physiognomy, see **138**
138	**Physiognomy**
	Determination of character from analysis of features
139	**Phrenology**
	Determination of mental capacities from skull structure

140   Specific philosophical viewpoints

Class specific philosophers in 180–190, a specific branch of philosophy with the subject

141   Idealism and related systems and doctrines

Spiritualism, panpsychism, subjectivism, voluntarism, Platonism, Neoplatonism, transcendentalism, individualism, personalism, romanticism

142   Critical philosophy

Existentialism [*formerly* 111], Kantianism, neo-Kantianism, phenomenalism, phenomenology

143   Intuitionism and Bergsonism

For mysticism, see 149

144   Humanism and related systems and doctrines

Pragmatism, instrumentalism, utilitarianism

145   Sensationalism and ideology

146   Naturalism and related systems and doctrines

Dynamism, energism, materialism, positivism (Comtism), atomism, mechanism, evolutionism

147   Pantheism and related systems and doctrines

Panentheism, animism, vitalism, parallelism, occasionalism, monism, pluralism, dualism

148   Liberalism, eclecticism, syncretism, traditionalism, dogmatism

149   Other philosophical systems and doctrines

Nominalism, conceptualism, realism, neorealism, critical realism, mysticism, anthroposophy, optimism, meliorism, pessimism, rationalism, intellectualism, innatism, nativism, agnosticism, skepticism, nihilism, fatalism, semantics

For existentialism, see 142

150   Psychology

This schedule is completely new, prepared with little reference to earlier editions and assigning new meanings to many numbers. Such numbers are italicized

[.13]   Applied psychology

Class in **158**

.19   Systems, schools, viewpoints

Psychoanalytic systems [*formerly* **131.34**], speculative systems, functionalism, reductionism, Gestalt psychology, field theory

[151]   Intelligence and aptitudes

Class in **153.9**

[.3]   Comparative psychology

Class in **156**

152   Physiological [*formerly* 131] and experimental psychology

Class perceptual processes [*formerly* **152**] in **153.7**

.1   Sensory perception

Attributes, thresholds, discrimination, tests of visual, auditory, olfactory, gustatory, cutaneous, proprioceptive perceptions

.3   Movements and motor functions [*formerly* 158]

Automatic movements, e.g., reflexes, instinctive movements; habits and habit formation, e.g., motor learning, handedness, laterality, voluntary movements; special motor functions, e.g., locomotion, vocal and graphic expressions, coordination

.4   Emotions and feelings [*formerly* 157]

Including conation and feeling [*formerly* **158**], sentiments, attitudes, moods, dispositions

.5   Motivation (Drives) [*formerly* 159]

152.8	Quantitative psychology

Threshold, discrimination, reaction-time studies based on psychophysical methods

Class a specific application with the subject

153 Intelligence, intellectual and conscious mental processes

.1 Memory and learning [*formerly* 154]

.2 Ideation

Association of ideas, concepts and concept formation, abstraction, inspiration

.3 Imagination and imagery [*formerly* 155]

Eidetic imagery, creativity

.4 Cognition (Knowledge)

Intuition [*formerly* **156**], thought and thinking, reasoning, value, judgment

For ideation, see **153.2**

.7 Perceptual processes [*formerly* 152]

Perceptual apprehension and understanding

Including basic elements, e.g., attention, apperception, preperception, subliminal perception; perceptual errors (normal illusions); types of perception, e.g., space, time, rhythm, movement

For sensory perception, see **152.1**; *extrasensory perception,* **133.8**

.8 Volition (Will) [*formerly* 159]

Class depth psychology [*formerly* **153.8**] in **154**

.9 Intelligence and aptitudes [*formerly* 151]

Factors affecting intelligence, intelligence and aptitude tests, superior intelligence

For exceptional children, see **155.45**

154	**Subconscious states and processes**
	Depth psychology [*formerly* 153.8]
	Class memory and learning [*formerly* 154] in 153.1
.2	**The subconscious**
.3	**Secondary consciousness**
	Daydreams [*formerly* 135], fantasies, reveries
.6	**Sleep phenomena** [*formerly* 135]
	Sleep, dreams, somnambulism
.7	**Hypnotism** [*formerly* 134]
155	**Differential and genetic psychology** [*formerly* 136]
	Class imagination and imagery [*formerly* 155] in 153.3
.2	**Individual psychology**
	Personality [*formerly* 137], character, individuality
	Including adaptability [*formerly* 159], individual differences, personality traits and determinants, typology
.28	**Appraisals and tests**
	Diagnostic graphology (handwriting analysis), inventories and questionnaires, projective techniques, e.g., Rorschach, Szondi, thematic apperception tests
.3	**Sex psychology**

▶ _____

155.4–155.7 Developmental psychology

For sex psychology, see 155.3

.4	**Child psychology**
	Thru age eleven
.41	**Basic behavior patterns**
	Motor, adaptive, personal-social behavior

▶ ────────

155.42–155.45 Specific groupings

Observe the following table of precedence, e.g., preschool boys **155.42**

> Exceptional children
> By class, type, relationships
> By age groups
> By sex

155.42   By age groups

> Infants, preschool children, school children

.43   By sex

.44   By class, type, relationships

> The only child, brothers and sisters, adopted and foster children, institutionalized children

.45   Exceptional children

.5   Adolescents

> Ages twelve to twenty

.6   Adults and aged

.7   Evolutional psychology

> Influence of heredity on personal characteristics

.8   Ethnopsychology and national psychology

.9   Psychology of influence, pattern, example

> Of physical, social, situational, housing and community, clothing, spatial and restrictive influences

156   Comparative psychology [*formerly* 151.3]

> Ontogenic and phylogenic studies of behavior mechanisms in lower organisms
>
> Class intuition [*formerly* **156**] in **153.4**

157 Abnormal and clinical psychologies [*both formerly* 132]

> Behavior patterns, psychodiagnoses, rehabilitation of psychotic, psychoneurotic, mentally deficient individuals
>
> Class emotions and feelings [*formerly* 157] in **152.4**
>
> *For exceptional children, see* **155.45**

158 Applied psychology [*formerly* 150.13]

> Including successful living, interpersonal relations, interviewing, leadership, cooperation
>
> Class specific applications with the subject
>
> Class movements and motor functions in **152.3**, conation and feeling in **152.4** [*both formerly* 158]

.6 Vocational interests

.7 Industrial psychology

159 Other aspects

> Class volition (will) in **153.8**, adaptability in **155.2**, motivation (drives) in **152.5** [*all formerly* 159]

160 Logic

> Science of reasoning processes

161 Induction

> *For hypothesis, see* **167**; *analogy,* **169**

162 Deduction

> *For syllogism, see* **166**

164 Symbolic and mathematical logic

───────

► 165–169 Specific topics

165 Fallacies and sources of error

> Contradictions, paradox, fictions

166 Syllogism

167 Hypothesis

168   Argument and persuasion

169   Analogy

170   Ethics (Moral philosophy)

.202   Practical ethics (Conduct of life)

Guides for specific groups and classes of people

171   Systems and doctrines

Based on authority, self-realization, fulfilment of personality, conscience, evolution, education, altruism, egoism, achievement of happiness or pleasure

Class morals and duties in comparative religion in **291.5**; in a specific religion with the religion, e.g., Christian moral theology **241**

►
172–179 Applied ethics

Inherent rightness and wrongness of specific human qualities, relationships, activities

Class comprehensive works on practical ethics in **170.202**

172   Ethics of political relationships

Citizenship, public office, international relations

173   Ethics of family relationships

Marriage, separation, divorce, responsibilities of parents for children and home life, of children to parents

174   Professional and occupational ethics [*formerly* standard subdivision 069]

If preferred, class in standard subdivision **01**

175   Ethics of recreation

Sportsmanship, fair play, other ethical concepts concerning entertainment

176   Sexual ethics

Chastity, celibacy, continence, adultery, artificial insemination, prostitution, obscenity in art and literature

177 Ethics of social relations

Friendship, courtship, philanthropy, slavery, discriminatory practices, kindness, courtesy, hospitality, conversation, slander, personal appearance

Class etiquette in **395**

For sexual ethics, see **176**

178 Ethics of temperance and intemperance

In use of alcoholic beverages, tobacco, narcotics, food

179 Other applications of ethics

Cruelty to animals and children, courage, respect for human life, other vices, faults, virtues

---

► **180–190 Historical and geographical treatment of philosophy**

Scope: development, description, critical appraisal, collected writings, biographical treatment of individual philosophers regardless of viewpoint

Class historical treatment not limited by period or place in **109**

180 Ancient, medieval, Oriental philosophy

Do not use standard subdivisions

.1–.9 Standard subdivisions of ancient philosophy

181 Oriental

Not limited by period

Use **181.001–181.009** for standard subdivisions

► **182–188 Ancient Western**

► **182–185 Greek**

Class comprehensive works in **182**

For Skeptic and Neoplatonic philosophy, see **186**

182 Pre-Socratic

73

183	Sophistic, Socratic and related philosophies
184	Platonic
185	Aristotelian
186	Skeptic and Neoplatonic

▶ 187–188 Roman

For Skeptic and Neoplatonic philosophy, see **186**

187	Epicurean
188	Stoic
189	Medieval Western

Including early Christian philosophy

190 Modern Western philosophy

Scope: Christian philosophy

Class here comprehensive works on modern philosophy, on Western philosophy

For ancient, medieval, Oriental philosophy, see **180**

191	United States and Canada
192	British Isles
193	Germany and Austria
194	France
195	Italy
196	Spain and Portugal
197	Russia and Finland
198	Scandinavia
199	Other

200 Religion

Class comparative religion in **291**

.1–.3	Philosophy, theory, miscellany, dictionaries, encyclopedias
.4	Religious mythology
.5–.9	Other standard subdivisions

► 201–209 Standard subdivisions of Christian religion

201 Philosophy and theory

202 Miscellany

203 Dictionaries, encyclopedias, concordances

205 Serial publications

206 Organizations

207 Study and teaching

Class religious training and instruction in Sunday schools, church schools, vacation Bible schools in **268**

208 Collections and anthologies

209 Historical and geographical treatment

Class historical and geographical treatment of Christian church in **270**

210 Natural religion

Religious belief attained thru observation and interpretation of evidence in nature, speculation, reasoning

211 Knowledge of God

Theism, rationalism (Free thought), deism, agnosticism, atheism, skepticism, humanism, secularism, humanitarianism

212 Nature of God

Polytheism, dualism, monotheism, pantheism, theosophy, anthropomorphism

213 Creation

By fiat, by evolutionary growth and change

214 Theodicy

Vindication of God's justice and goodness in permitting evil and suffering

Including Providence

215 Science and religion

Antagonism and reconciliation

For creation, see **213**

216 Good and evil

For theodicy, see **214**

217 Worship and prayer

218 Immortality and eternity

219 Analogy

Religious belief based on correspondences

► **220–280 Christian religion**

220 **Bible**

For Biblical theology, see **230**

.01 Philosophy and theory

Including value [*formerly* 220.6]

.02–.09 Other standard subdivisions

Class concordances in 220.2, dictionaries and encyclopedias in 220.3

.1 Origins and authenticity

Canon, inspiration, authorship, prophetic message

220.2	Concordances and indexes
.3	Dictionaries and encyclopedias

▶ ### 220.4–220.5 Texts and versions

Scope: textual criticism

For commentaries, see **220.7**

.4 **Original texts and early versions**

Codices and translations into modern languages from Chaldee, Syriac, Hebrew, Samaritan, Ethiopic, Arabic, Latin, Greek, other early versions

Class translations of Vulgate text into modern languages [*formerly* **220.4**] in **220.5**

For translations of Hebrew and Greek texts into modern languages, see **220.5**

.5 **Modern versions**

Translations into modern languages from Vulgate [*formerly also* **220.4**], Hebrew, Greek texts

.52 **In English**

.53–.59 **In other languages**

Divide like **430–490**, e.g., German-language versions **220.53**

.6 **Interpretation and higher criticism**

Class value of Bible [*formerly* **220.6**] in **220.01**

For commentaries, see **220.7**

.7 **Commentaries**

Criticism and interpretation arranged in textual order with or without text

.8 **Special subjects treated in Bible**

[.88] **Bible as literature**

Class in **809.9**

220.9	Geography, history, chronology of Bible lands in Bible times
.91	Geography (Description and civilization)
.92	Collective biography
.93	Archeology (Material remains)
.95	History of events

Including Bible stories retold

Use **220.950 01 – 220.950 09** for standard subdivisions

▶   221–229 Specific parts of Bible

221   Old Testament

For specific parts of Old Testament, see **222–224**

.1–.9   General principles

Divide like **220.1–220.9**, e.g., commentaries **221.7**; but class individual and collective biography in **221.92**

▶   222–224 Specific parts of Old Testament

Do not use standard subdivisions

222   Historical books

Pentateuch (Torah), Joshua (Josue), Judges, Ruth, Samuel, Kings, Chronicles (Paralipomena), Ezra (Esdras 1), Nehemiah (Esdras 2, Nehemias), Esther

(Optional: Tobit (Tobias), Judith, deuterocanonical part of Esther; prefer **229**)

223   Poetic books

Job, Psalms, Proverbs, Ecclesiastes, Song of Solomon (Canticle of Canticles)

(Optional: Wisdom of Solomon (Wisdom), Ecclesiasticus (Sirach); prefer **229**)

224   Prophetic books

> Isaiah (Isaias), Jeremiah (Jeremias), Lamentations, Ezekiel (Ezechiel), Daniel, Hosea (Osee), Joel, Amos, Obadiah (Obdias), Jonah (Jonas), Micah (Micheas), Nahum, Habakkuk (Habacuc), Zephaniah (Sophonias), Haggai (Aggeus), Zechariah (Zacharias), Malachi (Malachias)
>
> (Optional: Baruch, Song of the three children, Susanna, Bel and the dragon, Maccabees 1 and 2 (Machabees 1 and 2); prefer 229)

225   New Testament

> *For specific parts of New Testament, see* 226–228

.1–.9   General principles

> Divide like 220.1–220.9, e.g., modern versions 225.5; but class individual and collective biography in 225.92
>
> > *For life of Jesus, see* 232.9

────────────

▶   226–228 Specific parts of New Testament

> Do not use standard subdivisions

226   Gospels and Acts

227   Epistles

> Epistles of Paul to Romans, Corinthians, Galatians, Ephesians, Philippians, Colossians, Thessalonians, Timothy, Titus, Philemon, Hebrews; Epistles of James, Peter, John, Jude

228   Revelation (Apocalypse)

229   Apocrypha, pseudepigrapha, deuterocanonical works

> Esdras, Tobit (Tobias), Judith, Esther, Wisdom of Solomon (Wisdom), Ecclesiasticus (Sirach), Baruch, Epistle of Jeremy, Song of the three children, Susanna, Bel and the dragon, Prayer of Manasses, Maccabees (Machabees), pseudo gospels, other Old and New Testament pseudepigrapha
>
> If preferred, class Tobit (Tobias), Judith, deuterocanonical part of Esther in 222; Wisdom of Solomon (Wisdom), Ecclesiasticus (Sirach) in 223; Baruch, Song of the three children, Susanna, Bel and the dragon, Maccabees 1 and 2 (Machabees 1 and 2) in 224
>
> Use 229.001–229.009 for standard subdivisions

► ## 230–270 Specific elements of Christian religion

If preferred, class specific elements of specific denominations and sects in **280**

230 Doctrinal theology (Dogma)

Scope: Biblical theology

Use 230.01–230.09 for standard subdivisions

.1–.9 Doctrines of specific denominations and sects

Divide like **281–289**, e.g., Methodist doctrines **230.7**

(Optional: specific doctrines of specific denominations and sects; prefer **231–236**. If option is chosen, add **0** to number resulting from division like **281–289** and divide further like **231–236**, e.g., Methodist doctrines on salvation **230.704**)

► ## 231–236 Specific doctrines

Scope: specific doctrines of specific denominations and sects; if preferred, class in **230.1–230.9**

Class doctrines on church government, organization, nature in **262**

231 God, Trinity, Godhead

For Jesus Christ, see **232**

232 Jesus Christ and his family

Including Christology

.9 Doctrines on family and life of Jesus

Do not use standard subdivisions

.91 Mary, mother of Jesus (Mariology [*formerly* 232.93])

Immaculate Conception, annunciation, virginity, assumption, sanctity and virtues, spiritual powers

232.92 **Infancy of Jesus**

Nativity, adoration of the shepherds, Magi, circumcision, massacre of innocents, flight into Egypt, childhood in Nazareth, presentation in temple, among doctors in temple

Including Holy Family [*formerly* **232.93**]

.93 **Mary's husband and parents**

Joseph, Joachim, Anne

Class Mariology in **232.91**, Holy Family in **232.92** [*both formerly* **232.93**]

.94 **John the Baptist**

.95 **Public life of Jesus**

Baptism, temptation, teachings, transfiguration, Last Supper, last words to disciples

.96 **Passion and death of Jesus**

Betrayal by Judas, trial and condemnation, crucifixion and death, burial, descent into hell

.97 **Resurrection, appearances, ascension of Jesus**

233 **Man**

Creation and fall, sin, accountability, soul, freedom of choice between good and evil

For eschatology, see **236**

234 **Salvation (Soteriology)**

Grace, faith, redemption, regeneration, repentance, obedience, justification, sanctification, predestination and free will

Including sacraments as means of grace

235 **Invisible world**

Saints, angels, devils, demons

236 **Eschatology**

Including future state of man (life after death) [*formerly* **237**]

[237]   Future state of man (Life after death)

        Class in **236**

238   Creeds, confessions of faith, covenants, catechisms

        Class a specific doctrine with the subject

239   Apologetics and polemics

        Exposition of Christian doctrines refuting alleged errors in other systems

        Do not use standard subdivisions

        Class apologetics and polemics on a specific doctrine with the subject

240   **Moral and devotional theology**

241   Moral theology

        Including conscience, moral laws

        For conduct of Christian life, see **248.4**

    .3   Sins and vices

    .4   Virtues

    .5   Codes of conduct

        Ten Commandments, Golden Rule, precepts of church

▶   242–245 Devotional texts

242   Prayers [*formerly* 248], meditations, contemplations

        Class value of contemplation in **248.3**, devotional sermons in **252** [*both formerly* **242**]

▶   242.2–242.4 For specific times and occasions

    .2   Daily

    .3   For religious occasions

        Feast and fast days of liturgical year

    .4   For consolation in times of illness, troubles, bereavement

▶   242.7–242.8 Prayers

Class prayers for specific times and occasions in **242.2–242.4**

242.7   Specific prayers and groups of prayers

To God and specific saints

.8   Collections of prayers

For specific groups of prayers, see **242.7**

243   Evangelistic writings

Works designed to convert readers, promote repentance

Class evangelistic sermons [*formerly* **243**] in **252**

245   Hymns

Without music

Class metrical versions of Psalms in **223**

▶   246–247 Art, artifacts, places

246   Symbolism and symbolic objects and places

Art and decoration in services and buildings

247   Sacred furniture, vestments, insignia

▶   248–249 Practice of religion in personal and family life

248   Personal religion

Christian religion as an inner experience and guide to daily living

Class prayers [*formerly* **248**] in **242**

Class devotional texts in **242–245**

.2   Religious experience

Mysticism, conversion, moral rearmament, self-discipline

.3   Private worship, prayer, meditation, contemplation

Including value of contemplation [*formerly* **242**]

248.4	Conduct of Christian life
	Application of Christian virtues to everyday living

.5	Witness bearing
.8	Personal Christianity for specific classes of persons
	Including religious and monastic life [*formerly* 271]
	Class a specific aspect with the subject

249	Christian worship in family life

► **250–260 Practical theology**

250 Pastoral theology, parishes, religious orders

Do not use standard subdivisions

For public worship, see 264; *missions,* 266; *religious training and instruction,* 268

.1–.9 Standard subdivisions of pastoral theology

► 251–253 Pastoral theology

251 Preaching (Homiletics)

Use 251.001–251.009 for standard subdivisions

For sermons, see 252

252 Sermons

Scope: devotional sermons [*formerly* 242], evangelistic sermons [*formerly* 243]

Use 252.001–252.009 for standard subdivisions

Class sermons on a specific subject with the subject

.01–.09 By specific denominations and sects

Divide like 281–289, e.g., Anglican sermons 252.03

253 **Pastor**

Including life and person

▶ 253.5–253.7 Duties and responsibilities

For preaching, see **251**

.5 Counseling

.7 Evangelism

254 **Parish government and administration**

Including membership, programs, buildings and equipment

Use **254.001–254.009** for standard subdivisions

Class parish office methods [*formerly* **254**] in **651**

.2 In specific kinds of communities

Urban, suburban, rural

.3 Radio and television work

.4 Public relations and publicity

For radio and television work, see **254.3**

.8 Finance

Budget, income, methods of raising money, expenditures

Class compensation of clergymen [*formerly* **254.8**] in **331.2**

255 **Religious congregations and orders (Monasticism)**

Government, organization, administration

Use **255.001–255.009** for standard subdivisions

258 **Parochial welfare work**

Provision by parish and religious orders of assistance, guidance, cheer to disadvantaged members of parish

259 **Other parochial activities by parish and religious orders**

Recreation, work with children, soldiers, students, foreigners

► ## 260–280 Christian church

Class local church in 250

260   Social and ecclesiastical theology

Institutions, services, observances, discipline, work of
Christianity and Christian church

Including Christian church and the apostate and indifferent

261   Social theology

Attitude of Christianity toward and influence on secular matters
and other religions

.2   Christianity and other religions

.5   Christianity and intellectual development

[.6]   Christianity and world order

Class in **261.8**

.7   Christianity and civil government

Attitude toward and influence on political activities and
ideologies

Including religious freedom, theocracy

.8   Christianity and socioeconomic problems

Attitude toward and influence on social problems, the
economic order, international affairs

Including Christianity and world order [*formerly* **261.6**]

**262   Church government, organization, nature
(Ecclesiology)**

Governing leaders, parishes and religious orders in church
organization, specific administrative systems, general
(ecumenical) councils, church and ministerial authority

Including ecumenicalism [*formerly* **280.1**]

.7   Nature of the church

Attributes, marks, notes

262.9   Church law [*formerly* 348] and discipline

        Canon or ecclesiastical law

263   Days and times of religious observance

        Sundays, Sabbath (seventh-day observance), events of Church year, specific saints' days

        Class Sunday laws [*formerly* 263] in 340

264   Public worship

        Divine services, religious ceremonies, their conduct and texts

        Use 264.001–264.009 for standard subdivisions

        For Sunday schools, see 268; *other rites, ceremonies, ordinances,* 265

  .01–.09   By specific denominations and sects

        Divide like 281–289, e.g., Methodist services 264.07

265   Other rites, ceremonies, ordinances

        Preparation, instruction, performance

        Including sacraments

        Do not use standard subdivisions

        Class liturgy and ritual of sacraments in specific denominations in 264.01–264.09

  .01–.09   Standard subdivisions of sacraments

266   Missions [*formerly also* 274–279]

        Scope: missionary societies

        Use 266.001–266.009 for standard subdivisions

  .1–.9   Of specific denominations and sects

        Divide like 281–289, e.g., Presbyterian missions 266.5

267   Associations for religious work

        Salvation Army, Young Men's and Young Women's Christian Associations, denominational groups

        For missionary societies, see 266; *religious congregations and orders,* 255

268   Religious training and instruction

         In Sunday schools, church schools, vacation Bible schools

         For religious instruction in nonsectarian schools, see **377.1**

269   Organized spiritual renewal

         Revivals, camp meetings, retreats

270   **Historical and geographical treatment of Christian church**

         Use **270.01–270.08** for standard subdivisions

         For denominations and sects, see **280**

►   270.1–270.8 Historical periods

.1   Apostolic period to 325

.2   Period of ecumenical councils, 325–787

.3   Struggle between papacy and empire, 787–1054

         Including great schism

.4   Period of papal supremacy, 1054–1200

.5   Late Middle Ages to Renaissance, 1200–1517

.6   Reformation and Counter-Reformation, 1517–1648

.7   Peace of Westphalia to French Revolution, 1648–1789

.8   Modern church, 1789–

►   271–273 Specific topics of church history

271   Religious congregations and orders

         Use **271.001–271.009** for standard subdivisions

         Class religious and monastic life [*formerly* **271**] in **248.8**

272   Persecutions

273   Heresies

▶   *274–279* Treatment by continent, country,
         locality

        Class missions [*formerly* 274–279] in **266**

        Class geographical treatment of a specific element of the
        Christian church with the subject

274   Europe

        Add area notation **4** to **27**, e.g., Christian church in France
        274.4

275   Asia

        Add area notation **5** to **27**, e.g., Christian church in Japan **275.2**

276   Africa

        Add area notation **6** to **27**, e.g., Christian church in South Africa
        276.8

277   North America

        Add area notation **7** to **27**, e.g., Christian church in
        Pennsylvania **277.48**

278   South America

        Add area notation **8** to **27**, e.g., Christian church in Brazil **278.1**

279   Other parts of world

        Add area notation **9** to **27**, e.g., Christian church in Australia
        279.4

280   **Denominations and sects**

        Scope: general historical and geographical treatment of,
        comprehensive works on specific denominations and sects and
        their individual local churches

        Including Protestantism [*formerly* 284]

        Use **280.01–280.09** for standard subdivisions

        (Optional: specific elements of specific denominations and sects;
        prefer **230–270**)

  [.1]   Ecumenicalism

        Class in **262**

281	**Primitive and Oriental churches**

Including Apostolic Church, Monophysite, Coptic, Abyssinian, Nestorian churches

.9   **Eastern Orthodox**

Add area notations 4–9 to **281.9**

282   **Roman Catholic Church**

Class Oriental churches in communion with Rome in **281**

Add area notations 4–9 to **282**

283   **Anglican churches**

284   **Protestant denominations of Continental origin**

Lutheran churches, Calvinistic and Reformed churches in Europe, Hussites, Anabaptists, Albigenses, Waldenses, Huguenots, Moravians, modern schisms in Catholic Church, Arminianism, Remonstrants

Class Protestantism [*formerly* 284] in **280**

> *For Baptist churches, see* **286**; *Church of the New Jerusalem,* **289.4**; *Mennonites,* **289.7**

285   **Presbyterian, American Reformed, Congregational churches**

Do not use standard subdivisions

> *For United Church of Canada, see* **287**; *Christian Church,* **286**

286   **Baptist, Disciples of Christ, Adventist churches**

Do not use standard subdivisions

Including Christian Church

287   **Methodist churches**

Including United Church of Canada

288   **Unitarianism**

Unitarian Church, Unitarian Universalist Association

> *For Universalist Church, see* **289.1**

289	Other denominations and sects
.1	Universalist Church
.2	[Permanently unassigned]

If it is desired to give local emphasis and a shorter number to a specific denomination or sect not separately provided for, class it here

.3	Latter-Day Saints (Mormons)
.4	Church of the New Jerusalem (Swedenborgianism)
.5	Church of Christ, Scientist (Christian Science)
.6	Society of Friends (Quakers)
.7	Mennonites

Including Amish, Church of God in Christ

.8	Shakers

United Society of True Believers in Christ's Second Appearing

.9	Others

Including Assemblies of God, Churches of God, Church of the Nazarene, Jehovah's Witnesses, Pentecostal Assemblies, New Thought, United Brethren, Unity School of Christianity

If desired, class a specific denomination or sect requiring local emphasis in 289.2

For Salvation Army, see 267

290 Other religions and comparative religion

Scope: ecclesiastic laws [*formerly* 348]

291	Comparative religion
.2	Doctrinal theologies (Dogmas)

Divinities, man, his soul, salvation, invisible world, eschatology

.3	Forms of worship and other rites and ceremonies

Divination, witchcraft, sacred places and times, liturgy, public prayer, other public acts

For personal religion, see 291.4

291.4   Personal religion
            Religion as an inner experience and guide to daily living
            For moral theology, see **291.5**

.5   Moral theology
            Conscience, sins, vices, virtues, duties

.6   Leaders and organization

.7   Activities inspired by religious motives
            Religious wars, missions, religious training and instruction

.8   Sources
            Sacred books and scriptures, oral traditions, laws and
            decisions

.9   Sects and reform movements
            Class a specific aspect of a specific sect or reform movement
            with the subject

292   Classical (Greek and Roman) religion
            Divide like **291**, e.g., classical divinities **292.2**

293   Germanic religion

294   Brahmanism and related religions
            Including the Vedas

.3   Buddhism
.4   Jainism
.5   Hinduism

295   Zoroastrianism (Mazdaism, Parseeism)

296	Judaism
.1	Sources

Talmudic literature, Midrash, Haggadah, Cabala, Maimonides, Responsa, Halakah, other laws and decisions

For Old Testment, see **221**

.3	Doctrinal, moral, social theology
.4	Public services, rites, traditions

Liturgy, hymns, responsive readings, symbolism, ceremonies, comprehensive works on public and private worship and prayer

For personal and family religion, see **296.7**

.6	Leaders, organization, activities
.7	Personal and family religion

Religious experience, daily devotions and worship, observance of dietary laws, conduct of life

For moral theology, see **296.3**

.8	Sects and movements

Class a specific aspect of a specific sect or movement with the subject

297	Islam and religions derived from it

Do not use standard subdivisions

Including Islamic sects, religion of Black Muslims, Babism, Bahai faith

.01–.09	Standard subdivisions of Islam

298	[Permanently unassigned]

If it is desired to give local emphasis and a shorter number to a specific religion, class it here

299	Other religions

300 The social sciences

The sciences that deal with social activities and institutions

Use 300.1–300.9 for standard subdivisions

Class social, political, economic, diplomatic, welfare aspects of a specific war with the history of the war

▶ **301–309 General considerations**

301 Sociology

The science that deals comprehensively with social activities and institutions

.01–.09 Standard subdivisions

.1 Social psychology

Interaction between personality, attitudes, motivation of individuals and structure, dynamics, behavior of groups

.15 Group behavior

In opinion formation, for stability, change, leadership

Class behavior groups [*formerly* **301.15**] in **301.18**

.16 Mass communication processes

Including comprehensive works on mass communication [*formerly* **384**]

For group behavior for stability, see **301.15**; *effects of mass communication on cultural processes,* **301.2**

.18 Behavior groups [*formerly* 301.15]

Pressure groups [*formerly* **301.43**], the public at large, crowds, mobs, associations, meetings, cliques, gangs

301.2   Cultural processes

Progress and regress thru conflict, compromise, assimilation, acculturation, cooperation, communication, others

Including effects of invention, discovery, war, technology, automation, mass communication

[.209]   Historical and geographical treatment

Do not use; class in **301.29**

.29   Historical and geographical treatment

Add area notations **1–9** to **301.29**

Class cultural situation and progress in **901.9**

.3   Human ecology

Adaptation to spatial and temporal environment of populations within specific kinds of communities

Including migration within a country [*formerly* 325.1]

.4   Institutions and groups

Social characteristics and problems, impact on society as a whole

Use **301.400 1 – 301.400 9** for standard subdivisions

For behavior groups, see **301.18**

.41   The sexes [*formerly* 301.42]

Woman [*formerly* 396], man, celibacy, courtship, sex life outside marriage

.42   Marriage and family

Nature and forms of marriage, family and social change, husband-wife relationship, intrafamily relationships, family disorganization and adjustment

Class the sexes [*formerly* 301.42] in **301.41**

.43   Minors, middle-aged, aged

Class pressure groups [*formerly* 301.43] in **301.18**

301.44	**Systems and criteria of social distinction and stratification**
	By economic status, family and kinship, location and duration of residence, occupation, education, race, language
.45	**Nondominant groups**
	Scope: prejudice, discrimination, segregation, desegregation, integration, refugees and displaced persons
	Including socioeconomic, religious groups
.451	**Ethnic**
	Indigenous and nonindigenous
.453	**Of specific national origin**
.47	**Groups of persons with physical and mental illnesses and handicaps**
.5	**Sociology of everyday activities and preoccupations**
	Including securing housing [*formerly* 331.83]
309	**Social situation and conditions**
[.09]	**Historical and geographical treatment**
	Do not use; class in 309.1
.1	**Historical and geographical treatment**
	Add area notations 1–9 to 309.1
.2	**Planning**
	Development of programs on an international, national, state, provincial, local level to bring about desired change in conditions
	Including technical assistance, peace corps

► ### 310–390 Specific social sciences

The sciences that deal with specific social activities and institutions

310 Statistical method and statistics

Do not use standard subdivisions

.1–.9 **Standard subdivisions of statistics**

Class general statistics by continent, country, locality in modern world in **314–319**

311 Statistical method

Science of analysis and presentation of quantitative or qualitative data secured thru enumeration or experiment

Class mathematical calculations in **519**, statistical method applied to a specific subject in standard subdivision **01**

► ### 312–319 Statistics

Class statistics of a specific subject other than populations with the subject

312 Statistics of populations (Demography)

Vital statistics, somatology, population density, movement, other characteristics

► ### 314–319 General statistics by continent, country, locality in modern world

314 Europe

Add area notation **4** to **31**, e.g., general statistics of England **314.2**

315 Asia

Add area notation **5** to **31**, e.g., general statistics of Japan **315.2**

316 Africa

Add area notation **6** to **31**, e.g., general statistics of South Africa **316.8**

317   North America

> Add area notation **7** to **31**, e.g., general statistics of British Columbia **317.11**

318   South America

> Add area notation **8** to **31**, e.g., general statistics of Argentina **318.2**

319   Other parts of world

> Add area notation **9** to **31**, e.g., statistics of Australia **319.4**

320   **Political science**

> The science that deals with the institutions and processes of governmental regulation and control of men living in society
>
> *For public administration, see* **350**; *law,* **340**

.01   Philosophy and theory

> Class political theories and ideologies in **320.5**

.02–.09   Other standard subdivisions

.1   The state (The body politic)

.3   Comparative government

> Comparison of general structure of governments

.5   Political theories and ideologies

> Liberalism, conservatism, collectivism (socialism, communism, fascism)

.9   Political situation and conditions

> Add area notations **1–9** to **320.9**

321   Types and forms of states

> Including forms based on location of sovereignty in government, e.g., unitary state, federal state, empires, world state, ideal state (anarchy, Utopias), states with special limitations
>
> Do not use standard subdivisions

▶ ### 321.1–321.9 Types

Based on evolution of government

321.1   Primitive states and despotic states before 1500 A.D.

  .3   Feudal system

  .4   Pure democracy (Greco-Roman republicanism)

  .5   States controlled by select few

          Aristocracy, oligarchy, theocracy, plutocracy

▶ ### 321.6–321.9 Modern nation states

  .6   Monarchical absolutism

          16th–18th centuries

          Class totalitarian states [*formerly* 321.6] in 321.9

  .7   Modern constitutionalism

          Including constitutional or limited monarchy, socialistic state

          For representative democracy, see 321.8

  .8   Representative democracy

  .9   Totalitarian states [*formerly* 321.6]

          Bolshevik and fascist states

322   Relation of state to organized groups

        To Christian church and other religious bodies, labor, business, industry, protest and pressure groups

        Class relation of state to revolutionary and subversive groups in 323.2, to communities in 323.3, to education in 379, to political parties in 329

323   Relation of state to individuals and groups

        For relation of state to organized groups, see 322

  .1   Nondominant groups

          Ethnic, national, socioeconomic, religious

323.2	Revolutionary and subversive groups and individuals

Organized and unorganized groups

.3	Communities and social classes

Including slaves [*formerly* 326]

.4	Civil rights

.42	Equality before the law

.43	Rights of personal security

.44	Personal liberty and freedom of press

Including freedom of action, movement, conscience, religion, speech

For right of assembly and association, see **323.47**

.46	Right of private property

.47	Right of assembly and association

.48	Right of petition

.49	Limitation and suspension of individual rights and guarantees

.5	Political rights

Including representation

For suffrage, see **324**

.6	Citizenship

Duties and obligations of citizens, naturalization, nationality, expatriation, repatriation, passports and visas

324	Suffrage

Voting qualifications and procedures, elections

Add area notations **4–9** to **324**

325	International migration

.09   **Historical and geographical treatment**

Class treatment by continent, country, locality in modern world in **325.4–325.9**

.1   **Immigration**

Entrance into a country for the purpose of permanent residence

Class migration within a country [*formerly* **325.1**] in **301.3**

.2   **Emigration**

Departure from a country for residence elsewhere

Including political refugees, transfer of population

Do not use standard subdivisions

.3   **Colonization**

Do not use standard subdivisions

Class colonization in specific places in modern world in **325.4–325.9**

.4–.9   **International migration by continent, country, locality in modern world**

Migration to and colonization in specific places

Add area notations **4–9** to **325**

Class emigration from specific continents, countries, localities in **325.2**, colonization by specific countries in **325.3**

326	Slavery and emancipation

Class relation of state to slaves in **323.3**, slave trade in **380.1**, biographies of slaves associated with a specific subject in standard subdivision **092**, of slaves not so associated in **920** [*all formerly* **326**]

327   International relations

Affairs of the world political community

.09   Historical and geographical treatment

Class foreign policies of specific nations in 327.3–327.9

.3–.9   Foreign policies of specific nations

Attitudes, courses of action, objectives adopted by the government of a state in its relations with other states and regions

Add area notations 3–9 to 327

If desired, add 0 to 327.73 and again add area notations 4–9, e.g., foreign relations between United States and United Kingdom 327.730 42

328   Legislation

.1   Parliamentary rules and procedure

.3   Legislative branch of government

Parliaments, congresses, assemblies

.309   Historical and geographical treatment

Class treatment by continent, country, locality in modern world in 328.4–328.9

.4–.9   Legislative branch of government by continent, country, locality in modern world

Add area notations 4–9 to 328

329   Practical politics

Special-interest groups, study of public opinion, political propaganda, political parties and their organizations, nomination of party candidates, election campaigns, fund raising

Including political organizations and institutions [*formerly* 363]

Do not use standard subdivisions

For elections, see 324

───────────

►   **329.3–329.6 Specific political parties of United States**

          If preferred, class in **329.9**

329.3   Democratic Party

  .6   Republican Party

  .9   Political parties of other countries

         (Optional: specific parties of United States; prefer **329.3–329.6**)

         Add area notations 3–9 to **329.9**

330   **Economics**

      The science that deals with production, distribution, consumption of wealth

      For commerce, see **380**

 .01   Philosophy and theory

         Class general theories in **330.1**

 .02–.09   Other standard subdivisions

 .1   General systems, principles, theories

         Including theories of wealth, value, property

 .12   Systems of control

         Decentralized (free-enterprise economy), centralized (planned economy)

 .15   Integrated systems and schools

         Including capitalist and free-enterprise systems and schools

         (Optional: collectivist systems and schools; prefer **335**)

 .9   Economic situation and conditions

 .91–.99   Geographical treatment (Economic geography)

         If preferred, class in **910.1**

         Add area notations 1–9 to **330.9**

▶ ## 331–333 Specific factors of production

For entrepreneurship, see **338.7**

331   Labor

Utilization of manpower resources for production

.1   Industrial relations

Relations between labor and management

Including obtaining employment [*formerly also* **371.42**], labor force, labor stability and instability, unemployment and reemployment

Class labor courts [*formerly* **331.1**] in **347.9**

For industrial relations of special classes of workers, see **331.3–331.6**; *disputes between labor and management,* **331.89**

[.109]   Historical and geographical treatment

Do not use

.15   Conciliation practices

Settlement of labor-management differences thru discussions, deliberations, recommendations of third party

.2   Wages

Compensation in money, goods, services, computed on hourly, weekly, monthly, annual, piece basis; fringe benefits, e.g., pensions

Including compensation of Christian clergymen [*formerly also* **254.8**], teachers' compensation and pensions [*both formerly* **371.1**]

Class laws [*formerly* **331.2**] in **340**

For wages of special classes of workers, see **331.3–331.6**

.201   Philosophy and theory

Do not use for theories

[.209]   Historical and geographical treatment

Do not use

► ## 331.3–331.6 Special classes of workers

Industrial relations, wages, work periods, training and re-habilitation programs, organizations, disputes, specific occupations

Observe the following table of precedence, e.g., aged Negro women **331.3**

> Minors, middle-aged and aged people
> Women
> Substandard wage earners
> Other groups

331.3 **Minors, middle-aged and aged people**

.4 **Women**

.5 **Substandard wage earners**

Convicts, contract workers, apprentices, drafted workers, slaves, political and war prisoners, workers with physical and mental handicaps

.6 **Other groups**

Immigrants, ethnic groups, seasonal workers

.7 **Labor by occupation**

The professions, skilled crafts, public service, unskilled work, specific occupations

(Optional: specific subjects as professions or occupations; prefer standard subdivision **023**)

Do not use standard subdivisions

> *For a specific element of labor, see the subject, e.g., wages 331.2*

.702 **Choice of vocation**

331.8	Other topics

Class these topics in relation to special classes of workers in 331.3–331.6

.81	Occurrence and duration of work periods

Length of day and week, rest periods, shift systems, night work, overtime, leaves of absence

[.810 9]	Historical and geographical treatment

Do not use

[.82]	Industrial hygiene and accidents

Class industrial hygiene in 613.6, accidents in industry in 614.85

[.83]	Welfare services to and housing for laboring classes

Class welfare services in 362.8, housing in 301.5

[.85]	Workers' supplementary education

Class in 374

.86	Training and rehabilitation programs

Including apprenticeship and journeymen programs

.88	Labor organizations (Labor unions)

Trade, industrial, craft, company unions

Use 331.880 01 – 331.880 08 for standard subdivisions

.880 9	Historical and geographical treatment

Add area notations 3–9 to 331.880 9

.881	In specific occupations
.889	Open, union, closed shop

.89	Disputes between labor and management

Retaliatory measures by labor and management, e.g., strikes, sabotage, boycotts, lockouts, injunctions, political action

Including government intervention

332   Lucrative capital

     Former heading: Financial economics

     Theory, formation, manipulation, utilization, exchange of money, deposits, credit, evidences of ownership

     For public finance, see **336**; *cooperative systems,* **334**

.06   Organizations

     Class financial institutions in **332.1–332.3**

    ▶   332.1–332.3 Financial institutions and their functions

     For clearinghouses, see **332.7**

.1   Banks and banking

     Central, commercial, private, international

     Including safe-deposit services [*formerly* **332.2**]

     For savings banks and banking, see **332.2**

.2   Savings banks and banking

     Including savings departments of commercial banks

     Class safe-deposit services [*formerly* **332.2**] in **332.1**

.3   Credit and loan institutions and their functions

     Land banks, building and loan associations, pawnshops, personal loan and sales finance institutions

    ▶   332.4–332.8 Forms of lucrative capital

     Instruments and functions

.4   Money

     As a standard of value [*formerly also* **332.5**], a medium of exchange; theories, foreign exchange, minting practices and policies

[.409]   Historical and geographical treatment

     Do not use

332.5	Noncommodity money and other mediums of exchange

Fiat and paper money, barter instruments, managed currency, social credit money

Class money as a standard of value [*formerly* 332.5] in **332.4**

.6	Investment finance

Including securities exchanges, brokerage firms, exchange of securities (trading procedures), investment banking, lotteries

.63	Securities (Evidences of ownership)

Description and evaluation of stocks, bonds, mortgages, mutual funds, commodities

.67	Investment and investments

Investment practices and techniques, foreign and domestic investments

.7	Credit

Personal loans, credit instruments, credit collapse and restrictions, clearinghouses; commercial, agricultural, real estate, industrial credit

.8	Interest and discount

Class interest and discount tables in **511.802 1**

.9	Counterfeiting, forgery, alteration

Of currency, securities, credit instruments

333	Land (Natural resources)
.001	Philosophy and theory

Class theories in **333.01**

.002–.009	Other standard subdivisions

.01	Theories

Including Ricardo's theory of economic rent

333.1–333.6 Specific forms of control

For control of specific types of natural resources, see **333.7–333.9**

333.1   Public land (Public domain)

Land over which government exercises sole rights of control

.2   Common land

Land over which each member of an association exercises equal rights of control

.3   Private land

Land over which single owner exercises right of control

Including land tenure, real estate

Class management of real estate business [*formerly* **333.3**] in **658**

For absentee ownership, see **333.4**

.4   Absentee ownership

.5   Rent

Tenancy, landlordism, agricultural rent

For urban rent, see **333.6**

.6   Urban rent

Ground and building rent

333.7–333.9 Specific types of natural resources

Ownership, control, economic importance, settlement, utilization, conservation policies

.7   Surface resources and general conservation policies

Including arid, semiarid, pasture, forest, agricultural, urban, recreational lands

Class conservation policies of other specific types of terrestrial resources in **333.8–333.9**

.8   Subsurface (Mineral) resources

.9   Other natural resources

Shorelands, submerged lands, water, air, space

▶   334–335 Special methods of organization for production, distribution, consumption

334   Cooperative systems

Joint ownership and operation of economic enterprises and activities by voluntary groups for their own benefit

335   Collectivist systems and schools

Integrated assertions, theories, aims of economic and politicoeconomic ideologies

Including utopian, humanitarian, Christian socialist, anarchist systems

If preferred, class in **330.15**

Use **335.001–335.009** for standard subdivisions

For political theories and ideologies of collectivism, see **320.5**

.4   Marxian systems

.401   Philosophy and theory

Class basic concepts in **335.41**

.41   Basic concepts

Philosophic foundations and aims

.42   Scientific socialism

Including First International, Second International, Vienna International

.43   Revolutionary socialism (Communism)

For communist international organizations, see **335.44**

.44   Communist international organizations

.5   State socialism and social democracy

Nationalization of key industries

.6   Nationalist socialism

Including fascism, nazism, Falangism

336   Public finance

Financial transactions of governments and their units

Scope: local government finance [*formerly* 352]

Use 336.001–336.008 for standard subdivisions

Class financial administration of governments in 350

.09   Historical and geographical treatment

Class treatment by continent, country, locality in modern world in 336.4–336.9

―――――――

336.1–336.3 Specific elements

.1   Nontax revenues (Commercial and voluntary revenues)

Income from rents, franchises, sales of government property, deposits, investments, loans, gifts, fines, lotteries, grants

For revenues from fees and licenses, see 336.2

.2   Taxation (Compulsory revenues)

Direct and indirect taxes, revenues from fees and licenses, customs duties

Use 336.200 1 – 336.200 9 for standard subdivisions

.3   Credit, borrowing, expenditure

.4–.9   Public finance by continent, country, locality in modern world

Add area notations 4–9 to 336

[337]   Tariff

Class comprehensive works in 382, government regulation and control of international trade in 350

338   Production

Creation of wealth as form utility thru extraction and manufacture, as place utility thru transportation, as time utility thru storage, as ownership (possession) utility thru exchange, as personal service utility

Scope: specific firms and enterprises

Use **338.001–338.008** for standard subdivisions

Class marketing in **380.1**, public administration aspects of government control and regulation of production in **350** [*both formerly* **338**]

.09   Historical and geographical treatment

Industrial situation, existing and potential resources for production

Scope: industrial surveys, location of industries, productivity

Class a specific resource with the subject, e.g., water **333.9**

▶   338.1–338.4 Specific kinds of industries

Production of specific kinds of goods and services

For systems and organization of production, see **338.6–338.8**

▶   338.1–338.3 Primary (Extractive) industries

Scope: machines in production [*formerly* **338.4**], control, financial considerations, maladjustments in production

.1   Agricultural

Including food supply [*formerly* **641.3**]

.2   Mineral

.3   Other

Hunting and fishing industries

.4   Secondary industries

Service, professional, manufacturing, construction industries

Class machines in production in primary industries [*formerly* **338.4**] in **338.1–338.3**

112

| 338.5 | Prices and business cycles in relation to production |

For specific kinds of goods and services, see **338.1–338.4**

| .52 | Prices |

Class price control legislation [*formerly* **338.52**] in **340**

| .54 | Business cycles |

338.6–338.8 Systems and organization of production

| .6 | Systems |

Cottage industries, handicrafts, skilled trades, modern guilds, factory systems utilizing assembly-line and continuous methods

| .7 | Organization and structure |

Entrepreneurships, proprietorships, partnerships, corporations

For organization and structure of combinations, see **338.8**

| .8 | Combinations |

Organization and structure for massive production and control of production, e.g., monopolies, trusts, holding companies

| .9 | Production programs and policies |

Scope: control, subsidies, grants by government; nationalization

Use **338.900 1 – 338.900 9** for standard subdivisions

For specific kinds of industries, see **338.1–338.4**

| .91 | International |

Foreign economic policies, relations, assistance

| .93–.99 | National, state, provincial, local |

Add area notations **3–9** to **338.9**

339   **Distribution of capital goods and consumption of consumer goods**

   Former heading: Income and wealth

   For special methods of organization for distribution and consumption, see **334–335**

.2   **Distribution and accounting of income and wealth**

   Social and national accounting, economic budget

   For personal income, see **339.41**; *national income accounts,* **339.3**

.3   **National income accounts**

   Gross and net national product by expenditure or cost; valuation of income, wealth, capital

.4   **Consumption and conservation of income and wealth**

   Including deferred consumption (savings), underconsumption (poverty and hoarding), control of consumption, consumption of specific commodities

   Class consumer education [*formerly* **339.4**] in **640.73**

.41   **Personal income**

.42   **Cost and standard of living**

.49   **Conservation of national resources**

   For conservation policies for natural resources, see **333.7–333.9**

340   Law

Principles and regulations emanating from government and applicable to the people, in the form of legislation, custom, policies recognized and kept in force by judicial decision

Use 340.01–340.09 for standard subdivisions

Class here the following topics formerly provided for as indicated:

Library laws	[021.8]
Sunday laws	[263]
Wage laws	[331.2]
Price control legislation	[338.52]
Administrative law	[351.9]
Correctional courts	[364.5]
School laws and regulations	[379.1]
Legal status of woman	[396]
Laws and regulations of public health	[614]
Copyright	[655.6]
Building laws and codes	[692]

If preferred, class law of a specific subject in standard subdivision 026

341   International law (Law of nations)

Laws, procedures, institutions that govern public relations between sovereign states, private relations between their citizens, in peace and war; international cooperation and international responsibility of states

Including jurisdiction on land and sea, in air and space

.1   Cooperation to promote peace and order

For pacific settlement of disputes, see **341.6**

[.106]   Organizations

Do not use; class specific organizations in **341.12–341.18**

▶   341.12–341.18 Specific organizations

Class divisions dealing with a specific subject with the subject

.12   League of Nations

341.13	United Nations
.132	Charter
.133	General Assembly and general committees
.135	Security Council and its committees
.137	Secretariat
	Executive office, departments, personnel
.139	Relationship to specific countries and regions
	Add area notations 1–9 to **341.139**
.18	Regional associations
.2	Treaties
	Process of treaty making, texts of treaties
.3	Law of war
	Law of land, sea, air warfare
.4	Criminal law
	Including law of extraterritorial crime, trials of war criminals
	For extraterritoriality, see **341.7**
.5	Special topics
	Including commercial law [*formerly also* 380], law of outer space, private international law
	For law of war, see **341.3**
.6	Pacific settlement of disputes
	Negotiation, good offices, conciliation and commissions of inquiry, outlawry of war, arbitration and mediation, compulsive measures short of war; armaments reduction, limitation, control
.7	Diplomacy
	Laws, rules, customs governing conduct of official relations between governments
	Including capitulations, extraterritoriality, diplomatic privileges and immunities, protocol
.8	Consular systems

►   342–349 Municipal (Internal) law

342   **Constitutional law**

           Fundamental law of states

           Use **342.001–342.007** for standard subdivisions

           Add area notations **1–9** to **342**

343   **Criminal law**

           Including punishments, specific kinds of offenses

  .09   **Historical and geographical treatment**

                Scope: penal codes, reports, procedure, trials, evidence, handbooks and outlines

                Add area notations **1–9** to **343.09**

344   **Martial law**

           Military authority to carry on government functions in times of war or emergency

►   345–346 United States and British statutes and cases

           Session laws and statutes at large, codes and revised statutes, law digests, reports, digests of cases

           If preferred, class in **349**

345   **United States**

346   **British**

           United Kingdom and all parts of Commonwealth

347   **Private law and judicial system**

           Including common law, law of persons, property equity (chancery)

           Do not use standard subdivisions

  .01–.09   **Standard subdivisions of private law**

───────────

►   347.4–347.7 Private law

347.4   Contract and quasi contract

.5   Tort, negligence, damage

.6   Domestic relations and succession

.7   Commercial law [*formerly also* 380]

      Including agency law, maritime law

.9   Judicial system

      Procedure, trials, rules

      Scope: courts of limited jurisdiction, e.g., labor courts [*formerly* 331.1]

      Class criminal system in **343**, administrative system in **340**

.99   Historical and geographical treatment of courts

      Organization, jurisdiction, history, procedure, trials, rules

      Scope: specific courts and court systems

      Add area notations **1–9** to **347.99**

[348]   Religious law

      Class Christian church law in **262.9**, ecclesiastic laws in other religions and in comparative religion in **290**

349   Statutes and cases other than United States and British

      (Optional: United States and British statutes and cases; prefer **345–346**)

      Add area notations **1–9** to **349**

350 Public administration

Structure and operation of agencies charged with conduct of governmental affairs

Including regulation and control of public utilities [*formerly* 380], of international trade [*formerly* 337], of public health [*formerly* 614], of production [*formerly* 338], of education [*formerly* 379.1]; administration of civil defense [*formerly* 355.23], of reformatories [*formerly* 364.7], of prisons [*formerly* 365]

Do not use standard subdivisions

> *For legislative branch of government, see* 328.3; *judicial system*, 347.9

351 Central government

National, state, provincial

Do not use standard subdivisions

> *For administration of specific national, state, provincial governments, see* 353–354; *military administration*, 355–359

351.1–351.3 Civil service

.1 **Personnel management**

Procedures by which employees are hired, managed, replaced

.3 **Civil service examinations**

Class examinations of local governments in 352, on a specific subject in standard subdivision 076 [*both formerly* 351.3]

.5 **Pensions**

► ### 351.7–351.9 Specific administrative activities and responsibilities

.7 **Finance and public welfare**

Financial administration, police organization and management, maintenance of public order and security, regulation and control of public morals and public health, fire and accident protection

Class United States Coast Guard [*formerly* 351.7] in 359.9

351.8   Other regulations and controls

> Of production, commerce, consumption, labor, social welfare, education, culture, religion, public works, public utilities, justice, foreign affairs, defense

.9   Governmental accountability

> Liability of state for officials and of officials to the state, control of internal administration
>
> Class administrative law [*formerly* 351.9] in 340

352   Local units of government

> Counties, urban and rural municipalities, special districts
>
> Including building codes [*formerly* 692], civil service examinations [*formerly* 351.3]
>
> Use 352.000 1 – 352.000 8 for standard subdivisions
>
> Class local government finance [*formerly* 352] in 336

.000 9   Historical and geographical treatment

> Class specific local units in 352.03–352.09

.03–.09   General administration of specific local units

> Add area notations 3–9 to 352.0, e.g., administration of New York City 352.074 71

───────

►   353–354 Administration of specific national, state, provincial governments

353   United States federal and state governments

> If preferred, class in 354
>
> Do not use standard subdivisions

.000 1–.000 9   Standard subdivisions of federal government

.001–.009   Civil service, specific administrative activities, governmental accountability in federal government

> Divide like 351.1–351.9, e.g., finance 353.007

353.03	Executive branch

Including relationship to legislature, judiciary, constitution

---

► 353.032–353.036 The presidency

.032	Powers, functions, privileges
.034	Term of office
.035	Executive messages, speeches, writings
.036	Impeachment and resignation

► 353.1–353.8 Specific executive departments in federal government

.1	Department of State
.2	Department of the Treasury
.3	Department of the Interior
.4	Post Office Department
.5	Department of Justice
.6	Department of Defense

Including Department of the Air Force [*formerly* **358.4**]

Class Department of the Navy in **353.7**

.7	Department of the Navy
.8	Other departments
.81	Department of Agriculture
.82	Department of Commerce
.83	Department of Labor
.84	Department of Health, Education, and Welfare
.85	Department of Urban Affairs and Housing (Proposed)
.9	State governments

Add area notations **4–9** to **353.9**, e.g., administration of government of Hawaii **353.996 9**

354   Other central governments

Scope: administration of air force departments [*formerly* 358.4]

(Optional: United States federal and state governments; prefer 353)

Add area notations 3–9 to 354

►   355–359 Military administration

Military art and science and their application to conduct of defense and warfare

Class general principles in 355, administration of defense departments, civil-military relations in 350

355   General principles

Scope: application to land warfare, to combined warfare

Use 355.000 1 – 355.000 9 for standard subdivisions

Class applications of general principles to air warfare in 358.4, to space warfare in 358.8, to sea warfare in 359, to specific kinds of land forces in 356–357

►   355.02–355.07 Basic considerations underlying military administration

.02   War and warfare

Types, sociology, economics, causes, results of war and warfare

.03   Defense

Mutual security pacts, military missions and assistance, military situation and policy

.07   Military research and development

.1   Military life and postmilitary benefits

Service periods and their termination, veterans' rights and benefits, living conditions, discipline, honor, remuneration, etiquette, rewards, uniforms, ceremonials

355.2 **Military resources**

Value, availability, mobilization, demobilization of manpower, womanpower, raw materials, industrial resources, transportation, communication, other power facilities

[.23] **Civil defense**

Class administration in 350, services in 363.35

.3 **Organization and personnel of military forces**

Units organized for administrative purposes, hierarchy, combat units, reserves, special services

.4 **Attack and defense plans and operations**

Logistics, tactics, strategy, deception, technical analyses of military events

.409 **Historical treatment**

Class geographical treatment in 355.47

.47 **Tactical and strategic geography**

.5 **Training maneuvers, exercises, drills**

Including grand maneuvers, basic training of units, maneuvers involving civil population, officers' maneuvers and exercises

.6 **Central administration**

Military administration at top level

For organization of military forces, see 355.3

.7 **Military installations and land reservations**

Description, operation, use

.8 **Military equipment and supplies (Materiel)**

Description, issue, operation, use, packing, shipping of ordnance, food, clothing, camp and transportation equipment

▶ ## 356–359 Specific kinds of technical and combat forces

Units and services

▶ ## 356–357 Land forces

Class conduct of air warfare in **358.4**, of sea warfare in **359**, comprehensive works on land warfare in **355**

For armored and technical land forces, see **358**

356   ## Foot forces

Infantry and specialized foot forces

357   ## Mounted forces

Horse and mechanized cavalry

358   ## Armored and technical land forces, air and space forces

Do not use standard subdivisions

.4   ### Air forces

Scope: conduct of air warfare

Including specific forces, e.g., bombing, pursuit and fighting, transportation, reconnaissance, communications

Use **358.400 1 – 358.400 9** for standard subdivisions

Class administration of United States Department of the Air Force in **353.6**, of other air force departments in **354** [*all formerly* **358.4**]

Class conduct of land warfare in **355**, of sea warfare in **359**

.41   ### Functions and organization

Divide like **355**, e.g., air force installations and land reservations **358.417**

.8   ### Space forces

Conduct of space warfare

359   Sea (Naval) forces

Scope: conduct of sea warfare

Use 359.001–359.009 for standard subdivisions

Class conduct of land warfare in 355, of air warfare in 358.4

.1–.2   Naval life and resources

Divide like 355.1–355.2, e.g., naval resources 359.2

.3   Organization and personnel of naval forces

Including units organized for administrative purposes, hierarchy, combat units, reserves, special services

.32   Types of ships

.4–.8   Other elements

Divide like 355.4–355.8, e.g., naval ordnance 359.8

For specialist forces, see 359.9

.9   Specialist forces

Marine, coast guard, technical forces

Including United States Coast Guard [*formerly also* 351.7]

360   **Welfare and association**

Do not use standard subdivisions

▶   361–365 General welfare

Public and private services, activities, methods intended to promote social well-being

Class a specific activity of general welfare not provided for here with the subject, e.g., education 370

▶   361–362 Social welfare

Assistance to the disadvantaged

361   Organization and practice of social welfare work

Use 361.001–361.008 for standard subdivisions

[.009]   Historical and geographical treatment

Do not use

125

361.2	Planning
.3	Casework
.4	Group work

> Social adjustment of individuals promoted by participation in voluntary groups and with assistance of group leader

.5	Disaster relief
.6	Public welfare work

> Class a specific subject or kind of public welfare work with the subject

.7	Private welfare work

> Including fund raising
>
> Class a specific subject or kind of private welfare work with the subject
>
> *For parochial welfare work, see* **258**

.8	Community organization

> Coordination thru social service exchanges, community chests, united charities

362	Welfare services to special groups

> Scope: rehabilitation
>
> Class welfare services to criminals and delinquents in **364.6–364.8**

[.09]	Historical and geographical treatment

> Do not use

───────────

► 362.1–362.4 To those suffering illnesses and handicaps

> Services of general and special hospitals, clinics, sanitariums, nursing and custodial homes; medical social work; preparation and maintenance of records
>
> *For services to the aged and infirm, see* **362.6**; *to the young,* **362.7**

.1	To the physically ill

362.2	To the mentally ill
.3	To the mentally retarded
.4	To those suffering physical handicaps and disablements

> Services to the blind, partially sighted, deaf, deaf-mute, hard-of-hearing, crippled

.5	To the poor

> Including legal aid
>
> Class other specialized services with the subject

.6	To the aged and infirm, to survivors and dependents
.7	To the young (Child welfare)

> Aid to infants, children, adolescents thru aid to mothers, adoption and placement services, child guidance clinics, junior republics

.8	To other groups

> To laboring classes [*formerly* 331.83], families, unmarried mothers, minority groups, victims of crimes of violence

363	Other services

> Class political organizations and institutions [*formerly* 363] in 329

.2	Police services

> *For services in support of order and security, see* 363.3

.3	Services in support of order and security

> Including protection of freedom of information and association, control of explosives and firearms, disaster and emergency planning, prevention of violence
>
> *For services for control of public morals, see* 363.4

.35	Civil defense [*formerly* 355.23]
.4	Services for control of public morals

> Control of liquor traffic, gambling, prostitution, drug traffic

363.5   Public works services

> Class a specific service with the subject

.6   Public utility services [*formerly* 380]

> Water supply, electric power, gas
>
> Class communication and transportation services in **380**

364   Criminology

> Scope: comprehensive works on criminology and criminal law
>
> *For criminal law, see* **343**; *penology,* **365**

[.09]   Historical and geographical treatment

> Do not use

.1   Offenses

> Class offenders [*formerly* **364.1**] in **364.3**

.12   Detection

> Investigation of crime, collection and interpretation of evidence, identification of criminals

---

►   364.13–364.17 Specific kinds of offenses

> Scope: case studies
>
> Class military offenses in **355.1**

.13   Against constituted authority

> Treason, espionage, graft, bribery, illegal voting, counterfeiting, smuggling, bootlegging, tax evasion, perjury, lynching, piracy, war crimes

.14   Against public health, safety, order

> Rioting, disorderly conduct, vagrancy, traffic violations

.15   Against the person

> Genocide, homicide, sex offenses, abduction, robbery, assault and battery, criminal abortion, libel, drug traffic

364.16	Against property

364.16   **Against property**
Larceny, frauds, vandalism

.17   **Against public morals**
Gambling, public drunkenness, obscenity and pornography, cruelty to animals

.2   **Causes of crime and delinquency**
Physical, mental, social, economic factors

.3   **Offenders** [*formerly also* 364.1]
Including criminal types
Class causes of crime and delinquency in **364.2**, prevention in **364.4**, correction in **364.6–364.8**

.35   **Predelinquents**
Potential, near, quasi-delinquents

.36   **Juvenile delinquents**

.37   **Adults**

.4   **Prevention of crime and delinquency**
Thru control of population and economic conditions, law enforcement, preventive police work

[.5]   **Correctional courts**
Class in **340**

▶   **364.6–364.8 Correction of crime and delinquency**
Scope: welfare services

.6   **Punishment and other methods**
Deprivation of liberty and other rights, capital punishment, conditional release
For correctional courts, see **340**

364.7	**Institutions**

Reformatories and houses of correction, treatment of their inmates

Class administration of reformatories [*formerly* 364.7] in 350

.8	**Discharged offenders**

Rehabilitation, other welfare services

365	**Penology**

Prisons, penitentiaries, jails, concentration camps, treatment of their inmates

Class administration of prisons [*formerly* 365] in 350

For reformatories and houses of correction, see 364.7

[.09]	**Historical and geographical treatment**

Do not use

► **366–369 Association**

Organization for common purposes of a fraternal nature or for mutual assistance

For cooperative systems for production and distribution, see 334

366	**Comprehensive works**

Including esoteric (secret and semisecret) associations and societies

Use 366.001–366.008 for standard subdivisions

For orders of knighthood, see 929.7

[.009]	**Historical and geographical treatment**

Do not use

367	**Social clubs**
[.09]	**Historical and geographical treatment**

Do not use

368   Insurance

> Association to spread risk
>
> Including insurance of libraries [*formerly also* 022]

.001–.009   Standard subdivisions

> Do not use for treatment by continent, country, locality in modern world

.1   Against damage to and loss of property

> Fire, disaster, riot, war risk insurance
>
> *For transportation insurance, see* 368.2; *liability insurance,* 368.5

.2   Against damage to and loss of property in transit (Transportation insurance)

> Marine, automobile, railroad, air transportation, postal insurance
>
> Including insurance against damage to and loss of instrumentalities of transportation

.3   Against death, old age, illness, injury

> Life insurance, annuities, accident and health insurance
>
> *For government-sponsored social insurance, see* 368.4

.4   Against poverty

> Government-sponsored social insurance: social security
>
> Including workmen's compensation, accident and health, old-age and survivors', unemployment insurance

.5   Liability

> Miscellaneous lines and instrumentalities of transportation

369   Other kinds of associations and societies

       Including hereditary, military, patriotic societies

   .4   Young people's societies

   .42   Boys'

       For Boy Scouts, see **369.43**

   .43   Boy Scouts

   .46   Girls'

       For Camp Fire Girls, see **369.47**

   .463   Girl Scouts and Girl Guides

   .47   Camp Fire Girls

   .5   Service clubs

       Including Rotary, Kiwanis, Lions

370   **Education**

       Class study and teaching of a specific subject at elementary level in 372.3–372.8, at higher levels with the subject

   .1   Philosophy, theories, principles

   .11   Aims, objectives, value

       Humanistic, moral, ethical, character education

   .12   Classification and other philosophical foundations

       Including idealism, realism, pragmatism

   .15   Educational psychology

       Investigation of psychological problems involved in education, together with practical application of psychological principles to education

   .19   Sociological aspects

       Educational sociology, fundamental education, comparative and intercultural education

       Including integration and segregation of racial groups [*formerly* 371.9]

371   The school

Organization and administration

Use 371.001–371.009 for standard subdivisions

For organization and administration of the school at a specific level, see the level, e.g., the elementary school 372.1

.1   Teaching and teaching personnel

Including classroom control [*formerly* 371.5]

Use 371.100 1 – 371.100 9 for standard subdivisions

Class personnel management in 658.3

Class nonteaching personnel in 371.2, teachers' compensation and pensions in 331.2 [*all formerly* 371.1]

.2   Educational administration

Including nonteaching personnel [*formerly* 371.1], matriculation, tuition, school day and year, grouping of pupils for instruction, promotion, commencement, dropouts, transfers

.26   Educational tests and measurements

Measurement of students' growth in subject areas by use of standardized achievement tests

Administration, interpretation, use

.27   Evaluation of pupils' progress

Measurement of growth in subject areas by examination based on specific courses of study or curriculums

Including tests, examinations, marking systems

.3   Methods of instruction and study

.32   Textbooks

Value and use

.33   Audio-visual materials for teaching

Methods and use of radio, phonograph and phonograph records, tape recorder and recordings, still and motion pictures, television, bulletin boards

Class lecture method [*formerly* 371.33] in 371.39

▶   371.36–371.39 Methods of organizing learning experiences

371.36   Project or unit method

.37   Discussion methods

> Seminars, buzz groups, conferences

.38   Laboratory method

> Field trips, work-study programs, field work

.39   Other methods

> Including lecture method [*formerly* 371.33], student exchange programs, individualized instruction

.4   Guidance and counseling

> Formal and informal

.42   Educational and vocational guidance

> Class comprehensive works on obtaining employment in 331.1, trade and vocational education in secondary schools in 373.2, adult vocational education in 374 [*all formerly* 371.42]

.46   Social guidance

.48   Group guidance

.5   School discipline

> Rewards, punishments, student government
>
> Class classroom control in 371.1, prizes in 371.89 [*both formerly* 371.5]

.6   Physical plant

> Including equipment, supplies, furnishings, facilities

.7   School hygiene

> Promotion and maintenance of health and safety programs
>
> Class physical education in 613.7, intramural and interscholastic athletics and games in 796, intramural and interscholastic sports programs in 371.89 [*all formerly* 371.7]

371.8 The student

    Nonacademic life and welfare

    Including attitudes, behavior, organizations, transportation, housing

.85 Greek-letter societies and fraternities

.89 Activities

    Programs and events sponsored or formed by schools or student organizations, carrying partial or no academic credit

    Including intramural and interscholastic sports programs [*both formerly* 371.7], prizes [*formerly* 371.5], school journalism

.9 Special education

    Education employing nonstandard curriculums for exceptional students

    Including students exceptional because of class distinction, race, national origin

    Class integration and segregation of racial groups [*formerly* 371.9] in 370.19

.91 Students with physical handicaps

    Blind, partially sighted, deaf, deaf-mute, hard-of-hearing, speech defectives, crippled

.92 Students with mental deficiencies

.93 Delinquent and problem students

.94 Emotionally disturbed students

.95 Gifted students

372 Elementary education

    Scope: elementary education of girls [*formerly* 376]

    For special education, see 371.9

[.09] Historical and geographical treatment

    Do not use

372.1   The elementary school

Organization [*formerly* 372.2], administration, curriculums

Class courses of study in specific elementary school subjects in 372.3–372.8

[.109]   Historical and geographical treatment

Do not use; class in 372.9

.2   Levels of elementary education

Class elementary school organization [*formerly* 372.2] in 372.1

.21   Preschool education

Nursery schools and kindergartens

Class storytelling in 372.6, songs in 372.8 [*both formerly* 372.21]

.24   Elementary grades

Primary and upper elementary

Class grades 7 and 8 when part of junior high school in 373.2

372.3–372.8 Elementary school subjects

Methods of instruction, courses of study, textbooks

.3   Science and health

.4   Reading

Including readers, remedial reading

Class spelling [*formerly* 372.4] in 372.6

.5   Creative and manual arts

Drawing, painting, modeling, sculpturing, sewing, other handicrafts

Class handwriting [*formerly* 372.5] in 372.6

372.6	**Language arts (Communication skills)**

Storytelling [*formerly* 372.21], spelling [*formerly* 372.4], handwriting [*formerly* 372.5], grammar, phonetics and speech, foreign languages, drama

For reading, see 372.4

.7	**Mathematics**

.8	**Other studies**

Music (including songs [*formerly* 372.21], social studies, physical education, history, geography

.9	**Historical and geographical treatment of elementary education and schools**

Add area notations 1–9 to 372.9

373	**Secondary education**

For special education, see 371.9

.09	**Historical and geographical treatment**

Class treatment by continent, country, locality in 373.3–373.9

.1	**The secondary school**

Organization, administration, curriculums

Class courses of study in specific subjects in 375, educational programs of secondary schools of specific types in 373.2

.2	**Types of secondary schools**

Based on specialization, e.g., trade and vocational education [*formerly* 371.42], military academies; on control, e.g., private day schools and boarding schools, public schools; on organization, e.g., junior and senior high schools; on curriculum, e.g., college preparatory, classical, Latin grammar schools

For church-supported schools, see 377

.3–.9	**Secondary education and schools by continent, country, locality**

Add area notations 3–9 to 373

374   Adult education

Voluntary, purposeful efforts toward self-development of adults, conducted apart from formal education by public and private agencies

Scope: workers' supplementary education [*formerly* 331.85]

Including adult vocational education [*formerly* 371.42], correspondence schools and instruction

Use 374.001–374.008 for standard subdivisions

For special education, see 371.9

[.09]   Historical and geographical treatment

Do not use; class in 374.9

.1   Self-education

.2   Group education

Including institutes and workshops [*both formerly* 374.8], special interest groups, group use of radio, television, other similar mediums

.8   Continuation schools

Schools above elementary level enabling young people in trade or industry to continue schooling in spare time

Class institutes and workshops [*both formerly* 374.8] in 374.2

.9   Historical and geographical treatment of adult education

Add area notations 1–9 to 374.9

375   Curriculums

Programs of study offered to students by schools

Use 375.000 1 – 375.000 8 for standard subdivisions

Class comprehensive works on curriculums at a specific level with the level

.009   Historical and geographical treatment

376   **Education of women**

> Including coeducation versus separate education for women
>
> Class specific colleges for women in 378.4–378.9, elementary education of girls in 372 [*both formerly* 376]

[.09]   **Historical and geographical treatment**

> Do not use

377   **Schools and religion**

> Monastic, mission, church-supported schools, and religious instruction in nonsectarian schools

378   **Higher education**

> *For special education, see* 371.9

.001–.009   **Standard subdivisions**

> Class directories of institutions, historical and geographical treatment by continent, country, locality in modern world in 378.4–378.9

.1   **Colleges and universities**

> Organization, administration, curriculums
>
> Including types and levels of institutions, e.g., senior, junior, evening colleges, graduate schools, extension
>
> Use 378.100 1 – 378.100 9 for standard subdivisions

[.2]   **Preparation of theses**

> Class in 808.02

.3   **Student costs and finances**

> Including educational exchanges, student loans and employment
>
> Class veterans' education benefits in 355.1
>
> Class endowment of research [*formerly* 378.3] in 001.4

.33   **Fellowships**

.34   **Scholarships**

378.4–.9   Higher education and institutions by continent, country, locality in modern world

> Scope: specific colleges for women [*formerly* 376]
>
> Add area notations 4–9 to 378
>
> If preferred, arrange specific colleges and universities alphabetically under each continent, and under specific countries requiring local emphasis, e.g., University of South Africa 378.6 S6
>
> (Optional: publications of specific colleges and universities; prefer specific subjects)

379   Governmental supervision and financial support of education

[.1]   School laws and regulations

> Class laws in 340, regulation and control of education in 350

.4–.9   Public education by continent, country, locality in modern world

> Add area notations 4–9 to 379

380   **Commerce**

> Publicly and privately owned and administered activities and facilities for human intercourse thru exchange of goods and services, communication, transportation
>
> Use 380.01–380.09 for standard subdivisions
>
> Class comprehensive works on public utility services in 363.6, public regulation and control in 350, management in 658, international commercial law in 341.5, domestic commercial law in 347.7 [*all formerly* 380]

.1   Exchange of goods and services (Trade) [*formerly* 382]

> Including marketing [*formerly* 338], slave trade [*formerly* 326], specific commodities and services
>
> Class specific kinds in 381–382

380.3   Communication services

> Class specific kinds in **383–384**

.5   Transportation services [*formerly* 385]

> Class specific kinds in **385–388**

▶   381–382 Exchange of goods and services (Trade)

> Scope: marketing, commercial policy, specific commodities and services
>
> Class comprehensive works in **380.1**

381   Internal commerce (Domestic trade)

382   International commerce (Foreign trade)

> Including tariff [*formerly* 337], trade between nations, between nations and their colonies, protectorates, trusts
>
> Class comprehensive works on exchange of goods and services [*formerly* 382] in **380.1**

▶   383–384 Communication services

> Class comprehensive works in **380.3**

383   Postal communication

.09   Historical and geographical treatment

> Do not use for national systems

.2   Use of postage stamps

> Class philately [*formerly* 383.2] in **769**

384   Other systems of communication

> Class comprehensive works on communication in **001.5**, on mass communication in **301.16** [*both formerly* 384]

▶   384.1–384.7 Telecommunication

.1   Wire telegraphy

> *For submarine cable telegraphy, see* **384.4**

384.4	Submarine cable telegraphy
.5	Wireless communication

Including radiotelegraphy, radiotelephony

.54	Radiobroadcasting [*formerly also* 791.44]
.55	Television

Broadcasting [*formerly* **791.45**] and closed circuit communication

.6	Wire telephony
.7	Alarms and warning systems

Against fires, air raids, storms, floods

.8	Motion pictures [*formerly* 791.43]
.9	Visual signaling

────────────

▶   **385–388 Transportation services**

Class comprehensive works in **380.5**

For postal communication, see **383**

385	Railroad transportation

Including transportation by standard and light railway systems, inclined and mountain railway systems, unitized cargo and ship railway systems

Class comprehensive works on transportation services [*formerly* **385**] in **380.5**

For local rail transit systems, see **388.4**

[.9]	Pipeline transportation

Class in **388.5**

386	Inland waterway transportation

Including ships and ports

387   Water, air, space transportation

> Do not use standard subdivisions
>
> *For inland waterway transportation, see* **386**

.01–.09   Standard subdivisions of ocean (marine) transportation

---

▶   387.1–387.5 Ocean (Marine) transportation

Class standard subdivisions in **387.01–387.09**

.1   Ports

.2   Ships

.5   Activities of merchant marine (Maritime transport)

> Including seaways (trade lanes), salvage operations

.7   Air transportation

.8   Space transportation

388   Ground transportation

> Other than nonlocal rail transportation

.1   Roads and highways

> Including vehicular bridges and tunnels

.3   Vehicular transportation

> Including traffic flow and maintenance, terminal and parking facilities

---

▶   388.34–388.35 Vehicles

.34   Conventional

> Carts, wagons, carriages, cycles, motor cars

.35   Air-cushion

.4   Local rail and trolley transit systems

> Underground (subways) and elevated systems, trolleycars and trolleybuses

.5   Pipeline transportation [*formerly* 385.9]

389   Metrology and standardization

> Weights and measures, standards for interchangeability and performance

390   Customs and folklore

> Scope: cultural anthropology [*formerly also* 572]
>
> Including food customs [*formerly also* 641.3]
>
> Do not use standard subdivisions

.01–.08   Standard subdivisions of customs

.09   Historical and geographical treatment of customs

> Scope: customs of specific continents, countries, localities in modern world [*formerly* 914–919]

▶   391–395 Specific customs

> Origin, description, comparison of customs, practices [*both formerly also* 398.3], taboos, manners, habits, conventions, rituals
>
> *For customs of war, see* 399

391   Costume

> Garments, hair styles, body contours, bathing, tattooing, use of cosmetics, perfume, jewelry
>
> Including fashion [*formerly also* 646]
>
> Use 391.001–391.009 for standard subdivisions
>
> Class art aspects of costume [*formerly* 391] in 746.9

392   Customs of life cycle

> Customs attendant upon birth, puberty, majority, family and home, sex, treatment of aged
>
> *For death customs, see* 393

393   Death customs

> Burial, cremation, embalmment, mummification, exposure, mourning customs

394	Public and social customs

Including eating and drinking customs, pageants, parades, fairs, games, dances, official ceremonies and observances, knightly customs, dueling, suicide

.2	Festivals and anniversaries

Including carnivals, e.g., Mardi gras celebrations

.26	Holidays

[.260 9]	Historical and geographical treatment

Do not use; class in **394.269**

.268	Specific holidays

.269	Historical and geographical treatment

Add area notations **1–9** to **394.269**

395	Etiquette

Codes of social and formal conduct

Including etiquette for special groups and occasions, of social letter writing, of hospitality and table manners

For military etiquette, see **355.1**; *protocol of diplomacy,* **341.7**

[396]	Woman

Class sociological aspects in **301.41**, legal status in **340**

[397]	Gipsies

Class in area **174**

398 Folklore

      Class belles-lettres in **800**

  .2 Tales and legends

  .21 Fairy tales

  .22 Tales and legends of heroes

  .23 Tales and legends of places

      Including tales of haunted places [*formerly* **398.3**]

  .24 Tales and legends of animals and plants

398.3–398.4 Subjects of folklore

History and criticism

  .3 The real

      Places, special seasons and days, persons, nature and natural phenomena, superstitions

      Class customs, practices in **391–395**, tales of haunted places in **398.23** [*all formerly* **398.3**]

  .4 The unreal

      Supernatural beings, e.g., demons, ogres, fairies, ghosts; imaginary places, minerals, animals, plants

---

▶ **398.5–398.9 Specific forms of folklore**

For tales and legends, see **398.2**

  .5 Chapbooks

  .6 Riddles

  .8 Rimes and games

      Nursery rimes, counting-out rimes, street cries and songs

  .9 Proverbs

399 Customs of war

      Weapons, dances, treatment of captives, e.g., scalping, cannibalism

400 Language

Expression and comprehension of ideas thru systematic symbolism
Class language of a specific subject with the subject

401 Philosophy and theory

Including universal languages [*formerly* 408.9],
psycholinguistics

402 Miscellany

403 Dictionaries, encyclopedias, concordances

405 Serial publications

406 Organizations

407 Study and teaching

408 Collections and anthologies

[.7] Dialectology

Class in 417

[.9] Universal and artificial languages

Class universal languages in 401, artificial languages in 499.9

409 Historical and geographical treatment

410 Linguistics and nonverbal language

Do not use standard subdivisions
Class translation [*formerly* 410] in 418

.1–.9 Standard subdivisions of linguistics

▶

411–418 Linguistics

Science and structure of spoken and written language

Scope: comprehensive works on Indo-European languages
[*formerly* 491]

Class linguistics of specific languages in 420–490

411   Notations (Alphabets and ideographs)

Including hieroglyphics [*formerly* 419]

Class phonetic transcription [*formerly* 411] in 414

412   Etymology

Phonetic, graphic, semantic development of words and morphemes

For notations, see 411; *phonology,* 414

413   Polyglot dictionaries and lexicography

414   Phonology

Including phonetic transcription [*formerly* 411], intonation

415   Structural systems

Former heading: Grammar

Morphology and syntax

416   Prosody

417   Dialectology [*formerly* 408.7] and paleography

418   Usage (Applied linguistics)

Including translation [*formerly* 410] and interpretation

Use 418.001–418.009 for standard subdivisions

For polyglot dictionaries, see 413

419   Nonverbal language

Class hieroglyphics [*formerly* 419] in 411

▶ ## 420–490 Specific languages

Scope: comprehensive works on specific languages and their literatures

For literatures of specific languages, see **810–890**

▶ ## 420–480 Indo-European languages

Class comprehensive works in **411–418**

For East Indo-European and Celtic languages, see **491**

420 English and Anglo-Saxon

Do not use standard subdivisions

.1–.9 ### Standard subdivisions of English

Class dictionaries of the language in **423**

▶ ## 421–426 Description and analysis of standard English

Class standard English usage in **428**

421 Written and spoken codes

Abbreviations, acronyms, punctuation, notation, capitalization, spelling, pronunciation, intonation, paleography

▶ ## 422–423 Lexicology

Scope: synonyms, antonyms, hononyms [*all formerly* **424**]

422 Etymology

Phonetic, graphic, semantic development of words and morphemes

Including foreign elements

For notation, pronunciation, intonation, spelling, see **421**

423 Dictionaries
.1 ### Specialized

Abbreviations, acronyms, synonyms, antonyms, homonyms

423.3–.9 Bilingual

Divide like **430–490**, e.g., dictionaries of German and English **423.3**

When dividing other languages as instructed under **430–490**, interpret this entry as **423.2–423.9** and divide like **420–490**

Class bilingual dictionaries with the language requiring local emphasis, e.g., libraries in English-speaking regions class dictionaries of German and English in **433.2**. If the two languages require equal emphasis, class with the language coming later in the sequence **420–490**

[424] Synonyms, antonyms, homonyms

Class lexicology in **422–423**, standard usage in **428**

425 Structural system

Former heading: Grammar

Morphology and syntax

426 Prosody

427 Nonstandard English

Description, analysis, usage

Including Middle English, regional variations

For Old English, see **429**

.09 Modern nonregional variations

Slang, ephemera, picturesque and exaggerated expressions

428 Standard English usage (Applied linguistics)

General English, formal English, informal English; synonyms, antonyms, homonyms [*all formerly* **424**]

Including translating and interpreting from other languages, spelling and pronunciation

Use **428.001–428.009** for standard subdivisions

For dictionaries, see **423**; *composition*, **808.04**

▶ 428.2–428.3 Expression

428.2 Structural approach

Formal presentation of grammar, vocabulary, reading selections

For reading, see **428.4**

.3 Audio-lingual approach

Informal presentation thru practice in correct usage

.4 Reading

Remedial and developmental

.6 Readers

Graded selections with emphasis on structure and vocabulary as needed

429 Anglo-Saxon (Old English)

▶ **430–490 Other specific languages**

Divide each language identified by * like 421–428, e.g., Hebrew language dictionaries **492.43**. Under languages having more than one entry in this table, divide each entry identified by * like the corresponding number or numbers under **421–428**, e.g., German language reading **438.4**

430 **Germanic languages [*formerly* 439]**

Do not use standard subdivisions

.1–.9 Standard subdivisions of German

Class dictionaries of the language in **433**

▶ **431–436 Description and analysis of standard German**

Class standard German usage in **438**

431 Written and spoken codes

Abbreviations, acronyms, punctuation, notation, capitalization, spelling, pronunciation, intonation, paleography

► ## 432–433 Lexicology

Scope: synonyms, antonyms, homonyms [*all formerly* **434**]

432   Etymology

Phonetic, graphic, semantic development of words and morphemes

Including foreign elements

For notation, pronunciation, intonation, spelling, see **431**

433   *Dictionaries

[434]   Synonyms, antonyms, homonyms

Class lexicology in **432–433**, standard usage in **438**

435   Structural system

Former heading: Grammar

Morphology and syntax

436   Prosody

437   Nonstandard German

Description, analysis, usage of Old High German, Middle High German, regional and nonregional variations

438   *Standard German usage (Applied linguistics)

General German, formal German, informal German; synonyms, antonyms, homonyms [*all formerly* **434**]

439   Other Germanic languages

Class comprehensive works on Germanic languages [*formerly* **439**] in **430**

   .3   Dutch, Flemish, Afrikaans
   .7   *Swedish
   .8   Danish and Norwegian languages

* Divide as instructed under **430–490**

440   French, Provençal, Catalan

Do not use standard subdivisions

.1–.9   Standard subdivisions of French

Class dictionaries of the language in **443**

► **441–446 Description and analysis of standard French**

Class standard French usage in **448**

441   Written and spoken codes

Abbreviations, acronyms, punctuation, notation, capitalization, spelling, pronunciation, intonation, paleography

---

► **442–443 Lexicology**

Scope: synonyms, antonyms, homonyms [*all formerly* **444**]

442   Etymology

Phonetic, graphic, semantic development of words and morphemes

Including foreign elements

For notation, pronunciation, intonation, spelling, see **441**

443   *Dictionaries

[444]   Synonyms, antonyms, homonyms

Class lexicology in **442–443**, standard usage in **448**

445   Structural system

Former heading: Grammar

Morphology and syntax

446   Prosody

447   Nonstandard French

Description, analysis, usage of Old French, Middle French, regional and nonregional variations

* Divide as instructed under **430–490**

153

448   *Standard French usage (Applied linguistics)

General French, formal French, informal French; synonyms, antonyms, homonyms [*all formerly* 444]

449   Provençal and Catalan

Do not use standard subdivisions

450   **Italian, Romanian, Rhaeto-Romanic**

Do not use standard subdivisions

.1–.9   Standard subdivisions of Italian

Class dictionaries of the language in 453

▶   451–456 Description and analysis of standard Italian

Class standard Italian usage in 458

451   Written and spoken codes

Abbreviations, acronyms, punctuation, notation, capitalization, spelling, pronunciation, intonation, paleography

▶   452–453 Lexicology

Scope: synonyms, antonyms, homonyms [*all formerly* 454]

452   Etymology

Phonetic, graphic, semantic development of words and morphemes

Including foreign elements

For notation, pronunciation, intonation, spelling, see 451

453   *Dictionaries

[454]   Synonyms, antonyms, homonyms

Class lexicology in 452–453, standard usage in 458

* Divide as instructed under 430–490

455   Structural system

> Former heading: Grammar
>
> Morphology and syntax

456   Prosody

457   Nonstandard Italian

> Description, analysis, usage of Old Italian, Middle Italian, regional and nonregional variations

458   *Standard Italian usage (Applied linguistics)

> General Italian, formal Italian, informal Italian; synonyms, antonyms, homonyms [*all formerly* 454]

459   Romanian and Rhaeto-Romanic

> Do not use standard subdivisions

460   **Spanish and Portuguese**

> Do not use standard subdivisions

  .1–.9   Standard subdivisions of Spanish

> Class dictionaries of the language in **463**

  ▶   461–466 Description and analysis of standard Spanish

> Class standard Spanish usage in **468**

461   Written and spoken codes

> Abbreviations, acronyms, punctuation, notation, capitalization, spelling, pronunciation, intonation, paleography

  ▶   462–463 Lexicology

> Scope: synonyms, antonyms, homonyms [*all formerly* 464]

462   Etymology

> Phonetic, graphic, semantic development of words and morphemes
>
> Including foreign elements
>
> *For notation, pronunciation, intonation, spelling, see* **461**

* Divide as instructed under 430–490

463   *Dictionaries

[464]   Synonyms, antonyms, homonyms
        Class lexicology in 462–463, standard usage in 468

465   Structural system
        Former heading: Grammar
        Morphology and syntax

466   Prosody

467   Nonstandard Spanish
        Description, analysis, usage of Old Spanish, Middle Spanish, regional and nonregional variations

468   *Standard Spanish usage (Applied linguistics)
        General Spanish, formal Spanish, informal Spanish; synonyms, antonyms, homonyms [*all formerly* 464]

469   *Portuguese

470   Italic languages
        Do not use standard subdivisions

    .1–.9   Standard subdivisions of Latin
            Class dictionaries of the language in 473

            ─────────────────

►   471–476 Description and analysis of standard Latin
            Classical Latin; classical revival (medieval and modern) Latin [*formerly* 479]
            Class standard Latin usage in 478

471   Written and spoken codes
        Abbreviations, acronyms, punctuation, notation, capitalization, spelling, pronunciation, intonation, paleography

* Divide as instructed under 430–490

► ## 472–473 Lexicology

Scope: synonyms, antonyms, homonyms [*all formerly* **474**]

472   ## Etymology

Phonetic, graphic, semantic development of words and morphemes

Including foreign elements

For notation, pronunciation, intonation, spelling, see **471**

473   ## *Dictionaries

[474]   ## Synonyms, antonyms, homonyms

Class lexicology in **472–473**, standard usage in **478**

475   ## Structural system

Former heading: Grammar

Morphology and syntax

476   ## Prosody

477   ## Old, Postclassical, Vulgar Latin

478   ## *Standard Latin usage (Applied linguistics)

Classical Latin; classical revival (medieval and modern) Latin [*formerly* **479**]; synonyms, antonyms, homonyms [*all formerly* **474**]

479   ## Romance and other Italic languages

Including Osco-Umbrian languages

Class description and analysis of classical revival (medieval and modern) Latin in **471–476**, standard usage in **478** [*both formerly* **479**]

For Etruscan, see **499**

.1   ## Romance languages

Class specific Romance languages in **440–460**

* Divide as instructed under **430–490**

480 Classical languages [*formerly* 489.1] and modern Greek

Class Latin in **471–478**

.01–.09 Standard subdivisions of classical languages

.1–.9 Standard subdivisions of classical Greek

Class dictionaries of the language in **483**

▶ **481–486 Description and analysis of standard classical Greek**

Class standard classical Greek usage in **488**

481 Written and spoken codes

Abbreviations, acronyms, punctuation, intonation, capitalization, spelling, pronunciation, paleography

Including Minoan Linear B

▶ **482–483 Lexicology**

Scope: synonyms, antonyms, homonyms [*all formerly* **484**]

482 Etymology

Phonetic, graphic, semantic development of words and morphemes

Including foreign elements

For notation, pronunciation, intonation, spelling, see **481**

483 *Dictionaries

[484] Synonyms, antonyms, homonyms

Class lexicology in **482–483**, standard usage in **488**

485 Structural system

Former heading: Grammar

Morphology and syntax

486 Prosody

* Divide as instructed under **430–490**

487	**Postclassical Greek**

Hellenistic and Byzantine Greek

Including Biblical Greek

488	***Standard classical Greek usage (Applied linguistics)**

Synonyms, antonyms, homonyms [*all formerly* **484**]

489	**Other Greek languages**
[.1]	**Classical languages**

Class in **480**

.3	***Modern Greek**

Katharevusa and Demotic

490 Other languages

491	**East Indo-European and Celtic languages**

Do not use standard subdivisions

Class comprehensive works on Indo-European languages [*formerly* **491**] in **411–418**

.01–.09	**Standard subdivisions of East Indo-European languages**

.1	**Indo-Iranian (Aryan) languages**

For Indo-Aryan (Indic) languages, see **491.2–491.4**; Iranian languages, **491.5**

▶ 491.2–491.4 Indo-Aryan (Indic) languages

.2	**Sanskrit**

Vedic (Old Indic) and classical

* Divide as instructed under **430–490**

▶ 491.3–491.4 Prakrits

Class nonstandard Sanskrit (Primary Prakrits) in **491.2**

491.3   Middle Indic languages (Secondary Prakrits)

Including Pali

.4   Modern Indic languages (Teritiary Prakrits)

Sindhi, Punjabi, Hindi, Urdu, Bengali, Assamese, Bihari, Oriya, Marathi, Gujarati-Rajasthani, Sinhalese, Dard, Pahari, Romany

.5   Iranian languages

Old and Modern Persian, Avestan (East Iranian), Pahlavi (Middle Persian), Ossetic, Kurdish, Pashto, Baluchi, Pamir, Tajiki

Class Armenian [*formerly* **491.5**] in **491.9**

.6   Celtic languages

Gaelic, Cornish, Welsh, Breton, Manx

.7   East Slavic languages

Do not use standard subdivisions

.701–.709   Standard subdivisions of Russian

Class dictionaries of the language in **491.73**

.71–.76   *Description and analysis of standard Russian

Class standard Russian usage in **491.78**

.77   Nonstandard Russian

Description, analysis, usage of Old Russian, Middle Russian, regional and nonregional variations

.78   *Standard Russian usage (Applied linguistics)

.79   Ukrainian and Belorussian

Do not use standard subdivisions

* Divide as instructed under **430–490**

491.8	Balto-Slavic languages

Common Slavic, Bulgarian, Macedonian, Serbo-Croatian, Slovenian, Polish, Czech, Slovak, Wendish

Do not use standard subdivisions

For East Slavic languages, see **491.7**; *Baltic languages,* **491.9**

.9	Baltic and other East Indo-European languages

Armenian [*formerly* **491.5**], Albanian, Old Prussian, Lithuanian, Latvian (Lettish), Anatolian, Tocharian, Thraco-Phrygian, Illyrian, Indo-Hittite

▶ ### 492–493 Afro-Asian languages

492	Semitic languages

Including Akkadian, Aramaic, Ethiopic, Samaritan, South Arabic, Canaanite-Phoenician, Minoan Linear A

.4	Hebraic languages

Do not use standard subdivisions

.401–.409	Standard subdivisions of Hebrew

Class dictionaries of the language in **492.43**

.41–.48	*Principles of Hebrew

.49	*Yiddish

.7	Arabic (North Arabic)

493	Hamitic and other languages

Old Egyptian, Coptic, Berber, Cushitic (Hamitic Ethiopian), Chad

For Hausa, see **496**

* Divide as instructed under **430–490**

▶   494–495 Asian and related languages

For East Indo-European languages, see 491; *Afro-Asian languages,* 492–493

494   Ural-Altaic, Paleosiberian, Dravidian languages

Altaic languages (Tungusic, Mongolic, Turkish); Uralic languages (Samoyedic, Hungarian, Finnish, Estonian, Lapp); Paleosiberian languages (Luorawetlin, Ainu, Gilyak, Ket); Dravidian languages (Tamil, Malayalam, Kanarese, Gondi, Khond, Telugu, Brahui)

495   Languages of East and Southeast Asia

Including Tibeto-Burman, Burmese, Thai, Vietnamese, Cambodian languages

.1   Chinese

Do not use standard subdivisions

.6   Japanese

.7   Korean

496   African languages

Including Hottentot, Bushman, Bantu, Hausa, Swahili

For Afro-Asian languages, see 492–493

497   North American Indian languages

498   South American Indian languages

499   Austronesian and other languages

Including Negrito, Papuan, Malayan, Polynesian, Melanesian, Micronesian, Australian, Basque, Elamitic, Etruscan, Sumerian, Caucasian languages

.9   Artificial languages [*formerly* 408.9]

Esperanto, Interlingua, Volapük

Do not use standard subdivisions

500   Pure sciences
   .1   Natural sciences
   .2   Physical sciences
   .9   Natural history

501   Philosophy and theory

502   Miscellany

503   Dictionaries, encyclopedias, concordances

505   Serial publications

506   Organizations

507   Study and teaching

508   Collections, anthologies, travels, surveys
   .3   Travels and surveys

   For geographical treatment of travels and surveys, see
   508.4–508.9

   .4–.9   Geographical treatment of travels and surveys

   Add area notations **4–9** to **508**

509   Historical and geographical treatment

510   Mathematics

   Use **510.01–510.09** for standard subdivisions

   .78   Computation instruments and machines

   Mathematical principles of mechanical,
   electromechanical, electronic calculating devices

   Including analog instruments and digital machines

511   Arithmetic
   .021   Tabulated and related materials

   Class tables in **511.9**

511.024		Works for specific types of users
		Class business arithmetic in **511.8**

.07   Study and teaching

        Class problems in **511.9**

.8   Business arithmetic

        Including mensuration, mercantile rules, calculation of interest

.9   Problems and tables

512   Algebra

    .021   Tabulated and related materials

        Class tables in **512.9**

.07   Study and teaching

        Class problems in **512.9**

.9   Problems and tables

▶   513–516 Geometries

513   Synthetic geometry

        For trigonometry, see **514**; *descriptive geometry,* **515**

.07   Study and teaching

        Class problems in **513.9**

.9   Problems

514   Trigonometry

.07   Study and teaching

        Class problems in **514.9**

.9   Problems

515   Descriptive geometry

516	Analytic (Coordinate) geometry
.07	Study and teaching

Class problems in **516.9**

.9	Problems

517	Calculus
.07	Study and teaching

Class problems in **517.9**

.9	Problems

519	Probabilities and statistical calculations

520	**Astronomy and allied sciences**

Do not use standard subdivisions

► **520.1–520.9 Standard subdivisions of astronomy**

.1	Philosophy and theory

Class natural astrology, ancient and medieval astronomy [*all formerly* **520.1**] in **520.9**

.2–.8	Miscellany, dictionaries, serial publications, organizations, study and teaching, collections

.9	Historical and geographical treatment

Including natural astrology, ancient and medieval astronomy [*all formerly* **520.1**]

521	Theoretical astronomy and celestial mechanics

Specific theories and their application to celestial bodies

522	Practical and spherical astronomy

Observatories, telescopes and other astronomical instruments, observational techniques, corrections

523   Descriptive astronomy

          Use **523.001–523.009** for standard subdivisions

  .01   Physical and chemical aspects

          Astrophysics, radio and radar astronomy

          Class spectroscopical methods in **522**

  .1   Physical universe (Cosmology)

          Origin, development, structure, destiny of universe

          Including astrobiology, Milky Way

  .2   Solar system

  .207   Study and teaching

          Do not use for planetariums

▶   **523.3–523.8 Specific celestial bodies**

          Physical features and constitutions, phases, orbits, distances, motions, eclipses, spectroscopy

          For transits, satellites, occultations, see **523.9**

  .3   Moon

  [.302 1]   Tabulated and related materials

          Do not use; class in **523.39**

  [.302 2]   Illustrations

          Do not use; class in **523.39**

  .39   Charts, photographs, tables

  .4   Planets

          For earth, see **525**

  [.402 1]   Tabulated and related materials

          Do not use; class in **523.49**

  [.402 2]   Illustrations

          Do not use; class in **523.49**

  .49   Charts, photographs, tables

523.5	Meteors and zodiacal light
.6	Comets
[.602 1]	Tabulated and related materials

Do not use; class in **523.69**

[.602 2]	Illustrations

Do not use; class in **523.69**

.69	Charts, photographs, tables
.7	Sun
[.702 1]	Tabulated and related materials

Do not use; class in **525**

[.702 2]	Illustrations

Do not use; class in **523.79**

.79	Charts and photographs
.8	Stars

For Milky Way, see **523.1**; *sun*, **523.7**

[.802 1]	Tabulated and related materials

Do not use; class in **523.89**

[.802 2]	Illustrations

Do not use; class in **523.89**

.89	Charts, photographs, tables

Including observers' atlases, star catalogs

.9	Transits, satellites, occultations

For moon, see **523.3**

525	Earth (Astronomical geography)

Constants, dimensions, heat, light, radiation, orbit and motions, seasons, tides, astronomical twilight and twilight tables, sun tables

For geodesy, see **526**; *physical and dynamic geology*, **551**

526   Mathematical geography
          Including geodesy

  .3   Geodetic surveying
          Surveys in which curvature of the earth is considered in
          measurement and computation

  .8   Map projections
          Networks of parallel lines and meridians for map drawing
          Class printing maps [*formerly* 526.8] in 655.3

  .9   Surveying
          Boundary, topographic, hydrographic surveying
          Including aerial and terrestrial photogrammetry
          Class engineering surveys in 622–628
              For geodetic surveying, see 526.3; *snow surveys,* 551.5

527   Celestial navigation
          Determination of geographic position and direction from
          observation of celestial bodies
          Class practical navigation with the subject
              For finding time, see 529

528   Ephemerides (Nautical almanacs)
          Class tables of specific celestial bodies in 523

529   Chronology
          Intervals of time, calendars, horology (finding and measuring
          time)
          Class extrameridional instruments, sidereal clocks and
          chronometers in 522

530   Physics

.01   Philosophy and logic

Class theories in **530.1**

.02–.09   Other standard subdivisions

.1   Theories

.11   Relativity theory

.12   Quantum theory

Matrix, quantum, wave mechanics

Class classical mechanics in **531–533**

.13   Statistical and kinetic theories

Statistical mechanics and quantum statistics

Class classical mechanics in **531–533**

.14   Field theories

Unified and quantum field theories, problem of many bodies

.15   Mathematical physics

.16   Measurement theory

.4   States of matter

Solids (solid-state physics), liquids, gases

Class plasma in **537.1**

531–538 Classical physics

531   Mechanics

Energetics, kinematics, dynamics, statics of solids and particles

Including simple machines

For mechanics of fluids, see **532**

.01–.09   Standard subdivisions

Class tables, review, exercise in **531.9**

.9   Tables, review, exercise

532   Mechanics of fluids

Hydrostatics, hydrodynamics, surface and transport phenomena, other mechanical properties of liquids

For mechanics of gases, see **533**

.001–.009   Standard subdivisions

Class tables, review, exercise in **532.9**

.9   Tables, review, exercise

533   Mechanics of gases

Statics, dynamics, surface and transport phenomena, other mechanical properties of gases

Including vacuum and vacuum production

.01–.09   Standard subdivisions

Class tables, review, exercise in **533.9**

.6   Aeromechanics (Aerostatics and aerodynamics)

.9   Tables, review, exercise

534   Sound and related vibrations

Including generation thru vibration, propagation (transmission), characteristics, measurement, analysis, synthesis of sound waves

.01–.09   Standard subdivisions

Class tables, review, exercise in **534.9**

.5   Related vibrations

Subsonic and ultrasonic vibrations

.9   Tables, review, exercise

535	Visible light and paraphotic phenomena

Former heading: Optics

Including theories, physical and geometrical optics, spectral regions, spectroscopy

.01–.09	Standard subdivisions

Do not use for theories

Class tables, review, exercise in **535.9**

.5	Beams and their modification

Polarization and amplification

Including amplification by stimulated emission of radiation (lasers)

.6	Color
.9	Tables, review, exercise

536	Heat

Theories, transmission (heat transfer), heat effects, temperature, cryogenics, calorimetry, thermodynamics

.01–.09	Standard subdivisions

Do not use for theories

Class tables, review, exercise in **536.9**

.9	Tables, review, exercise

537	Electricity and electronics

For magnetism, see **538**

.01–.09	Standard subdivisions

Class theories in **537.1**; tables, review, exercise in **537.9**

.1	Theories

Electromagnetic and corpuscular theories, plasma and plasma dynamics

.2	Electrostatics

Charge and potentials, generators, dielectrics

537.5   Electronics

> Emission, behavior and effects of electrons in gas and vacuum tubes, photoelectric cells and similiar mediums; spectroscopy, tubes, circuitry of radio waves, microwaves, X rays, gamma rays; electron and ion optics
>
> *For semiconductors, see* **537.6**

.6   Electric currents

> Direct and alternating currents, semiconductors, conductivity, thermoelectricity
>
> *For dielectrics, see* **537.2**

.9   Tables, review, exercise

538   Magnetism

> Magnets, magnetic materials and phenomena, magnetohydrodynamics, geomagnetism and allied phenomena
>
> *For atmospheric electricity, see* **551.5**

.01–.09   Standard subdivisions

> Do not use for theories
>
> Class tables, review, exercise in **537.9**

.9   Tables, review, exercise

539   Modern physics

> Molecular, atomic, nuclear physics
>
> Scope: interpretation of structure thru spectroscopy
>
> *For electronics, see* **537.5**

.01–.09   Standard subdivisions

> Class tables, review, exercise in **539.9**

.7   Nuclear physics

> Including fundamental radiations, subatomic particles, their acceleration, detection, measurement

───────────

► 539.75–539.76 Nuclear reactions

539.75 Transmutations

Natural (radioactive decay) and artificial transmutations

.76 High-energy reactions

.762 Fission

.764 Fusion

.9 Tables, review, exercise

540 Chemistry and allied sciences

Do not use standard subdivisions

───────────

► 540.1–540.9 Standard subdivisions of chemistry

.1 Early theories

Alchemy, phlogiston theory, philosopher's stone, other ancient and medieval philosophies

Class theoretical chemistry in **541**

.2–.9 Other

Class apparatus and equipment in **542**

───────────

► 541–547 Chemistry

541 Physical and theoretical chemistry

Systematic application of physical concepts and methods to chemical systems

Class physical and theoretical organic chemistry in **547**

542 Laboratories, apparatus, equipment

Including general procedures and manipulation of equipment

Class a specific application with the subject

───────────

► 543–545 Analytical chemistry

Class organic analytical chemistry in **547**

543   General analysis

> Use 543.001–543.009 for standard subdivisions
>
> *For qualitative analysis, see* **544**; *quantitative analysis,* **545**

544   Qualitative analysis

> Systematic macro and semiquantitative methods and procedures for detecting and identifying constituents of a substance
>
> Use 544.001–544.009 for standard subdivisions

545   Quantitative analysis

> Determination of the amount of a constituent in a substance
>
> Use 545.001–545.009 for standard subdivisions

546   Inorganic chemistry

> Elements and their inorganic compounds

547   Organic chemistry

> General, physical, analytical chemistry of nonpolar compounds

548   Crystallography

> Geometrical, chemical, mathematical, physical, structural, optical

549   Mineralogy

> Occurrence, description, classification, identification of naturally-occurring elements and compounds formed by inorganic processes
>
> *For economic geology, see* **553**

.09   Historical and geographical treatment

> Class geographical distribution of minerals in **549.9**

.1   Determinative mineralogy

> Determination by location, associations, and physical, chemical, crystallographic properties
>
> Class determinative mineralogy of specific minerals in **549.2–549.7**

▶ 549.2–549.7 Specific minerals

549.2 Native elements

Metals, semimetals, nonmetals

.3 Sulfides, selenides, tellurides, antimonides, sulfosalts

.4 Halides

.5 Oxides

.6 Silicates

.7 Other minerals

Phosphates, vanadates, arsenates, nitrates, borates, tungstates, molybdates, chromates, sulfates, carbonates

.9 Geographical distribution of minerals

Add area notations 1–9 to 549.9

550 Earth sciences

551 Physical and dynamic geology

Scope: geophysics and geochemistry of lithosphere, hydrosphere, atmosphere

For astronomical geography, see 525

.1 Gross structure and properties of the earth

Structure and properties of earth's interior and crust

For geomagnetism, see 538

.2 Plutonic phenomena

Volcanoes, earthquakes, fumaroles, hot springs, geysers

.3 Exogenous processes and their agents

Erosion, weathering, deposition, sedimentation, transport thru action of ice, water, wind, frost

551.4	Geomorphology

Origin, development, transformations of topographic features, e.g., continents, islands, mountains, valleys, caves, plains, oceans, inland waters

Class physical geography [*formerly* 551.4] in 910

► **551.5–551.6 Meteorology, climatology, weather**

.5   Descriptive and dynamic meteorology

Physics of atmospheric circulation, temperature, pressure, electricity, moisture

Including snow surveys

[.59]   Climatology and weather

Class in 551.6

.6   Climatology and weather [*formerly* 551.59]

Weather belts, forecasting, reports, artificial modification and control, microclimatology

.7   Historical geology (Stratigraphy)

Do not use standard subdivisions

For paleontology, see 560

.8   Structural geology (Tectonophysics)

Forms, position, deformation of rocks, e.g., stratifications, joints, cleavages, synclines, antisynclines, faults, folds, veins, dikes, necks, bosses, laccoliths, sills

.9   Geochemistry

Class chemical analysis of rocks and ores in 543

552   Petrology

Origin, occurrence, constitution, classification of rocks

Use 552.001–552.009 for standard subdivisions

For mineralogy, see 549; *economic geology,* 553

553   Economic geology

Quantitative occurrence and distribution of rocks, minerals, other geological materials of economic importance

> *For a specific aspect of specific geological materials, see the subject, e.g., prospecting 622*

▶   554–559 Regional geology

Geology of specific continents, countries, localities

Class a specific geological aspect of a region with the subject

554   Europe

Add area notation 4 to 55, e.g., geology of England **554.2**

555   Asia

Add area notation 5 to 55, e.g., geology of Japan **555.2**

556   Africa

Add area notation 6 to 55, e.g., geology of South Africa **556.8**

557   North America

Add area notation 7 to 55, e.g., geology of Ohio **557.71**

558   South America

Add area notation 8 to 55, e.g., geology of Brazil **558.1**

559   Other parts of world

Add area notation 9 to 55, e.g., geology of Australia **559.4**

560   **Paleontology**

  .1   Philosophy and theory

  .17   Stratigraphic paleobotany and paleozoology

Class specific fossils or groups of fossils in **561–569**

  .9   Regional and geographical treatment

Divide like **574.9**, e.g., hydrographic paleontology **560.92**

561   Paleobotany

          Descriptive and taxonomic

    .09   Historical treatment

              Do not use for regional and geographical treatment

▶   562–569 Taxonomic paleozoology

562   Invertebrate paleozoology

          For Protozoa, Parazoa, Metazoa, see 563; Mollusca and molluscoidea, 564; other invertebrates, 565

563   Protozoa, Parazoa, Metazoa

          Unicellular animals, sponges, corals, starfishes

564   Mollusca and molluscoidea

          Clams, mussels, oysters, chitons, toothshells, snails, slugs, whelks, octopuses, squids, devilfishes, moss animals, lamp shells

565   Other invertebrates

          Worms, cyclops, fish lice, barnacles, sand fleas, sow bugs, wood lice, sea mantles, squillas, sea onions, lobsters, crabs, shrimps, mites, ticks, spiders, harvestmen, scorpions, millipedes, centipedes, insects

566   Vertebrate paleozoology (Chordata)

          For Anamnia, see 567; Sauropsida, 568; Mammalia, 569

567   Anamnia (Cyclostomes, fishes, amphibians)

568   Sauropsida (Reptiles and birds)

569   Mammalia (Mammals)

570   **Anthropological and biological sciences**

[571]   Prehistoric archeology

          Class in 913

572 Human races (Ethnology)

> Origin, distribution, physical characteristics of races
>
> Including causes of racial differences
>
> Class cultural anthropology [*formerly* 572] in 390
>
> > *For ethnopsychology, see* 155.8

.8 Specific races

> Divide like 420–490, e.g., Semitic races 572.892

.9 Races in specific countries

> Add area notations 3–9 to 572.9

573 Somatology (Physical anthropology)

> Including prehistoric man, environmental effects on physique, pigmentation, anthropometry
>
> > *For ethnology, see* 572

.021 Tabulated and related materials

> Class statistical tables in 312

.2 Organic evolution of man

> Heredity and environment (genetics), variation as factors in evolution

574 Biology

> *For botanical sciences, see* 580; *zoological sciences,* 590; *special biological fields and techniques,* 575–579

.09 Historical treatment

> Class regional and geographical treatment in 574.9

.1 Physiology

> Circulation, respiration, nutrition, metabolism, secretion, excretion, reproduction, histogenesis, movements, biophysics, biochemistry

.2 Pathology

> Anomalies, malformations, deformations, diseases

574.3	Maturation

Embryology and gametogenesis

For histogenesis, see **574.1**

.4	Morphology and descriptive anatomy
.5	Ecology

Interrelation of organisms to environment and to each other

.6	Economic biology
.8	Histology and cytology

Study of minute structure of tissues, and structure and physiology of cells

For histogenesis, see **574.1**

.9	Regional and geographical treatment
.909	Zonal and physiographic treatment

Class insular biology in **574.91**, hydrographic biology in **574.92**

.91	Insular biology
.92	Hydrographic biology

Including marine biology

.929	Fresh-water biology (Limnetic biology)
.93–.99	Geographical treatment

Add area notations 3–9 to **574.9**

► **575–579 Special biological fields and techniques**

575   Organic evolution

Origin of species thru historic descent with modification

Including evolution thru sexual selection, evolutionary cycles, origin and evolution of sexes

Class organic evolution of man in **573.2**, of plants in **581**, of animals in **591**

.001–.009	Standard subdivisions

Class theories in **575.01**

| 575.01 | Theories |

Darwinian, neo-Darwinian, orthogenetic, mutation, Lamarckian, neo-Lamarckian theories

.1 Genetics

Heredity and variation as factors in evolution

For variation, see 575.2

.2 Variation

Physiological and environmental aspects, hybrids, mutations, sports

576 Microbiology

Including ultramicrobes (rickettsiae, viruses), microorganisms in relation to immunity and pathogenicity

For Thallophyta, see 589; Protozoa, 593

.1 General principles

Divide like **574**, e.g., fresh-water microorganisms **576.192 9**

577 General properties of living matter

Origin and beginnings of life, spontaneous generation, comparison of living and nonliving substances and processes, conditions necessary for life, vitalism versus mechanism, degeneration and death, sex in nature

For biophysics and biochemistry, see 574.1

578 Microscopes and microscopy

Slide preparation, description and use of microscopes

Class a specific application with the subject

579 Collection and preservation of biological specimens

Preparation and preservation of skeletons and total specimens, taxidermy, techniques of collecting and transporting, arrangement and maintenance in museums

580   Botanical sciences

> *For paleobotany, see* **561**; *arrangement in museums,* **579**

581   Botany

> Class specific classes, orders, families in **582–589**

   .09   Historical treatment

> Class regional and geographical treatment in **581.9**

   .1–.9   General principles

> Divide like **574.1–574.9**, e.g., plants of United States **581.973**

►   582–589 Taxonomic botany

582   Spermatophyta (Seed-bearing plants)

> Use **582.001–582.008** for standard subdivisions
>
> *For Angiospermae, see* **583–584**; *Gymnospermae,* **585**

   .1   Special groupings

> Class specific classes, orders, families in **583–585**

►   582.13–582.14 Herbaceous plants

Seed plants without persistent woody tissue

   .13   Flowering plants

> Class here comprehensive works on herbaceous and woody flowering plants
>
> *For woody flowering plants, see* **582.16–582.18**

   .14   Shrubs and vines

> Succulent, carpet, mat, cushion, bush herbals

▶   582.16–582.18 Woody plants

Flowering and nonflowering woody plants

582.16	Trees (Dendrology)
.17	Shrubs
.18	Vines

▶   583–584 Angiospermae (Flowering plants)

Class comprehensive works in **582.13**

583	Dicotyledones (Dicotyledons)
584	Monocotyledones (Monocotyledons)
585	Gymnospermae (Naked-seed plants)
586	Cryptogamia (Seedless plants)

         Use **586.001–586.008** for standard subdivisions

           For Pteridophyta, see **587**; *Bryophyta,* **588**; *Thallophyta,* **589**

587	Pteridophyta (Vascular cryptogams)

         Quillworts, ferns, club mosses, horsetail family

588	Bryophyta

         Mosses, liverworts, hornworts

589	Thallophyta

         Including lichens, fungi, molds, algae, diatoms, fission plants other than bacteria

.9	Schizomycetes (Bacteriology)

         Use **589.900 1 – 589.900 8** for standard subdivisions

590   Zoological sciences

For taxonomic paleozoology, see **562–569**; *arrangement in museums,* **579**

591   Zoology

Class specific classes, orders, families in **592–599**

.09   Historical treatment

Class regional and geographical treatment in **591.9**

.1–.9   General principles

Divide like **574.1–574.9**, e.g., animals of United States **591.973**

For human physiology, see **612**; *human anatomy,* **611**

▶   592–599 Taxonomic zoology

592   Invertebrates

Use **592.001–592.008** for standard subdivisions

For Protozoa, Parazoa, Metazoa, see **593**; *Mollusca and molluscoidea,* **594**; *other invertebrates,* **595**

593   Protozoa, Parazoa, Metazoa

Unicellular animals, sponges, corals, starfishes, hydras, medusas, jellyfishes, sea urchins, sea walnuts, comb jellies, sea cucumbers

594   Mollusca and molluscoidea

Clams, mussels, oysters, shipworms, chitons, tooth shells, snails, slugs, whelks, octopuses, squids, devilfishes, moss animals, lamp shells

595   Other invertebrates

Including worms, cyclops, fish lice, barnacles, sand fleas, sow bugs, wood lice, sea mantles, squillas, sea onions, lobsters, crabs, shrimps, mites, ticks, spiders, harvestmen, scorpions, millipedes, centipedes

595.7	Insecta (Insects)

Use **595.700 1 – 595.700 8** for standard subdivisions

.76	Coleoptera (Beetles)
.77	Diptera and related orders

Midges, gnats, mosquitoes, flies, fleas

.78	Lepidoptera

Moths and butterflies

.79	Hymenoptera

Ants, wasps, bees

596	Chordata (Vertebrates)

Including Tunicata (sea squirts and sea grapes)

Use **596.001–596.008** for standard subdivisions

For Anamnia, see **597**; *reptiles and birds,* **598**; *Mammalia,* **599**

597	Anamnia (Cyclostomes, fishes, amphibians)

Including caecilians, frogs, toads, salamanders, newts, mud puppies

Use **597.001–597.009** for standard subdivisions

.2	Cyclostomata (Lampreys)
.3	Chondrichthyes

Sharks, skates, rays, torpedoes, guitarfishes, sawfishes, chimeras

---

597.4–597.5 Osteichthyes

.4	Actinopterygii and related orders

Bowfins, river dogfishes, ganoids, sturgeons, paddlefishes, spoonbills, lobe-finned fishes, gars, lung fishes

.5	Teleostei

Morays, carps, catfishes, top minnows, sea horses, herrings, salmon, trout, tarpons, snappers, basses, mackerels, pompanos, tunas, swordfishes, other bony fishes

598   Reptiles and birds

  .1   Reptilia (Reptiles)

           Scope: herpetology

           For amphibians, see **597**

  .11   Lepidosauria

           Lizards and tuataras

           For Serpentes, see **598.12**

  .12   Serpentes (Snakes)

  .13   Chelonia (Turtles, tortoises)

  .14   Crocodilia (Crocodiles, alligators)

  .2   Aves (Birds)

           For specific orders of birds, see **598.3–598.9**

  .209   History of ornithology

           Class regional and geographical treatment in **598.29**

  .29   Regional and geographical treatment

  .291   Zonal and physiographic treatment

  .293–.299   Geographical treatment

           Add area notations 3–9 to **598.29**

►   598.3–598.9 Specific orders of birds

  .3   Gruiformes and related orders

           Cranes, limpkins, rails, gallinules, coots, gulls, skimmers, terns, auks, oyster catchers, plovers, woodcock, sandpipers, curlews, phalaropes, herons, bitterns, egrets, storks, ibises, spoonbills, flamingos

  .4   Anseriformes and related orders

           Swans, geese, ducks, mergansers, screamers, albatrosses, shearwaters, fulmars, petrels, pelicans, gannets, cormorants, darters, penguins, loons, grebes

  .5   Palaeognathae

           Ostriches, rheas, cassowaries, emus, kiwis, tinamous

598.6	Galliformes and Columbiformes

Curassows, guans, grouse, quails, pheasants, turkeys, domestic chickens, hoatzins, sand grouse, pigeons, doves

.7	Psittaciformes, Trogoniformes, Cuculiformes

Parrots, parakeets, macaws, lories, jacamars, puffbirds, honey guides, toucans, woodpeckers, flickers, piculets, trogons, plantain eaters, cuckoos, roadrunners, anis

.8	Passeriformes (Passerine, perching birds)

Flycatchers, larks, swallows, titmice, nuthatches, wrens, mockingbirds, thrushes, wagtails, waxwings, crows, magpies, jays, shrikes, starlings, vireos, blackbirds, tanagers, grosbeaks, finches, sparrows, buntings

.89	Coraciiformes and Apodiformes

Kingfishers, rollers, todies, motmots, bee eaters, hoopoes, hornbills, swifts, hummingbirds

.9	Falconiformes (Birds of prey)

Hawks, falcons, buzzards, vultures, ospreys, eagles, owls, oilbirds, frogmouths, potoos, goatsuckers

599	Mammalia (Mammals)

Use **599.001–599.008** for standard subdivisions

.1	Monotremata

Spiny anteaters, platypuses

.2	Marsupialia

Opossums, opossum rats, kangaroos, marsupial mice, wallabies, bandicoots, phalangers, koalas, wombats

.3	Unguiculata and Glires

Edentates, lagomorphs, rodents, insectivores, dermopterans

For Chiroptera, see **599.4**; *Primates,* **599.8**

.4	Chiroptera (Bats)

599.5   Cetacea and Sirenia

        Whales, dolphins, porpoises, sea cows

   .6   Paenungulata

        Elephants, conies, dassies, hyraxes

        For Sirenia, see **599.5**

   .7   Mesaxonia, Paraxonia, Ferungulata

        Perissodactyls (horses, asses, tapirs, rhinoceroses), artiodactyls (pigs, hippopotamuses, ruminants, camels), carnivores

   .8   Primates

        Lemurs, monkeys, marmosets, tamarins, apes

        For Hominidae, see **599.9**

   .9   Hominidae (Man)

600 Technology (Applied sciences)

601   Philosophy and theory

602   Miscellany

       Class patents and inventions in **608.7**

603   Dictionaries, encyclopedias, concordances

605   Serial publications

606   Organizations

  [.4]   Fairs, expositions, temporary exhibits, competitions

       Class in **607**

607   Study and teaching

       Including fairs, expositions, temporary exhibits, competitions [*all formerly* **606.4**]

  .4–.9   In specific continents, countries, localities

       Add area notations **4–9** to **607**

608   Collections, anthologies, patents, inventions

  .7   Patents and inventions

       Add area notations **1–9** to **608.7**

609   Historical and geographical treatment

610 Medical sciences

  .6   Organizations and professions

  .69   Medical professions

       Physicians, surgeons, medical technicians, physician-patient relationships

       For nursing profession, see **610.73**

610.7   Study, teaching, nursing practice

> Class experimental medicine in **619**

.73   Nursing profession

> Duties and practices of professional and practical nurses, attendants, aides, orderlies
>
> If preferred, class a specific kind of nursing with the subject, e.g., Red Cross and other public health nursing **614.073**
>
> *For home nursing, see* **649.8**

611   Human anatomy

> Abnormal, prenatal, microscopic, gross
>
> Use **611.001–611.009** for standard subdivisions
>
> *For pathology, see* **616.07**

612   Human physiology

> Functions, biophysics, biochemistry, innervation of human body, its specific systems and organs
>
> Use **612.001–612.009** for standard subdivisions
>
> *For pathology, see* **616.07**

.6   Reproductive system and developmental periods

> Use **612.600 1 – 612.600 9** for standard subdivisions

.61   Male reproductive system

.62   Female reproductive system

.63   Pregnancy

> *For embryology, see* **612.64**

.64   Embryology

> Use **612.640 01 – 612.640 09** for standard subdivisions

.65   Child development

.66   Adult development

> From adolescence thru climacteric
>
> *For aging, see* **612.67**

.67   Aging (Physical gerontology)

613	General and personal hygiene

Health and its preservation

For public health, see **614**

.07	Study and teaching

Including health education [*formerly also* **371.7**]

.1	Environment and health

Effects of climate, air, light, temperatures, humidity, air conditioning on health

For housing and health, see **613.5**

.2	Food and health

Food programs for general well-being and improved appearance

For beverages and health, see **613.3**

.3	Beverages and health

For alcohol, see **613.8**

.4	Care of person

Cleanliness and comfort thru bathing and adequate clothing

.5	Housing and health

.6	Health and well-being under unusual conditions

Industrial hygiene [*formerly* **331.82**], self-defense, military and camp hygiene, shipboard hygiene, survival instructions

.7	Rest, exercise, physical fitness

Including physical education [*formerly* **371.7**]

.8	Addictions and health

Habit-forming stimulants and narcotics as factors deleterious to health, e.g., alcohol, opiates, tobacco

613.9   Factors relating to heredity, sex, age
>   Including inherited mental and physical disorders

.94   Eugenic practices
>   Sterilization and birth control

.95   Sex hygiene

.97   Hygiene for specific age groups
>   *For a specific aspect, see the subject, e.g., cleanliness*
>   **613.4**

614   Public health
>   Safeguarding public health by registering, certifying, reporting
>   births, deaths, diseases; by inspecting, standardizing,
>   certifying, labeling common commodities; by providing
>   programs for disease control, sanitation and environmental
>   comfort
>
>   Class vital statistics in **312**, forensic medicine in **340**, medical
>   social work in **362**, toxicology in **615.9**
>
>   Class laws, regulations, legal aspects in **340**, public
>   administration aspects in **350** [*both formerly* **614**]

.07   Study, teaching, nursing practice

.073   Red Cross and other public health nursing
>   (Optional; prefer **610.73**)

.4   Control of disease
>   *For control of specific diseases, see* **614.5**

.5   Control of specific diseases
>   Including control of specific infectious diseases and
>   noncommunicable diseases, e.g., heart diseases, cancer

.58   Mental hygiene [*formerly* 131.3]

614.8	Accidents and their prevention
	Safety thru regulation, inspection, other protective measures
	Including first aid
.83	By machinery and hazardous materials
	Flammable materials, explosives, fireworks, electrical equipment and appliances, radioactive materials
.84	By fire
.85	In industry [*formerly* 331.82]
615	Therapeutics and pharmacology
	Class therapies applied to specific diseases in **616**
.9	Toxicology
	Source, composition, physiological effects, tests, antidotes of poisons
	Use **615.900 1 – 615.900 9** for standard subdivisions
616	Medicine
	Use **610.1–610.9** for standard subdivisions
	For specialized medicine, see **617–618**
.01	Medical microbiology
	Pathogenic microorganisms and their relation to disease
.07	Pathology
	Symptomatology and diagnoses
.08	Psychosomatic medicine

▶ 616.1–616.8 Diseases of specific systems and organs

.1	Diseases of cardiovascular system
	Diseases of heart, blood vessels, blood

| 616.2 | Diseases of respiratory system |

Otorhinolaryngology, diseases of trachea, bronchi, lungs, pleura, mediastinum

Use **616.200 1 – 616.200 9** for standard subdivisions

For otology, see **617**

| .3 | Diseases of digestive tract |

Nutritional and metabolic diseases; diseases of mouth, throat, pharynx, esophagus, stomach, intestines, rectum, anus, biliary tract, pancreas, peritoneum

Class laryngology in **616.2**

For diseases of endocrine system, see **616.4**; *dentistry,* **617**

| .4 | Diseases of blood-forming, lymphatic, endocrine systems |

Diseases of spleen, bone marrow, lymphatics, breast, pancreatic internal secretion; of thymus, thyroid, parathyroid, adrenal, pituitary, pineal glands

For diseases of blood, see **616.1**; *of urogenital system,* **616.6**; *nutritional and metabolic diseases,* **616.3**

| .5 | Diseases of integument, hair, nails (Dermatology) |

For allergies, see **616.9**

| .6 | Diseases of urogenital system |

Diseases of kidneys, ureters, bladder, urethra, prostate, penis, scrotum, testicles and accessory organs

For gynecology, see **618.1**

| .7 | Diseases of musculoskeletal system |

Diseases of bones, joints, muscles, tendons, fasciae, bursae, sheaths of tendons, connective tissue

For nutritional and metabolic diseases, see **616.3**

616.8	Diseases of nervous system (Neurology and psychiatry)

Use **616.800 1 – 616.800 9** for standard subdivisions

.801–.809   Standard subdivisions of neurology

616.85–616.86 Psychoneuroses

Class comprehensive works in **616.85**

.85   General works

Chorea, hysterias, epilepsy, speech and language disorders, cutaneous sensory disorders, migraine, disorders of personality, character, intellect

.86   Psychoneurotic addictions and intoxications

Alcoholism, metallic intoxications, addictions to narcotics, stimulants, tobacco

.89   Psychiatry

Functional diseases (psychoses) of nervous system, e.g., general paresis, manic-depressive psychoses, paranoia and paranoid conditions, schizophrenia, senile dementias

Including psychoanalysis as therapy [*formerly* 131.34]

Class puerperal psychoses in **618.7**

For psychoneuroses, see **616.85–616.86**

.890 073   Psychiatric nursing

(Optional; prefer **610.73**)

.9   Other diseases

Communicable diseases, allergies and anaphylaxis, diseases due to physical and climatic conditions, rheumatic fever, neoplastic diseases

Use **616.900 1 – 616.900 9** for standard subdivisions

Class communicable diseases predominantly affecting a specific part of the body with the part affected

.907 3   Communicable disease nursing

(Optional; prefer **610.73**)

──────────

► ### 617–618 Specialized medicine

For neoplastic diseases, see **616.9**

617   Surgery

Orthopedic, systemic, regional, plastic surgery; dentistry, ophthalmology and optometry, otology and audiology

Use **617.001–617.008** for standard subdivisions

618   Other branches of specialized medicine

──────────

► ### 618.1–618.8 Gynecology and obstetrics

Medical and surgical treatment

.1   Gynecology

Class malignant neoplasms of genital tract in **616.9**

.107 3   Gynecological nursing

(Optional; prefer **610.73**)

.2   Obstetrics

Symptomatology, diagnosis, prenatal care, multiple pregnancy

.207 3   Obstetrical nursing

(Optional; prefer **610.73**)

──────────

► ### 618.3–618.8 Diseases, disorders, management of pregnancy, parturition, puerperium

.3   Diseases of pregnancy

Ectopic pregnancy, fetal abnormalities, abortion, prematurity

.4   Normal labor (Parturition)

Mechanism and management of normal labor and childbirth

.5   Complicated labor (Dystocia)

.6   Normal puerperium

Postpartum management and care

618.7   Puerperal diseases

.8   Obstetrical surgery

.9   Patients by age groups

Class surgical treatment in **617**

.92   Pediatrics

General and specific diseases of children and their treatment

Use **618.920 001 – 618.920 009** for standard subdivisions

.920 007 3   Pediatric nursing

(Optional; prefer **610.73**)

.97   Geriatrics

General and specific diseases of the aged and their treatment

.970 73   Geriatric nursing

(Optional; prefer **610.73**)

619   Comparative and experimental medicine

Study of diseases and their treatment in laboratory animals

For veterinary sciences, see **636.089**

620   **Engineering, and allied operations and manufactures**

Including fine particle technology, systems engineering

Use **620.001–620.009** for standard subdivisions

▶   620.1–620.4 Applied mechanics (Engineering mechanics)

For principles of flight, see **629.132**; *automatic control engineering,* **629.8**; *air conditioning engineering,* **697.9**

.1   Engineering materials, properties, tests

Class sound and related vibrations in **620.2**, mechanical vibration in **620.3** [*both formerly* **620.1**]

197

620.2	Sound and related vibrations [*formerly* 620.1]
	Applied acoustics and ultrasonics

.3	Mechanical vibration [*formerly* 620.1]
	For sound and related vibrations, see **620.2**

.8	Human engineering (Biotechnology)
	Designing for optimum man-machine and man-equipment relationships

621   Applied physics

Mechanical, electrical, electronic, electromagnetic, heat, light, nuclear engineering

Use **621.001–621.009** for standard subdivisions

.01–.09	Standard subdivisions of mechanical engineering
	Class thermodynamics [*formerly* **621.01**] in **621.4**

▶   621.1–621.2 Fluid-power engineering

For aerodynamics, see **629.132**; *air compression,* **621.5**

.1	Steam
	Engines, boilers, locomotives, tractors, rollers, steam generation and transmission, boiler-house practices

.2	Power derived from liquids
	Hydraulic-power and other liquid-pressure mechanisms
	Use **621.200 1 – 621.200 9** for standard subdivisions

.201–.209	Standard subdivisions of hydraulic power

.3	Electrical, electronic, electromagnetic engineering
	Use **621.300 01 – 621.300 09** for standard subdivisions

.301–.309	Standard subdivisions of electrical engineering

621.31	Generation, transmission, modification of electrical energy

Including transformers, condensers, details and parts of generators, control devices at central stations

Class electricity derived from nuclear power in **621.48**, by chemical methods in **621.35**, electric motors as prime movers in **621.4**

.312   Central stations

For dynamoelectric (generating) machinery, see **621.313**

.313   Dynamoelectric (Generating) machinery

Direct-current, alternating-current, synchronous, asynchronous machinery

.319   Transmission

.32   Light and illumination engineering

Illumination systems regardless of source, other branches of light engineering, e.g., lasers

Do not use standard subdivisions

For municipal lighting, see **628**

.320 01–.320 09   Standard subdivisions of illumination engineering

.320 1–.320 9   Standard subdivisions of electric lighting

.33   Traction

Electric-power transmission for railways

Including electrification of railway systems

.35   Applied electrochemistry

Primary and storage batteries, fuel cells

.36   Paraphotic engineering

Infrared and ultraviolet technology

Class heat radiation in **621.4**

.37   Electrical measurements

Meters, instruments, measurement of electric and nonelectric quantities by electrical means

621.38   Electronic and communication engineering

.381   Electronic engineering

Including microwave, circuit, X-ray, gamma-ray electronics

Class electroacoustical devices [*formerly* 621.381] in 621.389

For communication engineering, see **621.382–621.389**

.381 7   Miniaturization and microminiaturization

.381 9   Special developments

Including computers

► 621.382–621.389 Communication engineering

Electrical, electroacoustical, electronic devices

► 621.382–621.383 Wire telegraphy

.382   Codes, systems, types

Acoustic and automatic systems; printing, writing, facsimile, submarine cable types

.383   Specific instruments and apparatus

Keys, transmitters, receivers, calling apparatus, relays, repeaters, switches, recorders

.384   Radio- and microwave communication

► 621.384 1 – 621.384 6 Radio

.384 1   General principles

Including wave propagation and transmission, circuitry, instruments and apparatus, stations, manufacture of receiving sets

.384 19   Special developments

Radio beacons, radio compasses, loran, telecontrol, space communication

►   621.384 2 – 621.384 3 Radiotelegraphy

621.384 2   Systems, stations, types

                Including radiofacsimile

.384 3   Specific instruments and apparatus

►   621.384 5 – 621.384 6 Radiotelephony

.384 5   Systems, stations, types

.384 6   Specific instruments and apparatus

.384 8   Radar

                General principles, specific instruments and apparatus, systems, stations, scanning patterns, special developments, e.g., racon, shoran

►   621.385–621.387 Wire telephony

.385   Analysis, systems, stations

►   621.386–621.387 Instruments, apparatus, transmission

.386   Terminal instruments and apparatus

.387   Central station equipment and transmission

.388   Television

                Black-and-white and color television

                Including relay and satellite systems; measurements and standardization of impedance, frequency, wavelength, modulation, signal intensity

                Use **621.388 001 – 621.388 009** for standard subdivisions

.388 1   General principles

                Wave propagation and transmission, circuitry, optics

.388 3   Instruments and apparatus

                Transmitters, valves, cameras, antennas, receivers, supplementary instrumentation

621.388 6	Stations
.388 8	Manufacturing and servicing of receiving sets
.388 9	Special developments

> Including space communication

.389   Other communication devices

> Including electroacoustical devices [*formerly* 621.381], sound recording and reproducing systems [*formerly* 681.8], public address systems, language translators, underwater devices, e.g., projectors, hydrophones, sonar

.39   Other branches of electrical engineering

> Including thermoelectricity, rural and household electrification, conduction and induction heating

> Class generation and transmission of electricity regardless of method or purpose in **621.31**

.4   Heat and prime movers

> Including thermodynamics [*formerly* 621.01], electric motors, external-combustion engines (hot-air engines), air engines (air motors), wind engines

> Do not use standard subdivisions

> *For steam, see* **621.1**

.43   Internal-combustion engines

> Gas-turbine, spark-ignition, jet, rocket, diesel, semidiesel engines

.47   Solar-energy engineering

> Solar engines, batteries, furnaces

.48   Nuclear engineering

> Fission and fusion technology, their by-products (radioactive isotopes), treatment and disposal of radioactive waste

621.5   Pneumatic and low-temperature technology

> Including air compression, refrigeration, ice manufacture, cryogenic techniques
>
> *For fans, blowers, pumps, see* **621.6**

.55   Vacuum technology

.6   Mechanical fans, blowers, pumps

> Class hydraulic pumps in **621.2**

.7   Factory operations

> Automatic factories, machine-shop practice
>
> Class manufacture of a specific product with the subject, machine tools in **621.9**

.8   Mechanical power transmission and related equipment

> Mechanisms, transmission elements, materials-handling equipment, fastenings, lubrication
>
> *For pneumatic technology, see* **621.5**; *power derived from liquids,* **621.2**

.9   Tools

> Design, maintenance, repair, operations of machine, pneumatic, hand tools
>
> Use **621.900 1 – 621.900 9** for standard subdivisions
>
> Class special-purpose machinery in **681**

.97   Fastening machinery

> Hammers and riveting machinery

622   Mining engineering and operations

> Prospecting, surface and underground mining, ancillary equipment and operations, ore dressing, hazards and accidents

623   Military and naval engineering

Planning, structural analysis and design, construction methods, operations; maintenance, repairs

Including fortifications, demolition and defensive operations

.4   Ordnance

Class armored vehicles in **623.7**

.5   Ballistics and gunnery

.6   Transportation facilities

For vehicles, see **623.7**

.7   Other operations

Topography, communication facilities, vehicles, sanitation, power and light systems, camouflage

.8   Naval engineering

Including naval architecture, shipyards

.82   Ships and boats

Construction, maintenance, repairs of sailing craft, small and medium power-driven craft, merchant ships, warships and other government vessels, hand-propelled and towed craft

Do not use standard subdivisions

For parts and details of ships and boats, see **623.84–623.87**

▶   623.84–623.87 Parts and details of ships and boats

.84   Hull construction

.85   Special systems

Mechanical, electrical, electronic systems for lighting, air conditioning, temperature controls, water supply and sanitation, communication

.86   Equipment and outfit

.87   Power plants (Marine engineering)

Engines, fuels, engine auxiliaries

623.88   Seamanship

Art and science of handling ships

.89   Navigation

Selection and determination of course thru piloting, dead reckoning, use of electronic and other aids

For celestial navigation, see **527**

624   Civil engineering

Planning, structural analysis and design, construction methods, maintenance and repairs of foundations and other supporting structures, tunnels, bridges, roofs

For specific branches of civil engineering, see **625–628**

▶   **625–628 Specific branches of civil engineering**

For vehicles, see **629.1–629.4**

625   Railroads and their rolling stock, roads and highways

Planning, structural analysis and design, construction methods, maintenance, repairs

Including special-purpose railways, e.g., roadbeds, tracks and accessories, conveying apparatus, rolling stock of inclined, cable, ship, electric railways, and trolleybuses

.1   Railroads

Monorailroads, standard- and narrow-gage railroads

Including model railroads and trains

Do not use standard subdivisions

.2   Railroad rolling stock

Running gear, work cars, passenger cars, freight cars, accessory equipment, locomotives, mechanical operation of monorail rolling stock, standard- and narrow-gage railroads

For model trains, see **625.1**

.7   Roads and highways

For artificial road surfaces, see **625.8**

625.8   Artificial road surfaces

Design, construction, materials of vehicular thorofare and pedestrian pavements

Class maintenance and repairs in **625.7**

627   Hydraulic engineering and construction works

Planning, structural analysis and design, construction methods, maintenance, repairs of inland waterways, harbors, ports, roadsteads, dams and reservoirs, other measures for flood control, land and water reclamation

628   Sanitary and municipal engineering and construction works

Water supply, sewerage and sewage, garbage and refuse treatment and disposal, air pollution and countermeasures, fire-fighting technology, municipal lighting, insect and rodent extermination

629   Other branches

Planning, structural analysis and design, construction methods, operations, maintenance, repairs

————————

629.1–629.4 Vehicles

Self-propelled conveyances with directional independence

For ships and boats, see **623.82**

.1   Flight vehicles and engineering

For astronautics, see **629.4**

.13   Aeronautics

Do not use standard subdivisions

.132   Principles of flight

Aerostatics, aerodynamics, navigation, piloting, flight guides, wreckage studies, command systems for guided aircraft

629.133	Aircraft
	Lighter-than-air and heavier-than-air aircraft, their models
	For aircraft details, see **629.134**

.134	Aircraft details
	For aircraft instruments and equipment, see **629.135**

.135	Aircraft instruments and equipment
	Instruments for navigation, flight operations, power-plant monitoring; electrical, electronic, other equipment

.136	Airports

[.138]	Astronautics
	Class in **629.4**

.2	Motor land vehicles
	Including design and construction of automobiles, trucks, tractors, trailers, bicycles, motorcycles, and their parts

.22	Types
	Passenger automobiles, trucks, tractors, trailers, cycles, racing cars, their models
	Do not use for specific details

.28	Tests, operation, maintenance, repairs

.282	Tests and related topics
	Road tests, periodic inspection and roadability tests, wreckage studies

▶ 629.283–629.284 Operation

Methods of driving, factors in safe driving

.283	Of passenger cars
.284	Of other types of motor vehicles
.3	Ground-effect machines (Air-cushion vehicles)

629.4	Astronautics [*formerly* 629.138]
.42	Propulsion systems

Power plants (rockets) and ancillary instrumentation and equipment

.43	Flight of unmanned vehicles
.44	Space stations
.45	Flight of manned vehicles

►
_____

629.46–629.47 Spacecraft

Structural analysis and design, construction methods, maintenance, repairs

For propulsion systems, see **629.42**

.46	Unmanned vehicles

Including expandable space structures

.47	Manned vehicles

Including life-support and ground-support systems

.8	Automatic control engineering

Open-loop and closed-loop (feedback) systems

630	**Agriculture and agricultural industries**
.1	Philosophy and theory

Including agricultural life

Class scientific aspects in **630.21–630.29**

.2	Miscellany

Class here without further subdivision miscellany provided for in standard subdivisions **021–029**

.21–.29	Scientific aspects

Divide like **510–590**, e.g., agricultural chemistry **630.24**

631–632 General principles

Class general principles applied to specific crops in **633–635**

631   Farming

[.1]   Business management of farms

         Class in **658**

.2   Farm structures

         Description, maintenance, use and place in farming of farmhouses, barns, granaries, silos, elevators, sheds, fences, walls, hedges, roads, bridges

.3   Farm tools, machinery, appliances

         Description, maintenance (farm mechanics), use and place in farming

         Class uses in a specific operation with the operation

.4   Soil and soil conservation

         For soil improvement, see **631.6–631.8**

[.409]   Historical and geographical treatment

         Do not use

.5   Crop production

631.6–631.8 Soil improvement

.6   Reclamation and drainage

         For irrigation and water conservation, see **631.7**

.7   Irrigation and water conservation

.8   Fertilizers and soil conditioners

632   Plant injuries, diseases, pests, and their control

►   633–635 Production of specific crops

633   Field crops

> Large-scale production of crops, other than fruit, intended for agricultural purposes and industrial processing
>
> Do not use standard subdivisions

634   Orchards, small fruit, forestry

  .9   Forestry

> Formation, maintenance, cultivation, exploitation of forests

635   Garden crops (Horticulture)

> Commercial and home gardening

►   635.1–635.8 Vegetables

> Crops grown primarily for human consumption without intermediate processing other than preservation

  .1   Edible roots

> Beets, turnips, carrots, parsnips, radishes, salsify, related crops

  .2   Edible tubers and bulbs

> Potatoes, sweet potatoes, yams, Jerusalem artichokes, onions and other alliaceous plants

  .3   Asparagus, artichokes, cabbages

  .4   Cooking greens and related vegetables

> Spinach, chard, rhubarb
>
> *For cabbages, see* **635.3**

  .5   Salad greens

  .6   Edible fruits and seeds

> Melons, squashes, pumpkins, cucumbers, tomatoes, green peppers, eggplants, okra, legumes, corn

635.9   Flowers and ornamental plants (Floriculture)

Class flower arrangement [*formerly* **635.9**] in **745.92**

.93   General and taxonomic groupings

Including annuals, biennials, perennials

.933–.939   By families, genera, species

Divide like **583–589**, e.g., dicotyledons **635.933**

Class families, genera, species of trees in **635.97**

►   635.96–635.97 Special groupings

Class specific families, genera, species, other than trees, in **635.933–635.939**

.96   By purpose

For flower beds, borders, edgings, ground cover, houseplants, rock gardens, water gardens, wild flower gardens

.97   Other groupings

Everlastings, vines, foliage plants, shrubs, hedges, trees

Including families, genera, species of trees

►   636–638 Animal husbandry

Class culture of cold-blooded animals other than insects in **639**

636   Livestock and domestic animals

Do not use standard subdivisions

.08   Stock production, maintenance, training

Including fur farming [*formerly* **636.9**]

.089   Veterinary sciences

Veterinary anatomy, physiology, hygiene, public health, pharmacology, therapeutics, diseases and their treatment

636.1 **Horses and other equines**

Including asses, mules, zebras

Do not use standard subdivisions

.2 **Cattle and other larger ruminants**

Including zebus, bison, antelopes, water buffaloes, eland, bongos, kudus, gazelles, musk-oxen, deer, elk, moose, reindeer, caribous, giraffes, okapis, camels, llamas, alpacas, vicuñas

Do not use standard subdivisions

.3 **Sheep and goats (Smaller ruminants)**

Do not use standard subdivisions

.4 **Swine**

Do not use standard subdivisions

.5 **Poultry**

Do not use standard subdivisions

.59 **Other domestic birds**

Turkeys, guinea fowl, pheasants, peafowl, pigeons, ducks, geese

.6 **Birds other than poultry**

Plumage, song and ornamental birds

.7 **Dogs**

Do not use standard subdivisions

————————

► **636.72–636.76 Specific breeds**

Class the miniature of any breed in **636.76**

.72 **Nonsporting dogs**

Boston terriers, English and French bulldogs, chow chows, Dalmatians, Keeshonden, poodles, schipperkes

For working dogs, see **636.73**

636.73	Working dogs

Alaskan malamutes, boxers, collies, Doberman pinschers, Eskimo dogs, German shepherds, Great Danes, Great Pyrenees, mastiffs, Newfoundlands, Samoyeds, schnauzers, sheepdogs, Siberian huskies, Saint Bernards, Welsh corgis

.75	Sporting dogs

Gun dogs, hounds, terriers

For Boston terriers, see **636.72**

.76	Toy and miniature dogs

Affenpinschers, Chihuahuas, English toy spaniels, Italian greyhounds, Maltese, Mexican hairless, papillons, Pekingese, Pomeranians, toy poodles, pugs, toy Manchester and Yorkshire terriers

.8	Cats

Domestic cats, ocelots, margays, cheetahs

.9	Other warm-blooded animals

Monotremes, marsupials, other mammals

Class fur farming [*formerly* **636.9**] in **636.08**

637	Dairy and related industries

Milk, butter, cheese, frozen desserts, eggs

638	Insect culture

Class culture of invertebrates other than insects [*formerly* **638**] in **639**

639	Nondomesticated animals

Hunting, fishing, culture, conservation practices

Including culture of invertebrates other than insects [*formerly* **638**]

Class hunting and fishing as sport in **799**, fur farming in **636.08**, insect culture in **638**

640   Domestic arts and sciences (Home economics)

Care of household, family, person

Class personal hygiene in **613**

.73   Consumer education [*formerly* 339.4]

Selection of consumer goods, guides to quality

Including reports on named products

641   Food and drink

For food service, see **642**

.1   Applied nutrition

Occurrence in food of nutrients required to meet needs of human body

.3   Foods and foodstuffs

Comprehensive works on production, manufacture, preservation, preparation, use

Do not use standard subdivisions

Class food customs in **390**, food supply in **338.1** [*both formerly* **641.3**]

Class production in **630**, manufacture (commercial preparation and preservation) in **663–664**, home preservation and preparation in **641.4–641.8**

▶   641.4–641.8 Preservation and preparation

.4   Preservation for later use

Canning, drying, dehydrating, cold storage, deep freezing, brining, pickling, smoking, use of additives

▶   641.5–641.8 Preparation for proximate use (Cookery)

With and without use of heat

Scope: cookbooks, recipes

641.5   General cookery

   .59   Characteristic of specific geographic environments

         Add area notations 3–9 to **641.59**

         Class general cookery, noncharacteristic recipes from specific places in **541.5** without subdivision

     ▶   641.6–641.8 Special cookery

     Limited by dish, material, process

     Observe the following table of precedence, e.g., roasting meats **641.6**

         Composite dishes
         Specific materials
         Specific processes and techniques

   .6   Specific materials

         Cookery using preserved foods, wines, beers, spirits, fruits, vegetables, meats, dairy products

   .7   Specific processes and techniques

         Baking, roasting, boiling, simmering, stewing, broiling, grilling, barbecuing, frying, sautéing, braising

   .8   Composite dishes

         Sauces, relishes, appetizers, savories, stews, meat pies, casserole dishes, salads, sandwiches, sugar products, desserts, beverages

         Including bartenders' manuals [*formerly* 663]

642   Food and meal service

         Menus, food services at public and private places, table service and decor

643   The home and its equipment

         Selection, purchase, rental, location, orientation, arrangement, improvement and remodeling

644   Household utilities

         Description, selection, operation, care of systems, appliances, fittings, fixtures, accessories for heating, lighting, ventilation, air conditioning, water supply

645   Household furnishings

Description, selection, installation, use, care, repair of floor, wall, ceiling coverings, of furniture and outdoor furnishings

Class design and decorative treatment of interior furnishings in **747**

646   Clothing and care of body

Including selection of clothing and materials

Do not use standard subdivisions

Class fashion [*formerly* **646**] in **391**

.01–.09   Standard subdivisions of clothing

Use **646.09** for Frigid Zones, cold weather, Tropics, hot weather clothing

.2   Plain sewing

Including mending, darning, reweaving, machine sewing

For clothing construction, see **646.4**

.4   Clothing construction

Patternmaking, cutting, fitting, remodeling

Do not use standard subdivisions

For construction of headgear, see **646.5**

.5   Construction of headgear

Do not use standard subdivisions

.6   Care of clothing

Including cleaning, dyeing

For mending, see **646.2**; *laundering,* **648**

.7   Care of body (Toilet)

Hairdressing, facial care, manicuring, pedicuring, barbering, reducing, slenderizing

647   Housekeeping

Private and public households of all types

Class a specific operation with the subject

648	Household sanitation

Laundering, housecleaning, control and eradication of pests, storage and preparation for storage

649	Child rearing and home nursing

Do not use standard subdivisions

.01–.09	Standard subdivisions of child rearing

649.1–649.7 Child rearing

.1	Care, training, supervision

Including works for expectant parents, baby-sitters

For specific elements of care, training, supervision, see **649.3–649.7**

649.3–649.7 Specific elements of care, training, supervision

.3	Feeding
.4	Clothing and care of body
.5	Supervised activities

Including play with dolls

.6	Manners and habits

Training in toilet, cleanliness, dressing and feeding self, good behavior

.7	Moral, religious, character training

.8	Home nursing

Care of sick and infirm

650   **Business and related types of enterprise**

Organization, activities, processes, techniques

Do not use standard subdivisions

651   Office services

Organization, equipment, supplies, personnel, operations, records management

Including parish office methods [*formerly* 254]

Class personnel management of office services [*formerly* 651] in 658.3

> *For accounting procedures, see* 657

.7   Communication

Internal and external transmission of oral and written information thru messenger, postal, telecommunication, other systems

Class business writing [*formerly* 651.7] in 808.06

.8   Data processing

652   Writing

Including handwriting

> *For shorthand, see* 653; *calligraphy* (*elegant handwriting*), 741

.3   Typewriting

Do not use standard subdivisions

[.4]   Duplicating

Class in 655.2–655.3

.8   Cryptography

653   Shorthand

655   Printing and related activities

Scope: bookmaking and book arts [*both formerly* 002]

Do not use standard subdivisions

.01–.08   Standard subdivisions of printing

Class historical and geographical treatment in **655.1**

▶   655.1–655.3 Printing

.1   Historical and geographical treatment

▶   655.2–655.3 Processes

Scope: duplicating [*formerly also* 652.4]

Class processes of specific establishments in **655.1**

.2   Typography and composition

For special printing, see **655.3**

.3   Other

Mechanical and photomechanical techniques, special printing, e.g., music, Braille and other raised characters

Including maps [*formerly* 526.8]

▶   655.4–655.5 Publishing

Production of books, periodicals, newspapers

Class standard subdivisions in **655.4**

Class bookselling (book trade) [*formerly* **655.4–655.5**] in **658.8**

For printing, see **655.1–655.3**; *bookbinding,* **655.7**

.4   Standard subdivisions

.401–.409   Specific standard subdivisions

Class geographical treatment in **655.4** without subdivision

655.5   **Specific elements**

Publishing processes, kinds of publications and publishers

Including music publishing [*formerly* 781]

Class specific establishments in 655.4, editorial techniques in 808.02

For journalism, see 070

[.6]   **Copyright**

Class in 340

.7   **Bookbinding**

657   **Accounting principles and procedures**

Scope: description, use, maintenance of equipment

▶   **657.2–657.6 General principles**

Class general principles applied to accounting for specific kinds of enterprises in 657.8

.2   **Constructive (Recording, Bookkeeping)**

.3   **Financial (Reporting)**

.4   **Administrative (Analytical)**

Cost analysis and internal auditing

.6   **Public accounting and auditing**

.8   **Accounting for specific kinds of enterprises**

658   **Management**

The executive function of planning, organizing, coordinating, directing, controlling, supervising a project or activity with responsibility for results

Scope: management of real estate business [*formerly* 333.3], of public utility services [*formerly* 380], business management of newspapers and periodicals [*formerly* 070.3], of farms [*formerly* 631.1]

Do not use standard subdivisions

For public administration, see 350

▶   658.1–658.8 Specific elements

658.1   Management by control of structure

Thru promotion and organization, legal counsel, financial direction and supervision, intercorporate relations, international operations

.2   Management of plants (Plant engineering)

Management of equipment and facilities

Do not use standard subdivisions

.3   Management of personnel (Personnel management)

Procedure by which employees are hired, managed, replaced

Scope: personnel management of office services [*formerly* 651]

Do not use standard subdivisions

Class managerial personnel policies [*formerly* **658.3**] in **658.4**

.31   Administration of employment policies

Selection, recruitment, placement, promotion, transfer, termination of service, employer-employee relationships, employee morale

Including in-service training, work schedules [*both formerly* **658.38**]

.32   Wage and salary administration

Payroll administration, compensation plans, pensions

Including classification and pay plans, pensions, retirement for library personnel [*formerly also* 023]

.37   Personnel management in specific kinds of enterprises and occupations

For a specific element of personnel management, see the subject, e.g., wage and salary administration **658.32**

658.38   **Promotion of personnel welfare, satisfaction, efficiency**

Health and safety programs, welfare services, counseling services, educational programs

Class work schedules, in-service training in **658.31**, internal organization in **658.4** [*all formerly* **658.38**]

.4   **Management at executive levels (Executive management)**

Including managerial personnel policies [*formerly* **658.3**], internal organization [*formerly* **658.38**], communication, use of consultants, security

Do not use standard subdivisions

Class a specific activity of executive management with the subject

▶ 658.42–658.43 Specific levels

.42   **Top management**

Direction and control of organization and functions, coordination of interdivisional relationships by senior officers

.43   **Middle management**

Direction and control of operations by junior officers

.5   **Management of production (Industrial engineering)**

Management of extraction, manufacture, transportation, storage, exchange (procurement and marketing) of goods and services

Do not use standard subdivisions

For plant engineering, see **658.2**; *materials control,* **658.7**; *marketing,* **658.8**

.7   **Management of materials (Materials control)**

Control of goods used and commodities produced

For marketing, see **658.8**

658.8	Management of distribution (Marketing)

Of goods and services

Including sales management and promotion techniques, channels of distribution

Scope: bookselling (book trade) [*formerly* **655.4–655.5**]

Do not use standard subdivisions

.83 Market research and analysis

[.830 9] Historical and geographical treatment

Do not use

.85 Personal selling (Salesmanship)

Class personal selling of specific kinds of goods and services in **658.89**

.86 Wholesale marketing

.87 Retail (Consumer) marketing

Do not use standard subdivisions

.88 Credit management

Mercantile and consumer (retail) credit

Including deferred payment plans

.89 Personal selling of specific goods and services

659 Other activities, processes, techniques

.1 Advertising

Promotion of organizations, products, services thru publicity

▶ 659.11–659.17 Specific elements

.11 Organization

Policies, agencies, campaigns

659.13   Visual and audio-visual advertising

Thru newspapers, magazines, direct mail, signs, entertainment, specialty features, e.g., blotters, calendars, programs, novelties

For advertising by display of goods and services, see 659.15; broadcast advertising, 659.14

.14   Broadcast advertising

.15   Advertising by display of goods and services

Including fashion modeling

.17   Contests and lotteries

.2   Public relations

Promotion of rapport and good will, assessment of public reaction

660   **Chemical technology and related industries**

Including chemical engineering, applied physical chemistry, industrial microbiology

Do not use standard subdivisions

For elastomers and elastomer products, see 678

.01–.09   Standard subdivisions of chemical technology

661   Industrial chemicals (Heavy chemicals)

Large-scale production of chemicals used as raw materials or reagents in the manufacture of other products

Including cyclic chemicals [*formerly 668.7*]

Do not use standard subdivisions

For industrial gases, see 665

662   Explosives, fuels, and related products

Including fireworks, propellants, detonators, matches, nonfuel carbons

Class fluid fossil fuels in 665

► ## 663–664 Food and drink

Manufacture (commercial preparation and preservation), packaging of edible products for human and animal consumption

Class comprehensive works in **664**

For dairy and related industries, see **637**

663 ## Drinks, stimulants, their substitutes

Alcoholic and nonalcoholic beverages, stimulants used in preparation of beverages, e.g., coffee, tea, herbals, cocoa, chocolate

Class bartenders' manuals [*formerly* 663] in **641.8**

664 ## Food technology

Do not use standard subdivisions

Class honey in **638**

665 ## Industrial oils, fats, waxes, gases

Nonvolatile, saponifying, lubricating oils, fats, waxes of organic and mineral origin; natural, derived, manufactured gases

Including petroleum

Class beeswax in **638**

666 ## Ceramic and allied industries

Glass, enameling and enamels, pottery, refractories, synthetic minerals, artificial stones, masonry adhesives

667 ## Cleaning, color and related industries

Cleaning and bleaching of textiles, furs, feathers, leather; dyes, pigments, process dyeing and printing, inks, paints, varnishes and allied products, surface finishing

Class a specific application of surface finishing with the subject

For nonfuel carbons, see **662**

668   Other organic products

Soaps, detergents, wetting agents, glycerin, glues, crude gelatin, gums, resins, sealants, plastics, perfumes, cosmetics, fertilizers, soil conditioners, pesticides

Class plastic fibers and fabrics in 677

For elastomers, see 678

[.7]   Cyclic chemicals

Class in 661

669   Metallurgy

Scope: comprehensive works on metals

Including scrap metals [*formerly* 671.9]

Use 669.001–669.009 for standard subdivisions

For a specific aspect of metals, see the subject, e.g., metal manufactures 671

▶   669.1–669.7 Extractive metallurgy of specific metals and their alloys

.1   Ferrous metals

▶   669.2–669.7 Nonferrous metals

Class comprehensive works in 669.7

.2   Precious and rare-earth metals

Gold, silver, platinum, radium, uranium, other rare-earth metals

.3   Copper

Brass, bronze, Muntz metal, gun metal, copper-aluminum alloys, copper-beryllium alloys, aluminum bronze

.4   Lead

.5   Zinc and cadmium

.6   Tin

.7   Other

669.8   Metallurgical furnaces
         Operation, maintenance, supplies

   .9   Physical and chemical metallurgy
         Assay practices, physical metallurgy, metallography

670–680 Manufactures

670   Products based on processible materials
         For chemical technology and related industries, see **660**

671   Metal manufactures
         Fabrication of metals and manufacture of primary products
         Class specific metals in **672–673**

   .2   Foundry practice (Hot-working operations)
   .3   Mechanical working and forming
         Cold-working operations, treatment and hardening,
         powder metallurgy

   .5   Joining and cutting
         Welding, flame and arc cutting, soldering, brazing, riveting

   .7   Finishing and surface treatment
         Buffing, polishing, coating

   .8   Primary products
         Sheet products, tubes, pipes, wires, cordage, cables, powder
         products

 [.9]   Scrap metals
         Class in **669**

672–673 Specific metals manufactures
Fabrication of specific metals and manufacture of primary
products

672   Ferrous metals
673   Nonferrous metals

674   Lumber, cork, wood-using industries

> Do not use standard subdivisions

675   Leather and fur industries

> Preliminary tanning, dressing, finishing operations

676   Pulp and paper industries

> Materials, machinery, manufacturing processes, properties, tests, recovery of waste products, primary and converted paper products, final paper and paperboard products

677   Textiles

> Production of fibers, and manufacture of fabrics and cordage
>
> Including primary products, e.g., carpets, rugs, felt hats, blankets, lap robes, coverlets
>
> Do not use standard subdivisions

678   Elastomers and elastomer products

> Natural and synthetic rubber and latexes, synthetic rubber and derivatives, elastoplastics
>
> Including primary products, e.g., tires, overshoes, heels, rubber bands, hose, sheeting

679   Other products

> Including ivory and feather products, brooms, brushes, mops, cigars, cigarettes, products derived from waste materials
>
> Class products manufactured from a specific waste material with the subject

680   **Handcrafted, assembled, final products**

> Class final paper and paperboard products in 676, rubber products in 678, other products based on processible materials in 679

681   Precision mechanisms and related machines

> Measuring instruments, cameras, business machines, printing and duplicating machines, timepieces, optical devices, conventional and mechanical musical instruments and devices
>
> Class hand construction of musical instruments in 786–789

[681.8]	Sound recording and reproducing systems

Class in **621.389**

682 Small forge work (Blacksmithing)

Horseshoeing, production of hand-forged tools and ironwork

683 Hardware

Locksmithing, gunsmithing, manufacture of household appliances

Class refrigerators and freezers in **621.5**

For heating, ventilating, air conditioning equipment, see **697**

684 Furnishings and wheeled supports

Do not use standard subdivisions

▶ 684.08–684.09 Home (Amateur) workshops

.08 Woodworking

.09 Metalworking

.1 Furniture

Do not use standard subdivisions

.3 Fabric furnishings

Draperies, hangings, slip covers, curtains

For carpets and rugs, see **677**

.7 Carriages, wagons, carts, wheelbarrows

For motor land vehicles, see **629.2**

685 Leather goods and their substitutes

Saddlery, harness making, leather and fur clothing, footwear, gloves, mittens, travel and camping equipment

For overshoes, see **678**

687 Clothing

For leather and fur clothing, see **685**

688   Other final products

> Including models, costume jewelry, smokers' supplies, accessories for personal grooming
>
> Class engineering models in **620**
>
> > *For brushes, see* **679**; *cosmetics,* **668**

.7   Recreational equipment

> Toys, equipment for games and sports
>
> > *For leather goods and their substitutes, see* **685**; *motor land vehicles,* **629.2**

690   **Buildings**

> Planning, structural analysis and design, construction methods, maintenance, repairs of habitable structures and their interior accessories
>
> Use **690.01–690.09** for standard subdivisions
>
> Class creative design and construction in **721**

.5–.8   Specific types of habitable structures

> > Divide like **725–728**, e.g., ranch houses **690.86**
> >
> > Class forts and fortresses in **623**, trailers in **629.22**

691   Materials

> Selection, preservation, construction properties of timber, natural and artificial stones, ceramic and clay materials, masonry adhesives, glass, structural metals, plastics, insulating materials, prefabricated housing materials, adhesives and sealants

692   Construction practices

> Interpretation and use of architects' drawings for construction purposes, construction specifications, contracting, estimates of materials and time
>
> Class drawing of plans [*formerly* 692] in **720**
>
> Class building laws in **340**, local government regulation in **352**

693   Systems of construction

For materials, see **691**

693.1–693.3 Solid block masonry

.1   Stone

.2   Stabilized earth

Brick, adobe, pisé, cob, tapia, tabby

.3   Tile and terra cotta

.4   Hollow block masonry

Concrete block, cinder block, hollow tile, hollow brick

.5   Solid concrete construction

Poured, precast, prestressed

.6   Plaster-, stucco-, lathwork

Internal and external application

.7   Metal construction

.8   Resistant construction

To fire, shock, pests, lightning, water, moisture, heat, sound

.9   Construction in other materials

Including ice, snow, sandwich panels, glass, prefabricated
materials

For wood construction, see **694**

694   Wood construction (Structural woodworking)

Including planning, structural analysis and design

Do not use standard subdivisions

.01–.09   Standard subdivisions of carpentry

─────────────

► **694.2–694.6 Carpentry**
For roofs, see **624**

694.2   **Rough carpentry (Framing)**

.6   **Finish carpentry (Joinery)**
Construction of details

695   **Roofing, auxiliary structures, and their materials**
Covering, maintaining, repairing roofs; installing, maintaining, repairing gutters, flashings, other weatherings

─────────────

► **696–697 Utilities**
For household electrification, see **621.39**

696   **Plumbing, pipe fitting, heating, ventilating**
Design, installation, maintenance, repairs
Do not use standard subdivisions
Class heating and ventilating in **697**

697   **Heating, ventilating, air conditioning engineering**
Principles, systems, equipment, installation, maintenance, repairs
Do not use standard subdivisions

─────────────

► **697.1–697.2 Local heating**
For chimneys and flues, see **697.8**

.1   **With open fires (Radiative heating)**
Including fireplaces, braziers

.2   **With space heaters (Convective heating)**

► 697.3–697.7 Central heating
For chimneys and flues, see **697.8**

697.3 Warm-air heating

.4 Hot-water heating

.5 Steam heating

Including district heating

Do not use standard subdivisions

.7 Other methods

Including radiant-panel, solar, nuclear heating

.8 Chimneys and flues

.9 Ventilation and air conditioning

698 Detail finishing

Application and installation of decorative and protective coatings and coverings

.1 Painting

Exteriors and interiors

For painting woodwork, see **698.3**

.2 Calcimining and whitewashing

.3 Finishing woodwork

By staining, polishing, varnishing, lackering, painting

.5 Glazing and leading windows

.6 Paperhanging

.9 Floor coverings

Measuring, cutting, laying linoleum, tiles, carpeting

700 The arts

Description and critical appraisal, materials and techniques of the fine, decorative, graphic, performing, recreational arts

Use 700.1–700.9 for standard subdivisions

For literature, see 800

► 701–709 Standard subdivisions of fine arts

701 Philosophy and theory

.1 Nature and character

.15 Psychology

Including fine arts as products of creative imagination

.17 Esthetics

.18 Criticism and appreciation

Theory and technique, history

Including criticism and appreciation thru use of audio-visual aids

Class works of critical appraisal in 709, audio-visual treatment of art in 702

.8 Techniques

Composition, color, decoration, perspective, use of models

Class research methodology in 701.9

For description, critical appraisal of artists, see 709

.9 Research methodology

Class psychological aspects in 701.15

702 Miscellany

Class techniques in 701.8

703 Dictionaries, encyclopedias, concordances

704	**Persons occupied with art, collections and anthologies, iconography**

Class development, description, critical appraisal, collections of works, biographical treatment of artists in **709**; art dealers in **706**

.9   Collections, anthologies, iconography

.94   Iconography

Development, description, critical appraisal, collections of works

Including human figures and their parts, natural scenes, still life, architectural subjects, symbolism and allegory

.945   Abstractions

.947   Mythology and legend

.948   Religion and religious symbolism

For mythology, see **704.947**

705   **Serial publications**

706   **Organizations**

707   **Study and teaching**

Class museums and permanent exhibits in **708**

708   **Galleries, museums, private collections**

Including museum economy

Do not use standard subdivisions

Class collections and anthologies of writings in **704.9**, temporary and traveling exhibits in **707.4**

▶   **708.1–708.9 Treatment by continent, country, locality**

Scope: guidebooks, catalogs of specific galleries, museums, private collections

.1   In North America

Class galleries, museums, private collections in Middle America in **708.972**

.11   Canada

708.13–.19	United States

Divide like area notations 73–79, e.g., galleries, museums, private collections in Pennsylvania 708.148

.2–.8   In Europe

Divide like area notations 42–48, e.g., galleries, museums, private collections in England 708.2

Class galleries, museums, private collections in countries not provided for in area notations 42–48 in 708.94

.9   In other countries

Add area notations 3–9 to 708.9

709   Historical and geographical treatment

Development, description, critical appraisal, collections of works, biographical treatment of artists

▶   709.01–709.04 Periods of development

.01   Primitive peoples and ancient times

.02   500–1500

Including art of 15th century [*formerly* 709.03]

.03   1500–1900

Class art of 15th century [*formerly* 709.03] in 709.02

.04   1900–

.3–.9   Geographical treatment

710   Civic and landscape art

711   Area planning (Civic art)

Design of physical environment for public welfare, convenience, pleasure on international, national, regional, local level

For landscape design, see 712

712   Landscape design (Landscape architecture)

Landscaping public, private, semiprivate, institutional parks and grounds

For specific elements in landscape design, see **714–717**; *design of trafficways,* **713**; *of cemeteries,* **718**

713   Landscape design of trafficways

► **714–717 Specific elements in landscape design**

714   Water features

Natural and artificial pools, fountains, cascades

715   Woody plants

Nonflowering and flowering

716   Herbaceous plants

Nonflowering and flowering

Class here comprehensive works on herbaceous and woody flowering plants

For woody flowering plants, see **715**

717   Structures

Relationship of buildings, terraces, fences, gates, steps, ornamental accessories to other elements of landscape design

718   Landscape design of cemeteries

719   Natural landscapes

Including public parks and natural monuments, wildlife reserves, forest and water-supply reserves

720   Architecture

Including drawing of plans [*formerly also* 692]

.9   Historical and geographical treatment

[.901–.904]   Periods of development

Do not use; class in **722–724**

237

[*720.93*]   In the ancient world

        Do not use; class in 722

721   Architectural construction

        Comprehensive works on design and construction of structural elements, e.g., foundations, walls, columns, arches, vaults, domes, roofs, floors, ceilings, doors, windows, stairs, balustrades

        For design of structural elements, see 729; *building construction,* 690; *specific types of structures,* 725–728

►   ### 722–724 Periods of development

        Chronological development of architectural styles

        Class development of specific types of structures in 725–728

        For architectual construction, see 721; *design and decoration of structures,* 729

722   Ancient period to ca. 300

        Oriental, classical, pre-Columbian American architectures

723   Medieval period, ca. 300–1400

        Early Christian, Byzantine, Saracenic, Romanesque, Norman, Gothic architectures, not limited geographically

724   Modern period, 1400–

        Not limited geographically

        Including Renaissance, classical revival, Gothic revival, Renaissance revival, neoclassical, Swiss timber and half timber, Romanesque revival architectures

  .9   20th century architecture

►   ### 725–728 Specific types of structures

        Comprehensive works on design and construction

        Scope: specific structures

        For building construction, see 690

725   Public structures

Government, military, commercial, transportation, storage, industrial, welfare, health, recreational, prison, reformatory, exhibition, memorial buildings; arches, gateways, walls, towers, bridges, tunnels, moats, vehicles

Including morgues and crematories [*both formerly* 726.8]

726   Buildings for religious purposes

Including temples, shrines, mosques, minarets, synagogues, parish houses, baptistries, churches, cathedrals, Sunday school buildings, monastic buildings, mortuary chapels, tombs, parsonages, missions

[.8]   Morgues and crematories

Class in 725

727   Buildings for educational and research purposes

Library, school, university, college, laboratory, botanical and zoological garden, observatory, museum, art gallery, community center, learned society buildings

728   Residential buildings

Not used primarily for public, religious, educational, research purposes

Including temporary buildings, multiple dwellings (other than hotels, motels, row houses), club houses, resort dwellings, accessory domestic structures, e.g., gatehouses, garages, conservatories, farm buildings

.3   Houses of urban type

Row and duplex houses, separate houses of two or more stories

For large and elaborate dwellings, see 728.8

.5   Hotels and motels

.6   Dwellings of suburban and rural types

Cottages, bungalows, ranch and split-level houses, farmhouses, solar houses

For large and elaborate dwellings, see 728.8

728.8   Large and elaborate dwellings

>   Castles, palaces, chateaux, mansions, manor houses, villas

729   Design and decoration of structures and accessories

>   Design in vertical and horizontal planes; design and decoration of structural elements, e.g., foundations, walls, columns, arches, vaults, domes, roofs, floors, ceilings, doors, windows, stairs, balustrades; decoration in specific mediums; built-in ecclesiastical furniture

>   *For specific types of structures, see 725–728; interior decoration, 747*

730   Sculpture and the plastic arts

>   Do not use standard subdivisions

▶   730.1–730.9 Standard subdivisions of sculpture

.1   Philosophy and theory

.2   Miscellany

>   Class techniques, apparatus, equipment in 731.3–731.4

.3–.8   Dictionaries, serial publications, organizations, study and teaching, collections

.9   Historical and geographical treatment

>   Class geographical treatment of sculpture of primitive peoples [*formerly* 730.9] in 732

[.901–.904]   Periods of development

>   Do not use; class in 732–735

[.93]   In the ancient world

>   Do not use; class in 732–733

731–735 Sculpture

Fine art of producing figures and designs in relief or the round by fashioning in plastic and rigid materials

731   Processes and representations

Including composition, materials

Class individual sculptors in **730.9**

.3   Equipment

Tools, machines, accessories

For techniques, see **731.4**

.4   Techniques

Modeling, molding, casting, carving, firing and baking, restoration

731.5–731.8 Representations

Development, description, critical appraisal, collections of works

.5   Styles and forms

Idealistic, naturalistic, realistic, grotesque styles; forms in relief, as mobiles and stabiles

For sculpture in the round, see **731.7**; *iconography,* **731.8**

.7   Sculpture in the round

Garden sculpture and fountains, vases, urns, busts, masks, monuments

For iconography, see **731.8**

.8   Iconography

Portrayal of specific subjects

► **732–735 Periods of development**

Chronological development of sculptural styles

► **732–733 Sculpture of primitive peoples and ancient world**

732 Nonclassical

Including geographical treatment of sculpture of primitive peoples [*formerly* 730.9]

733 Classical

Greek (Hellenic), Roman, Etruscan

Class sculpture of Greek Archipelago in 732

734 Medieval period, ca. 500–1400

Early Christian, Byzantine, Romanesque, Gothic styles not limited geographically

735 Modern period, 1400–

Not limited geographically

► **736–739 Other plastic arts**

Processes and products

For decorative and minor arts, see **745–749**

736 Carving and carvings

Including paper cutting and folding

Class seals, stamps, signets [*all formerly* 736] in 737

737 Numismatics

Including seals, stamps, signets [*all formerly* 736], medals, talismans, amulets, counters, tokens, jettons

.4 Coins

.49 Of specific countries

Add area notations 3–9 to 937.49

738 **Ceramic arts**

Class ceramic sculpture in **731–735**

For glass, see **748**

────────────

738.1–738.3 Pottery

.1 Processes

Materials, equipment, techniques, decorative treatments

.2 Porcelain (China)

.3 Earthenware and stoneware

.4 Enameling and enamels

Cloisonné, champlevé, basse-taille, surface-painted enamels

Class a specific application of enameling with the subject, e.g., nielloing **739**

.5 Mosaic ornaments and jewelry

.6 Ornamental bricks and tiles

.8 Other products

Lighting fixtures, candlesticks, stoves, braziers, figurines

739 **Art metalwork**

Decorative metallic forms other than sculpture

Including work in iron, steel, copper, bronze, brass, tin, pewter, nickel, aluminum, chromium

For numismatics, see **737**

.02 Miscellany

Do not use for techniques, apparatus, equipment

.2 Work in precious metals

Including goldsmithing, silversmithing, platinumwork

For watch- and clockcases, see **739.3**

.27 Jewelry

For mosaic ornaments and jewelry, see **738.5**

.3 Watch- and clockcases

.7 Arms and armor

740   Drawing and decorative arts
Do not use standard subdivisions

.1–.9   Standard subdivisions of drawing and drawings
Class techniques in **741.4**

► 741–744 Drawing and drawings

741   Freehand drawing and drawings
Scope: calligraphy (elegant handwriting), artistic lettering
For freehand drawing and drawings by subject, see **743**

.02   Miscellany
Class technique, apparatus, equipment in **741.2–741.4**

.09   Historical and geographical treatment
Class historical and geographical treatment of collections of drawings in **741.9**

.2   Drawing in specific mediums
Materials, equipment, processes
For drawing for specific purposes, see **741.5–741.7**

.4   Drawing processes
Composition, techniques
For perspective, see **742**; *drawing in specific mediums,* **741.2**; *for specific purposes,* **741.5–741.7**

► 741.5–741.7 Drawing and drawings for specific purposes
Mediums and processes

.5   Cartoons, caricatures, comics
Including materials and methods of drawing animated cartoons

.59   Collections

.593–.599   Geographical treatment
Add area notations 3–9 to **741.59**

741.6	Illustration (Commercial art)
.64	Books
	Including book jackets, children's books
.65	Magazines and newspapers
.67	Advertisements and posters
	Including fashion drawing
.68	Calendars, greeting and postal cards
.7	Silhouettes
.9	Collections of drawings
	Regardless of medium or process
	For collections of cartoons, caricatures, comics, see **741.59**
742	Perspective
	Theories, principles, methods
	For techniques of drawing specific subjects, see **743**
743	Freehand drawing and drawings by subject
	Including techniques of drawing specific subjects
744	Technical drawing
.4	Drafting procedures and conventions
	Engineering, mechanical, architectural, map drawing; production illustration, lettering, titling, dimensioning, shades, shadows, projections
	For perspective, see **742**
.5	Preparation and reading of copies
	Blueprints, photostats
	For blueprinting process, see **772**; *production of photostats*, **778.1**

► ## 745–749 Decorative and minor arts

Processes and products not provided for in **736–739**

Class comprehensive works in **745**

745 Design and crafts

Do not use standard subdivisions

.1 Antiques

Class a specific form of antiques with the subject

► ### 745.2–745.4 Design

.2 Industrial art and design

Creative design of mass-produced commodities

.4 Pure and applied design and decoration

For industrial design, see **745.2**; *design in a specific art form, the form, e.g., design in architecture* **729**

[.409] Historical and geographical treatment

Do not use

► ### 745.5–745.9 Crafts

Scope: folk art

.5 Handicrafts

Creative work done by hand with aid of simple tools or machines

► ### 745.51–745.57 In specific materials

For textile handicrafts, see **746**

.51 Woods

Marquetry, inlay trim, ornamental woodwork

For ornamental woodwork in furniture, see **749**

.53 Leathers and furs

745.54	Papers

End papers, gift wrappings, wallpaper

.55	Shells
.56	Metals
.57	Rubber and plastics
.59	Making specific objects

Handicrafts in composite materials

Including decorations for special occasions, artificial flowers, lampshades, candlesticks, toys

.6	Lettering, illumination, heraldic design
.7	Decorative coloring

Painting, lackering, japanning, stenciling, decalcomania, tolecraft

For printing, painting, dyeing textiles, see **746.6**

.8	Panoramas, cycloramas, dioramas
.9	Other decorative arts and crafts
.92	Floral arts

Selection and arrangement of plant materials and appropriate accessories

Including flower arrangement [*formerly* **635.9**]

746	Textile handicrafts
1	Weaving

For tapestry making, see **746.3**; *rug- and carpetmaking,* **746.7**

.2	Making laces and related fabrics

Needlepoint, bobbin, darned laces; passementerie

For knitting, crocheting, tatting, see **746.4**

.3	Tapestry making
[.309]	Historical and geographical treatment

Do not use

746.4	Other textile crafts

Braiding, matting, basketry, knitting, crocheting, tatting, embroidery, patchwork, quilting

For rug- and carpetmaking, see **746.7**

.5	Beadwork
.6	Printing, painting, dyeing

Block and silk-screen printing, resist-dyeing, hand decoration, stenciling

.7	Rug- and carpetmaking
[.709]	Historical and geographical treatment

Do not use

.9	Costume [*formerly* 391]

747	Interior decoration

Design and decorative treatment of interior furnishings

Including decoration of specific elements, e.g., ceilings, walls, doors, windows, floors; draperies and upholstery; decoration of specific rooms of residential and other types of buildings, for specific occasions

For furniture and accessories, see **749**

[.09]	Historical and geographical treatment

Do not use; class in 747.2

.2	Historical and geographical treatment

►   747.201–747.204 Historical treatment

Periods of development not limited geographically

.201	Ancient period to ca. 500 A.D.
.202	Medieval period, ca. 500–1400
.203	Renaissance period, 1400–1800
.204	Modern period, 1800–
.21–.29	Geographical treatment

Divide like 708.1–708.9, e.g., interior decoration in Pennsylvania 747.214 8

748 **Glass**

Including methods of decoration, specific articles other than glassware

.2 **Glassware**

Blown, prest, molded, cast, decorated products other than stained glass

[.209] Historical and geographical treatment

Do not use

.5 **Stained, painted, leaded, mosaic glass**

[.509] Historical and geographical treatment

Do not use

749 **Furniture and accessories**

Including built-in furniture, specific kinds of furniture, ornamental woodwork, heating and lighting fixtures, wall decorations

For upholstery, see 747

[.09] Historical and geographical treatment

Do not use; class in **749.2**

.2 **Historical and geographical treatment**

Scope: antiques and reproductions

.201–.204 Historical treatment

Divide like **747.201–747.204**, e.g., Renaissance period **749.203**

.21–.29 Geographical treatment

Divide like **708.1–708.9**, e.g., French furniture **749.24**

750 Painting and paintings

For commercial art, see 741.6; painting in a specific decorative art, the subject, e.g., painting textiles 746.6

.2 Miscellany

Class techniques, apparatus, equipment in 751.3–751.4

[.9] Historical and geographical treatment

Do not use; class in 759

751 Processes and forms

Class individual painters in 759.1–759.9

▶ 751.2–751.6 Processes

.2 Materials

Surfaces, pigments, mediums, fixatives, coatings

For techniques, see 751.4

.3 Equipment

Models, tools, accessories

For techniques, see 751.4

.4 Techniques

Painting with specific mediums

Class pastel in 741.2

.5 Reproduction and copying

Including forgeries, alterations, expertizing, determination of authenticity

For print making and prints, see 761–769

.6 Care, preservation, restoration

.7 Specific forms

Easel paintings, murals, panoramas, cycloramas, dioramas, theatrical scenery, miniatures

For specific subjects, see 753–758

752   Color theory and practice
       Including color symbolism

       ▶   753–758 Specific subjects
                Class individual painters in **759.1–759.9**

753   Abstractions, symbolism, mythology
       For religious symbolism, see **755**

754   Subjects of everyday life (Genre paintings)

755   Religion and religious symbolism

756   Historical events
       Battles, coronations, disasters

757   Human figures and their parts
       Not provided for in **753–756, 758**

758   Other subjects
       Landscapes, still life, marine scenes, animal and plant life,
       industrial and technical subjects, architectural subjects

759   Historical and geographical treatment

       ▶   759.01–759.06 Periods of development
                Not limited geographically

   .01   Primitive peoples and ancient times
          Including geographical treatment of paintings of primitive
          peoples [*formerly* **759.1–759.9**]

   .02   Medieval period, ca. 500–1400
   .03   1400–1600
   .04   1600–1800
   .05   1800–1900
   .06   1900–

► 759.1–759.9 Geographical treatment

Scope: individual painters regardless of process, form, subject

Class geographical treatment of paintings of primitive peoples [*formerly* 759.1–759.9] in 759.01

759.1 **North America**

Class painting and paintings of Middle America in 759.972

.11 **Canada**

.13 **United States**

Class comprehensive works on painting and paintings of specific states in 759.14–759.19

.14–.19 **Specific states of United States**

Divide like area notations 74–79, e.g., painting and paintings of California 759.194

Class individual painters in 759.13, painting and paintings of Hawaii in 759.996 9

.2–.8 **Europe**

Divide like area notations 42–48, e.g., painting and paintings of Wales [*formerly* 759.9] 759.29

Class painting and paintings of countries not provided for in area notations 42–48 in 759.94

.9 **Other parts of world**

Add area notations 3–9 to 759.9

Class painting and paintings of Wales [*formerly* 759.9] in 759.29

760 **Graphic arts**

Do not use standard subdivisions

For drawing and drawings, see 741–744; painting and paintings, 750; photography and photographs, 770

.1–.8 **Standard subdivisions of print making and prints**

[760.9]   Historical and geographical treatment of print making and prints

> Do not use; class in **769**

―――――――――――

► 761–769 Print making and prints

―――――――――――

► 761–767 Print making

761   Relief processes (Block printing)

> Printing from raised surfaces

763   Lithographic (Planographic) processes

> Printing from flat surfaces
>
> *For chromolithography, see* **764**

764   Chromolithography and serigraphy

―――――――――――

► 765–767 Intaglio processes

> Printing from incised surfaces

765   Metal engraving

> Class here comprehensive works on metal relief and metal intaglio processes
>
> Including line, stipple, criblé engraving
>
> *For relief processes, see* **761**; *mezzotinting and aquatinting,* **766**; *etching and drypoint,* **767**

766   Mezzotinting, aquatinting, related processes

> Including composite processes

767   Etching and drypoint

769   Prints

> Description, critical appraisal, collections regardless of process
>
> Including postage stamps (philately [*formerly* **383.2**]), paper money, other special forms

770   Photography and photographs

.1   Philosophy and theory

Class chemical aspects in **771**

.2   Miscellany

.28   Techniques

Including reversing negatives, recovery of waste
materials, preservation of negatives, transparencies,
positives

Class equipment in **771**

.282   Camera use

Loading, focusing, exposure, plate and film removal

►   770.283–770.284 Darkroom practice

.283   Preparation of negatives

Developing, desensitizing, reducing, intensifying,
rinsing, fixing, washing, drying exposed plates, films,
paper

.284   Preparation of positives (Contact printing)

Exposing, developing, rinsing, fixing, washing, drying,
retouching, toning, coloring, mounting

771   Equipment, supplies, chemistry

Class here comprehensive works on use and manufacture

Including studios, laboratories, darkrooms, furniture, fittings,
developing and printing apparatus, chemical supplies,
sensitometry

Class equipment and supplies used in special processes in
772–773, in specific fields of photography in **778**, manufacture
of a specific kind of equipment or supplies with the subject,
e.g., of cameras **681**

.3   Cameras and accessories

► **772–773 Special processes**

Equipment, supplies, methods

> *For processing techniques in color photography, see* **778.6**; *photomechanical printing techniques,* **655.3**

772 Metallic salt processes

Blueprinting (cyanotype), direct positive and printing-out, platinotype processes

773 Pigment processes of printing

Carbon, carbro, powder (dusting-on), imbibition, gum-bichromate, diazotype, photoceramic, photoenamel, oil processes

778 Specific fields of photography

Methods; comprehensive works on use and manufacture of equipment and supplies

Class manufacture of a specific kind of equipment or supplies with the subject, e.g., of cameras **681**

.1 Photoduplication (Photocopying)

Of photographs, sketches, paintings, drawings, documents, other printed and written matter thru production of facsimiles, photostats, projected prints

> *For microphotography, see* **778.3**; *blueprinting process,* **772**

.2 Photographic projection

Filmstrips and filmslides

> *For stereoscopic projection, see* **778.4**; *motion-picture projection,* **778.5**

.3 Scientific and technological applications

Photomicrography and microphotography in black-and-white and color, telephotography, radiography (X-ray photography), infrared, close-up, panoramic, aerial and space, high-speed photography

Class a specific application with the subject

> *For photogrammetry, see* **526.9**

255

778.4   Stereoscopic photography and projection

Production of effects of binocular vision

For stereoscopic motion-picture photography, see **778.5**

.5   Motion pictures

Photography (cinematography), editing, projection, photomicrography, preservation and storage of films, stereoscopic motion pictures

.6   Color photography and photography of colors

Orthochromatic and panchromatic photography, direct and indirect processing techniques in color photography

Class color motion-picture photography in **778.5**, color photomicrography and microphotography in **778.3**

.7   Photography under specific conditions

Outdoors, indoors, under water, under extreme climatic conditions

.8   Trick photography

Including tabletop photography; photography of specters, distortions, multiple images; silhouette photography

.9   Photography of specific subjects

Class photography of specific subjects by specific methods in **778.1–778.8**

779   Collections of photographs

780   **Music**

If preferred, distinguish scores and parts by prefixing **M** to number for treatises, e.g., scores and parts for string instruments **M787**

───────────

► 780.07–781.9 General works

Scope: instrumental music

.07   Music and society

Musicians, critics, musicologists, amateurs, support and regulation

780.1	**Philosophy and esthetics**
	Class general principles ("theory of music") in **781**
.15	**Criticism and appreciation**
	Analytical guides and program notes
	Class scientific aspects in **781.1**
.2	**Miscellany**
	Class techniques, apparatus, equipment in **781**
.7	**Study, teaching, performances**
.73	**Performances**
	Concerts and recitals
781	**General principles ("Theory of music") and techniques**
	Class principles and techniques of dramatic music in **782**, of sacred music in **783**, of music for specific mediums in **784–789**
	Class music publishing [*formerly* 781] in **655.5**
.1	**Scientific aspects**
	Mathematical, physical, physiological, psychological aspects
	For musical sound, see **781.2**
.2	**Basic considerations**
	Musical sound, nomenclature and systems of terms, notation
	For musical structure, see **781.3–781.4**

► **781.3–781.4 Musical structure**

For musical forms, see **781.5**

.3	**Harmony**
.4	**Melody and counterpoint**
	Including canon and fugue
.5	**Musical forms**
	Sonata, dance music, program music, jazz and related forms
	For canon and fugue, see **781.4**

781.6   Composition and performance

        For musical structure, see **781.3–781.4**

.7   Music of ethnic and national orientation

        Class geographical treatment of music in **780.93–780.99**

.9   Other topics

        Musical instruments, words to be sung or recited with music, bibliographies and catalogs of scores and parts

        Class bibliographies of treatises on music in **016.78**, catalogs and lists of recordings in **789.9**

782   Dramatic music and production of musical drama

.1   Opera

        Grand, comic, satiric, chamber

.12   Librettos
.13   Stories, plots, analyses
.15   Scores and parts

.8   Theater music

        Operettas, musical comedies, revues, secular cantatas and oratorios, incidental dramatic music; film, radio, television music

.9   Other forms of dramatic music

        Including music for pantomimes, masks, pageants, ballets

783   Sacred music

        Music composed for public and private worship or dedicated to a religious purpose

.1   Instrumental music

        Treatises on instrumental music and instrumental accompaniment to vocal music

        Class scores and parts in **785–789**

783.2	Liturgical and ritualistic music

Including works combining texts (librettos) with scores

Do not use standard subdivisions

Class texts used by a specific religion with the religion, e.g., liturgy and ritual of Christian church **264**

.3	Oratorios

Including Passions

.4	Nonliturgical choral pieces

Anthems, motets, choruses, cantatas

For oratorios, see **783.3**

.5	Nonliturgical chants

Gregorian, Ambrosian, Anglican, Jewish chants

.6	Songs

Including carols

.7	Evangelistic music

Treatises on mission, revival, Sunday school music

Class scores and parts in **783.6**, scores and parts for congregational singing in **783.9**

.8	Church choirs and vocal groups

Including training and conducting

Class scores and parts of music for choirs with the kind of music, e.g., anthems **783.4**

.9	Hymns

Songs for congregational singing

► 784–789 Individual mediums of musical expression

Scope: appreciation, composition, performance, concerts and recitals

Observe the following table of precedence for works combining two or more mediums, e.g., voice and piano **784**

Voice
String instruments
Wind instruments
Percussion instruments
Accordion
Organ
Harpsichord
Piano

For dramatic music, see **782**

784   Voice and vocal music

With or without instrumental accompaniment

Scope: comprehensive works on or combining words and music (texts and scores)

For sacred music, see **783**; *words to be sung or recited with music,* **781.9**; *music for orchestra with incidental vocal parts,* **785.2**

► 784.1–784.7 Specific kinds of vocal music

► 784.1–784.3 Vocal music according to number of voices

For vocal music according to origin, subject, special interest, see **784.4–784.7**

.1   Choruses and part songs

Madrigals, glees, rounds, catches, other choral pieces not originally composed for orchestral accompaniment

Do not use standard subdivisions

.2   Complete choral works

Originally composed for chorus and orchestra with or without solo voices

Do not use standard subdivisions

784.3   Songs for from one to nine parts

> Vocal chamber music, art songs, dance songs, ballads, ballades, canzonets
>
> Do not use standard subdivisions

▶   784.4–784.7 Vocal music according to origin, subject, special interest

.4   Folk songs

> Do not use standard subdivisions
>
> Class national airs, songs, hymns and songs of specific ethnic and cultural groups in **784.7**

.6   Songs for specific groups and on specific subjects

> Topical songs, songs for home, community, students, children, societies, service clubs
>
> Do not use standard subdivisions

.7   Other kinds of songs

> National airs, songs, hymns; songs of specific ethnic and cultural groups
>
> Do not use standard subdivisions

.8   Collections of vocal music

> Too general to be provided for in **784.1–784.7**

.9   The voice

> Training, performance, vocal ensemble

▶   785–789 Instruments and instrumental music

> *For treatises on sacred instrumental music, see* **783.1**

785   Instrumental ensembles and their music

.06   Organizations

> Including bands [*formerly* **785.1**], orchestras, chamber music ensembles

.1   Symphonies and band music

> Class bands [*formerly* **785.1**] in **785.06**

785.2	Music for orchestra with incidental vocal parts
.3	Miscellaneous music for orchestra

> Serenades and other romantic music, symphonic poems and other program music, variations

.4	Music for small ensembles

> Dance music, jazz, music for rhythm and percussion bands
>
> *For chamber music, see* **785.7**

.5	Independent overtures for orchestra
.6	Concertos

> Class music for organ, piano, orchestra in **786.8**

.7	Chamber music

> Compositions for two or more different solo instruments

.8	Suites for orchestra

▶ **786–789 Specific instruments and their music**

Scope: design, hand construction, care, tuning, repairing of instruments

786	Keyboard instruments and their music

> *For celesta, see* **789**

.1	Keyboard string instruments and their music

> *For instruments, see* **786.2**; *training and performance,* **786.3**; *music,* **786.4**

.2	Keyboard string instruments

> Pianoforte (piano) and its early forms, harpsichord, spinet, virginal, clavichord
>
> *For player pianos, see* **789.7**

.3	Training and performance on keyboard string instruments

786.4   Music for keyboard string instruments

              Class instructive editions in **786.3**

   .5   Keyboard wind instruments and their music

              For a specific instrument, see the subject, e.g., organ **786.6**; *training and performance,* **786.7**; *music,* **786.8**

   .6   Organ

              Class electronic organs and reed organs in **786.9**

   .7   Training in and performance on keyboard wind instruments

              For accordion and concertina, see **786.9**

   .8   Music for keyboard wind instruments

              Class instructive editions in **786.7**

                For accordion and concertina, see **786.9**

   .9   Other keyboard instruments

              Electronic organs, reed organs (harmoniums, melodeons, cabinet organs), accordions and concertinas and their music

              Class training and performance in electronic and reed organs in **786.7**, music in **786.8**

   ►   787–789 Other instruments and their music

787   String instruments and their music

              Bowed and plectral instruments and their music, e.g., violin, viola, violoncello, viols, harp, guitar, mandolin, lute, banjo, zither, ukulele

788   Wind instruments and their music

              Brass and woodwind instruments and their music, e.g., trumpet, cornet, bugle, trombone, horns, flute, piccolo, fife, clarinet, saxophone, oboe, basson, bagpipe, harmonica (mouth organ)

789   Percussion, mechanical, electrical instruments

              Including membranophones, cymbals, triangle, bells, carillons, chimes, glockenspiel, marimba, xylophone, celesta, vibraphone

►   789.7–789.9 Mechanical and electrical reproduction of music

789.7   Mechanical instruments and devices

Including barrel organ, reproducing and player pianos and orchestrion

.8   Music box

.9   Electronic musical instruments and music recording

790   Recreation (Recreational arts)

Materials, equipment, techniques

.01   Philosophy, theory, programs

.013   Value, influence, effect

Including psychological aspects of recreation, effective use of leisure

.019   Recreation for specific classes

Including recreational programs for families, children, senior citizens, invalids, persons with handicaps

.02   Miscellany

.023   Hobbies

Including collecting

.03–.09   Other standard subdivisions

.2   The performing arts

Including comprehensive works on stage, motion pictures, radio, television [*formerly* 791.4]

For music, see 780

791   Public entertainment

.06   Organizations

Including amusement parks

.1   Traveling shows

Including medicine shows, minstrel shows and skits

For circuses, see 791.3

791.3	Circuses

.4 Motion pictures, radio, television

Class comprehensive works on stage, motion pictures, radio, television in **790.2**, script writing for motion pictures, radio, television in **808.06** [*all formerly* **791.4**]

.43 Motion-picture entertainment

Class comprehensive works on motion-picture communication [*formerly* **791.43**] in **384.8**

.44 Radio

Class comprehensive works on radiobroadcasting [*formerly* **791.44**] in **384.54**

.45 Television

Class comprehensive works on television broadcasting [*formerly* **791.45**] in **384.55**

.5 Miniature, toy, shadow theaters

.6 Pageantry

Processions, festivals, illuminations, parades, floats for parades

For water pageantry, see **797.2**; *circuses,* **791.3**

.8 Animal performances

Including bullfighting, rodeos, cockfighting

For circuses, see **791.3**; *equestrian sports and animal racing,* **798**

792 Theater (Stage presentations)

For miniature, toy, shadow theaters, see **791.5**

[.02] Miscellany

Do not use

▶   792.1–792.8 Specific kinds of dramatic performance

For specific productions, see **792.9**

792.1	Tragedy and serious drama

          Including historical, Passion, morality, miracle plays

.2   Comedy and melodrama

.3   Pantomime

.7   Vaudeville, music hall, variety, cabaret, night club presentations

.8   Ballet

.809   Historical and geographical treatment

          Do not use for specific performances

.82   Ballet dancing

          Including choreography

.9   Specific productions

          Including production scripts (stage guides)

          Class specific ballets in **792.8**

793   Indoor games and amusements

          For indoor games of skill, see **794**; *games of chance,* **795**

.2   Parties and entertainments

          Charades, tableaux, children's and seasonal parties

.3   Dancing

          Including folk and national dances, theatrical dances, sword dances, cotillions, germans, balls

.33   Ballroom dancing (Round dances)

.34   Square dancing

.4   Games of action

.5   Forfeit and trick games

793.7	**Games not characterized by action**
	Puzzles, puzzle games, mathematical games and recreations
.73	**Crossword puzzles**
.8	**Magic**
	Scientific recreations, conjuring, juggling, ventriloquism
	For card tricks, see **795.4**

794 Indoor games of skill

For card games, see **795.4**

.1	**Chess**
.12	**Strategy and tactics**
	Combinations, sacrifices, traps, pitfalls, attack, counterattack, defense
.14	**Individual chessmen**
	Position, moves, power, value
.15	**Collections of games**
	Master matches, tournaments, championship games
.17	**Special forms of chess**
	Blind play, simultaneous play, living chess; automaton, mechanical, electronic chess players
.18	**Variants of chess**
	Chinese (chong-kie), Japanese (Shōgi), three-dimensional
.2	**Checkers and similar games**
.6	**Bowling**
.7	**Ball games**
	Billiards, pool
	Class table tennis [*formerly* **794.7**] in **796.34**
	For bowling, see **794.6**; *athletic games,* **796**

795   Games of chance
> Including dice games, wheel and top games, dominoes, mah-jongg, bingo, gambling and betting systems

.4   Card games
> Including card tricks

796   Athletic and outdoor sports and games
> Scope: intramural and interscholastic athletics and games [*both formerly 371.7*]
>
> *For aquatic and air sports, see* 797; *equestrian sports and animal racing,* 798; *fishing, hunting, shooting,* 799

.1   Miscellaneous games
> Singing and dancing games, leapfrog, hide and seek, puss in corner, prisoner's base, play with kites and similar toys
>
> *For active games requiring equipment, see* 796.2

.2   Active games requiring equipment
> Including roller skating, quoits, horseshoe pitching
>
> *For ball games, see* 796.3

.3   Ball games
.31   Ball thrown or hit by hand
> Handball, lawn bowling

.32   Inflated ball thrown or hit by hand
> Net ball, basketball, volleyball

.33   Inflated ball driven by foot
> Including pushball

.332   American football
.333   Rugby
> Union and League

.334   Soccer (Association football)
.335   Canadian football

796.34	Racket games

Table tennis [*formerly* 794.7], court tennis, paddle tennis, lawn tennis, rackets and squash, badminton, lacrosse

.35   Ball driven by club, mallet, bat

Including polo, croquet, field hockey

.352   Golf

.357   Baseball

.357 2   Strategy and tactics

Defensive and offensive play

.357 3   Umpiring

.357 6   Specific types of baseball

Night, sandlot, precollege, college, professional, semiprofessional

For specific games, see **796.357 7**; *strategy and tactics,* **796.357 2**

.357 7   Specific games

.357 8   Variants

Softball, baseball for girls and women, indoor baseball, one old cat

.358   Cricket

.4   Athletic exercises and gymnastics

Calisthenics, track and field athletics, jumping, vaulting, throwing, use of horizontal and parallel bars, trapeze work, rope climbing, wire walking, acrobatics, tumbling, trampolining, contortion, the Olympic games

.5   Outdoor life

Including walking, mountaineering, spelunking

.54   Camping

.56   Dude ranching and farming

796.6   Cycling
          Use of wheeled vehicles driven by manpower
          Including bicycle, soapbox racing

.7   Driving motor vehicles
          For racing, for pleasure

.8   Combat sports
          Wrestling, jujitsus, boxing, fencing

.9   Ice and snow sports
          Ice skating, snowshoeing, skiing, tobogganing and coasting, curling, ice hockey, iceboating

797   Aquatic and air sports
.1   Boating
          Canoeing, rowboating, sailboating, motorboating, yachting, surf riding, water skiing, boat racing and regattas

.2   Swimming and diving
          Including water pageantry, water games
          Do not use standard subdivisions

.21   Swimming
          For submarine swimming, see **797.23**

.23   Submarine swimming
          Skin diving, scuba diving

.24   Springboard and precision diving

.5   Air sports
          Aircraft racing, flying for pleasure, stunt flying, gliding and soaring, parachuting (skydiving)

798   Equestrian sports and animal racing
          Horsemanship, horse racing, driving and coaching, racing other animals

---

799   Fishing, hunting, shooting

   .1   Fishing

        Fresh- and salt-water

   .17   Fishing for specific kinds of fish

        Divide like **597.2–597.5**, e.g., trout fishing **799.175**

   .2   Hunting

        Small and big game

        Including falconry

 [.209]   Historical and geographical treatment

        Do not use; class in **799.29**

   .24   Birds

   .25   Small game other than birds

   .26   Big game other than birds

        For specific kinds, see **799.27**

   .27   Specific kinds of big game other than birds

   .29   Historical and geographical treatment

        Add area notations **1–9** to **799.29**

   .3   Shooting other than game

        With guns at stationary and moving targets, e.g.,
        trapshooting, skeet shooting; with bows and arrows
        (archery)

800 Literature (Belles-lettres) and rhetoric

Scope: literature itself, works about literature

Observe the following table of precedence for works combining two or more literary forms, e.g., English poetic drama 822

Drama
Poetry
Fiction
Essays
Speeches
Letters
Satire and humor
Miscellany

If preferred, give precedence to satire and humor over all other forms

► ### 801–807 Standard subdivisions of literature

Class collections and anthologies in 808.8, history, description, critical appraisal, biographical treatment in 809

801 Philosophy and theory

Including theory, technique, history of literary criticism

802 Miscellany about literature

Class techniques in 808.02–808.7

803 Dictionaries, encyclopedias, concordances

[804] Essays and lectures

Class in 809

805 Serial publications of and about literature

806 Organizations

807 Study and teaching

808	**Rhetoric, collections, anthologies**

Do not use standard subdivisions

► **808.02–808.06 Rhetoric (Composition)**

Techniques of oral and written communication for clarity and esthetic pleasure

Class rhetoric in specific literary forms in **808.1–808.7**

.02 **Authorship and editorial techniques [*formerly* 029.6]**

Preparation of manuscripts

Including preparation of theses [*formerly* **378.2**], plagiarism, writing for publication

.04 **Composition in specific languages**

For composition for specific purposes and types of readers, see **808.06**

.06 **Composition for specific purposes and types of readers**

Professional, technical, expository writing; writing for children in specific literary forms

Including news writing [*formerly* **070.4**], business writing [*formerly* **651.7**], script writing for motion pictures, radio, television [*all formerly* **791.4**]

If preferred, class techniques of writing on specific subjects in standard subdivision **01**

► **808.1–808.7 Rhetoric in specific literary forms**

Observe table of precedence under **800**

Class specific forms for children in **808.06**

.1 Poetry

.2 Drama

.3 Fiction

.31 Short stories

.4 Essays

808.5		**Speech**

Scope: voice, expression, gesture

.51 **Public speaking (Oratory)**

Platform, radio, after-dinner speaking

For debating and public discussion, see **808.53**; *preaching,* **251**

.53 **Debating and public discussion**

.54 **Recitation**

Storytelling, reading aloud

.55 **Choral speaking**

.56 **Conversation**

.6 **Letters**

.7 **Satire and humor**

.8 **Collections and anthologies of literature**

Scope: works emphasizing equally collections of literary texts and history, description, critical appraisal of literature

Class literatures of specific languages in **810–890**

For history, description, critical appraisal of literature, see **809**

▶ ──────────

808.81–808.88 In specific forms

Observe table of precedence under **800**

.81–.87 **In specific literary forms**

Divide like **808.1–808.7**, e.g., collections of public speeches **808.851**

.88 **Miscellany**

Quotations, epigrams, diaries, journals, reminiscences, prose literature

Class a specific form of prose literature with the form, e.g., essays **808.84**

.89 **For and by persons having common characteristics**

For literature in specific forms, see **808.81–808.88**

[808.9]   Literatures of artificial languages

        Class in **899.9**

809   History, description, critical appraisal, biographical treatment of literature

        Scope: essays and lectures [*both formerly* 804]

        Class theory, technique, history of literary criticism in **801**, literatures of specific languages in **810–890**

.1–.7   In specific forms

        Divide like **808.1–808.7**, e.g., poetry **809.1**

.8   For and by persons having common characteristics

        For literature in specific forms, see **809.1–809.7**; *displaying specific features,* **809.9**

.9   Displaying specific features

        Including Bible as literature [*formerly* 220.88]

        For literature in specific forms, see **809.1–809.7**

▶   ## 810–890 Literatures of specific languages

        By language in which originally written

        Scope: literature in dialect

        If preferred, class translations into a language requiring local emphasis with the literature of that language

810   **American literature in English**

        English-language literature of Western Hemisphere and Hawaii

        If desired, distinguish literature of a specific country by initial letter, e.g., literature of Canada **C810**, of United States **U810**; or, if preferred, class literatures not requiring local emphasis in **819**

.8   Collections and anthologies by more than one author

        Class collected works of single authors not limited to or chiefly identified with one specific form [*formerly* **810.81**] in **818**

810.9   History, description, critical appraisal, biographical treatment

> Class description, critical appraisal, biographical treatment of single authors not limited to or chiefly identified with one specific form in **818**

▶   ### 811–818 Specific forms

Observe table of precedence under **800**

Class under each form without further subdivision description, critical appraisal, biographical treatment, single and collected works of single authors; but, if preferred, class these regardless of form in **818**

Use **001–009** under each for standard subdivisions

811   Poetry

812   Drama

813   Fiction

> If preferred, do not class works of fiction

814   Essays

815   Speeches

816   Letters

817   Satire and humor

818   Miscellany

> Quotations, epigrams, diaries, journals, reminiscences, prose literature; collected works of single authors not limited to or chiefly identified with one specific form [*formerly* 810.81]
>
> (Optional: class here description, critical appraisal, biographical treatment, single and collected works of single authors regardless of form; prefer **811–818**)
>
> *For a specific form of prose literature, see the form, e.g., essays* **814**

819   Literatures not requiring local emphasis

> In libraries emphasizing United States literature: Canadian and other; in libraries emphasizing Canadian literature: United States and other
>
> (Optional; prefer **810**)

► **820–890 Other literatures**

820 **Of English and Anglo-Saxon languages**

Do not use standard subdivisions

If desired, distinguish English literature of a specific country by initial letter, e.g., literature of England **E820**, of Ireland **Ir820** (or of all British Isles **B820**), of Australia **A820**, of India **In820**; or, if preferred, class literatures not requiring local emphasis in **828.99**

For American literature in English, see **810**

.1–.7 Standard subdvisions of English literature

.8 Collections and anthologies of English literature by more than one author

Class collected works of single authors not limited to or chiefly identified with one specific form [*formerly* **820.81**] in **828**

.9 History, description, critical appraisal, biographical treatment of English literature

Class description, critical appraisal, biographical treatment of single authors not limited to or chiefly identified with one specific form in **828**

► 821–828 Specific forms of English literature

Observe table of precedence under **800**

Class under each form without further subdivision description, critical appraisal, biographical treatment, single and collected works of single authors; but, if preferred, class these regardless of form in **828**

Use **001–009** under each for standard subdivisions

821 Poetry

822 Drama

.3 William Shakespeare

823 Fiction

If preferred, do not class works of fiction

824 Essays

277

825   Speeches

826   Letters

827   Satire and humor

828   Miscellany

> Quotations, epigrams, diaries, journals, reminiscences, prose literature; collected works of single authors not limited to or chiefly identified with one specific form [*formerly* 820.81]
>
> (Optional: class here description, critical appraisal, biographical treatment, single and collected works of single authors regardless of form; prefer 821–828)
>
> *For a specific form of prose literature, see the form, e.g., essays* 824

.99   English-language literatures not requiring local emphasis

> In libraries emphasizing British literature: Australian, Indian, other; in libraries emphasizing Australian literature: British, Indian, other
>
> (Optional; prefer 820)

829   Anglo-Saxon (Old English)

830   Of Germanic languages

> Do not use standard subdivisions

.1–.7   Standard subdivisions of German literature

.8   Collections and anthologies of German literature by more than one author

> Class collected works of single authors not limited to or chiefly identified with one specific form [*formerly* 830.81] in 838

.9   History, description, critical appraisal, biographical treatment of German literature

> Class description, critical appraisal, biographical treatment of single authors not limited to or chiefly identified with one specific form in 838

▶ ## 831–838 Specific forms of German literature

Observe table of precedence under **800**

Class under each form without further subdivision description, critical appraisal, biographical treatment, single and
collected works of single authors; but, if preferred, class
these regardless of form in **838**

Use **001–009** under each for standard subdivisions

831   Poetry

832   Drama

833   Fiction

   If preferred, do not class works of fiction

834   Essays

835   Speeches

836   Letters

837   Satire and humor

838   Miscellany

   Quotations, epigrams, diaries, journals, reminiscences, prose
   literature; collected works of single authors not limited to or
   chiefly identified with one specific form [*formerly* 830.81]

   (Optional: class here description, critical appraisal, biographical
   treatment, single and collected works of single authors regardless
   of form; prefer **831–838**)

   *For a specific form of prose literature, see the form, e.g.,
   essays* **834**

839   Other Germanic languages

   Divide like **439**, e.g., Swedish **839.7**

▶ ## 840–860 **Of Romance languages**

Class comprehensive works in **879.9**

840 **French, Provençal, Catalan**

Do not use standard subdivisions

If desired, distinguish French literature of a specific country by initial letter, e.g., literature of Canada **C840**, of France **F840**; or, if preferred, class literature not requiring local emphasis in **848.99**

.1–.7 Standard subdivisions of French literature

.8 Collections and anthologies of French literature by more than one author

Class collected works of single authors not limited to or chiefly identified with one specific form [*formerly* **840.81**] in **848**

.9 History, description, critical appraisal, biographical treatment of French literature

Class description, critical appraisal, biographical treatment of single authors not limited to or chiefly identified with one specific form in **848**

▶ ## 841–848 Specific forms of French literature

Observe table of precedence under **800**

Class under each form without further subdivision description, critical appraisal, biographical treatment, single and collected works of single authors; but, if preferred, class these regardless of form in **848**

Use **001–009** under each for standard subdivisions

841 Poetry

842 Drama

843 Fiction

If preferred, do not class works of fiction

844 Essays

845 Speeches

846   Letters

847   Satire and humor

848   Miscellany

> Quotations, epigrams, diaries, journals, reminiscences, prose literature; collected works of single authors not limited to or chiefly identified with one specific form [*formerly* 849.81]

> (Optional: class here description, critical appraisal, biographical treatment, single and collected works of single authors regardless of form; prefer 841–848)

>> *For a specific form of prose literature, see the form, e.g., essays* 844

.99   French-language literatures not requiring local emphasis

> In libraries emphasizing Canadian literature: literature of France, Belgium, other; in libraries emphasizing literature of France: literature of Canada, Belgium, other

> (Optional; prefer 840)

849   Provençal and Catalan

850   Italian, Romanian, Rhaeto-Romanic

> Do not use standard subdivisions

.1–.7   Standard subdivisions of Italian literature

.8   Collections and anthologies of Italian literature by more than one author

> Class collected works of single authors not limited to or chiefly identified with one specific form [*formerly* 850.81] in 858

.9   History, description, critical appraisal, biographical treatment of Italian literature

> Class description, critical appraisal, biographical treatment of single authors not limited to or chiefly identified with one specific form in 858

▶ ### 851–858 Specific forms of Italian literature

Observe table of precedence under **800**

Class under each form without further subdivision description, critical appraisal, biographical treatment, single and collected works of single authors; but, if preferred, class these regardless of form in **858**

Use **001–009** under each for standard subdivisions

851	Poetry
852	Drama
853	Fiction

If preferred, do not class works of fiction

854	Essays
855	Speeches
856	Letters
857	Satire and humor
858	Miscellany

Quotations, epigrams, diaries, journals, reminiscences, prose literature; collected works of single authors not limited to or chiefly identified with one specific form [*formerly* 850.81]

(Optional: class here description, critical appraisal, biographical treatment, single and collected works of single authors regardless of form; prefer **851–858**)

For a specific form of prose literature, see the form, e.g., essays **854**

859	Romanian and Rhaeto-Romanic

860 Spanish and Portuguese

Do not use standard subdivisions

If desired, distinguish Spanish literature of a specific country by initial letter, e.g., literature of Chile **Ch860**, of Colombia **Co860** (or, of all American countries **A860**), of Spain **S860**; or, if preferred, class literature not requiring local emphasis in **868.99**

.1–.7   Standard subdivisions of Spanish literature

860.8	**Collections and anthologies of Spanish literature by more than one author**

Class collected works of single authors not limited to or chiefly identified with one specific form [*formerly* 860.81] in **868**

.9	**History, description, critical appraisal, biographical treatment of Spanish literature**

Class description, critical appraisal, biographical treatment of single authors not limited to or chiefly identified with one specific form in **868**

► **861–868 Specific forms of Spanish literature**

Observe table of precedence under **800**

Class under each form without further subdivision description, critical appraisal, biographical treatment, single and collected works of single authors; but, if preferred, class these regardless of form in **868**

Use 001–009 under each for standard subdivisions

861	**Poetry**
862	**Drama**
863	**Fiction**

If preferred, do not class works of fiction

864	**Essays**
865	**Speeches**
866	**Letters**
867	**Satire and humor**
868	**Miscellany**

Quotations, epigrams, diaries, journals, reminiscences, prose literature; collected works of single authors not limited to or chiefly identified with one specific form [*formerly* 860.81]

(Optional: class here description, critical appraisal, biographical treatment, single and collected works of single authors regardless of form; prefer **861–868**)

For a specific form of prose literature, see the form, e.g., essays **864**

868.99   Spanish-language literatures not requiring local
          emphasis

> In libraries emphasizing Mexican literature: literature of other
> Hispanic-American countries and of Spain, other; in libraries
> emphasizing literature of Spain: Hispanic-American and other
>
> (Optional; prefer 860)

869   Portuguese

> Scope: literature in Galician (Gallegan) dialect
>
> If desired, distinguish literature of a specific country by initial
> letter, e.g., literature of Brazil B869, of Portugal P869; or, if
> preferred, class literatures not requiring local emphasis in
> 869.899

.08   Collections and anthologies by more than one author

> Class collections of single authors not limited to or chiefly
> identified with one specific form [*formerly* 869.081] in
> 869.8

.09   History, description, critical appraisal, biographical
          treatment

> Class description, critical appraisal, biographical
> treatment of single authors not limited to or chiefly
> identified with one specific form in 869.8

► 869.1–869.8 Specific forms

Observe table of precedence under 800

Class under each form without further subdivision description, critical appraisal, biographical treatment, single and
collected works of single authors; but, if preferred, class
these regardless of form in 869.8

.1–.7   Specific literary forms

> Divide like 811–817, e.g., essays 869.4
>
> Use 001–009 under each for standard subdivisions

869.8   Miscellany

Quotations, epigrams, diaries, journals, reminiscences, prose literature; collected works of single authors not limited to or chiefly identified with one specific form [*formerly* 869.081]

(Optional: class here description, critical appraisal, biographical treatment, single and collected works of single authors regardless of form; prefer 869.1–869.8)

Use **869.800 1 – 869.800 9** for standard subdivisions

For a specific form of prose literature, see the form, e.g., essays **869.4**

.899   Literatures not requiring local emphasis

In libraries emphasizing Brazilian literature: literature of Portugal and other; in libraries emphasizing literature of Portugal: Brazilian and other

(Optional; prefer **869**)

870   Of Italic languages

Do not use standard subdivisions

.1–.7   Standard subdivisions of Latin literature

.8   Collections and anthologies of Latin literature by more than one author

Class collected works of single authors not limited to or chiefly identified with one specific form [*formerly* 870.81] in **878**

.9   History, description, critical appraisal, biographical treatment of Latin literature

Class description, critical appraisal, biographical treatment of single authors not limited to or chiefly identified with one specific form in **878**

►   871–878 Specific forms of Latin literature

Classical Latin; classical revival (medieval and modern) Latin [*formerly* 879]

Observe table of precedence under **800**

Class under each form without further subdivision description, critical appraisal, biographical treatment, single and collected works of single authors; but, if preferred, class these regardless of form in **878**

Use **001–009** under each for standard subdivisions

871   Poetry

For dramatic poetry, see 872; *epic poetry,* 873; *lyric poetry,* 874

872   Dramatic poetry and drama

873   Epic poetry and fiction

874   Lyric poetry

875   Speeches

876   Letters

877   Satire and humor

878   Miscellany

Quotations, epigrams, diaries, journals, reminiscences, prose literature; collected works of single authors not limited to or chiefly identified with one specific form [*formerly* 870.81]

(Optional: class here description, critical appraisal, biographical treatment, single and collected works of single authors regardless of form; prefer **871–878**)

For a specific form of prose literature, see the form, e.g., speeches 875

879   Other Italic languages

Class classical revival (medieval and modern) Latin literature [*formerly* 879] in **871–878**

.9   Romance languages

Including Osco-Umbrian languages

Class literatures of other specific Romance languages in **840–860**

880 Of classical languages and modern Greek

Do not use standard subdivisions

Class literature of Latin language in **870**

.1–.7 Standard subdivisions of classical Greek literature

.8 Collections and anthologies of classical Greek literature by more than one author

Class collected works of single authors not limited to or chiefly identified with one specific form [*formerly* **880.81**] in **888**

.9 History, description, critical appraisal, biographical treatment of classical Greek literature

Class description, critical appraisal, biographical treatment of single authors not limited to or chiefly identified with one specific form in **888**

▶ ### 881–888 Specific forms of classical Greek literature

Ancient Greek; medieval (Byzantine) Greek [*formerly* **889**]

Observe table of precedence under **800**

Class under each form without further subdivision description, critical appraisal, biographical treatment, single and collected works of single authors; but, if preferred, class these regardless of form in **888**

Use **001–009** under each for standard subdivisions

881 Poetry

For dramatic poetry, see **882**; *epic poetry,* **883**; *lyric poetry,* **884**

882 Dramatic poetry and drama

883 Epic poetry and fiction

884 Lyric poetry

885 Speeches

886 Letters

887   Satire and humor

888   Miscellany

Quotations, epigrams, diaries, journals, reminiscences, prose literature; collected works of single authors not limited to or chiefly identified with one specific form [*formerly* 880.81]

(Optional: class here description, critical appraisal, biographical treatment, single and collected works of single authors regardless of form; prefer 881–888)

> *For a specific form of prose literature, see the form, e.g., speeches* 885

889   Modern Greek

Katharevusa and Demotic

Class medieval (Byzantine) Greek literature [*formerly* 889] in 881–888

890   Of other languages

891   East Indo-European and Celtic languages

Divide like 491, e.g., literature of modern Persian language 891.5

892   Semitic languages

Divide like 492, e.g., literature of Yiddish language 892.49

893   Hamitic and other languages

Literatures of Old Egyptian, Coptic, Berber, Cushitic (Hamitic Ethiopian), Chad-family languages

> *For Hausa, see* 896

894   Ural-Altaic, Paleosiberian, Dravidian languages

Literatures of Altaic languages (Tungusic, Mongolic, Turkic families); Uralic languages (Samoyedic, Magyar, Permian, Finnish, Estonian, Lapp languages); Paleosiberian languages (Luorawetlin, Ainu, Gilyak, Ket); Dravidian languages (Kota, Toda, Kurukh, Tamil, Malayalam, Kanarese, Gondi, Khond, Telugu languages); Brahui

895   **Languages of East and Southeast Asia**

> Literatures of Chinese, Japanese, Korean, Tibeto-Burman, Burmese, Thai, Vietnamese, Cambodian languages
>
> Divide like **495**, e.g., literature of Chinese language **895.1**

896   **African languages**

> Literatures of Hottentot, Bushman, Bantu, Hausa, Swahili languages and dialects
>
> Class Afro-Asian literatures in **892–893**

897   **North American Indian languages**

898   **South American Indian languages**

899   **Austronesian and other languages**

> Including literatures of Negrito, Papuan, Malayan, Polynesian, Melanesian, Micronesian, Australian, Basque, Elamitic, Etruscan, Sumerian, Caucasian languages

.9   **Artificial languages** [*formerly* 808.9]

> Literatures in Esperanto, Interlingua, Volapük

900

900 General geography and history and related disciplines

Do not use standard subdivisions

Class historical and geographical treatment of a specific subject with the subject

▶ ### 901–908 Standard subdivisions of general history

Class history of specific continents, countries, localities in 930–990

901 Philosophy and theory

Class civilization of ancient world [*formerly* 901] in 913.03

.9 **Civilization**

Man's spiritual, intellectual, social, material situation and progress

If preferred, class in 909

Class areal treatment in 910

.92 In the years 500–1500

.93 In the years 1500–1900

.94 In the years 1900–

902 Miscellany

Including chronologies

903 Dictionaries, encyclopedias, concordances

904 Collected accounts of specific events

Including adventure [*formerly* 910.4]

905 Serial publications

906 Organizations

907   Study and teaching

908   Collections and anthologies

909   World history

> Use **909.001–909.009** for standard subdivisions
>
> (Optional: civilization; prefer **901.9**)
>
> Class history of ancient world to ca. 500 A.D. in **930**

.07   Medieval, to 1450/1500

> Comprehensive works only

.08   Modern, 1450/1500–

> Comprehensive works only
>
> Class history of 1700–1799 in **909.7**, of 1800–   in **909.8**

.7   1700–1799

.8   1800–

.81   1800–1899

.82   1900–

> *For World War I, see* **940.3**

.824   1940–1949

> *For World War II, see* **940.53**

.825   1950–1959

.826   1960–1969

910   **General geography**

> Areal differentiation and traveler's observation of the earth
> (physical geography [*formerly* **551.4**]) and man's civilization upon
> it
>
> Use **910.001–910.008** for standard subdivisions; but class charts
> and plans in **912**

.02   The earth (Physical geography)

.03   Man and his civilization

910.09   Historical and regional treatment

Including geography of regions not limited by continent, country, locality; discovery, exploration, growth of geographic knowledge

Class geography of specific continents, countries, localities in 913–919

.1   Topical geography

(Optional; prefer specific subject, e.g., economic geography 330.91–330.99)

Divide like 001–899, e.g., economic geography 910.133

.2–.3   Miscellany, dictionaries, encyclopedias, concordances of travel

.4   Accounts of travel

Trips around the world, ocean travel, seafaring life, shipwrecks, mutinies, buried treasure, pirates' expeditions

Class adventure [*formerly* 910.4] in 904

Class discovery and exploration in 910.09, collections and anthologies of travels in 910.8, scientific travels in 508.3

.5–.9   Other standard subdivisions of travel

Class travel in specific continents, countries, localities in 913–919

911   Historical geography

Growth and changes in political divisions

912   Graphic representations of earth's surface

Atlases, maps, charts, plans

For map projections, see 526.8

.1   Specific subjects

.3–.9   Specific continents, countries, localities

Add area notations 3–9 to 912

▶ ## 913–919 Geography of specific continents, countries, localities

Scope: comprehensive works on geography and history of specific continents, countries, localities

If preferred, class in **930–990**

Class history of specific continents, countries, localities in **930–990**, geography of regions in **910.09**

For historical geography, see **911**; *graphic representations of earth's surface,* **912**

913 ## Geography of ancient world

Including prehistoric archeology [*formerly* **571**]

Use **913.001–913.008** for standard subdivisions

.02 ### The earth (Physical geography)

.03 ### Man and his civilization [*formerly also* 901]

Including archeology (study of man's past civilizations thru discovery, collection, interpretation of his material remains)

.04 ### Travel

.3 ### Continents, countries, localities

Add area notation 3 to **913**, e.g., geography of ancient Italian peninsula **913.37**

▶ ## 914–919 Geography of modern world

Class customs of specific continents, countries, localities [*formerly* **914–919**] in **390.09**

914 ## Europe

Add area notation **4** to **91**, e.g., geography of British Isles **914.2**; then add **001–008** for standard subdivisions

915 ## Asia

Add area notation **5** to **91**, e.g., geography of Japan **915.2**; then add **001–008** for standard subdivisions

916   Africa

>   Add area notation 6 to 91, e.g., geography of South Africa 916.8; then add 001–008 for standard subdivisions

917   North America

>   Add area notation 7 to 91, e.g., geography of Ohio 917.71; then add 001–008 for standard subdivisions

>   Class Indians and their civilization in 970.1

918   South America

>   Add area notation 8 to 91, e.g., geography of Brazil 918.1; then add 001–008 for standard subdivisions

>   Class Indians and their civilization in 980.1

919   Other parts of world

>   Add area notation 9 to 91, e.g., geography of Australia 919.4; then add 001–008 for standard subdivisions

920   **General biography, genealogy, insignia**

>   Including biography of Indians of North America [*formerly* 970.2], of South America [*formerly* 980.2], of slaves [*formerly* 326]

>   Do not use standard subdivisions

>   Class biography of persons associated with a specific subject with the subject

.001–.008   Standard subdivisions of biography

.009   Historical and geographical treatment of biography

>   Class treatment by continent, country, locality in 920.03–920.09

▶   920.02–920.09 General collections of biography

.02   Not limited geographically

.03–.09   By continent, country, locality

>   Add area notations 3–9 to 920.0, e.g., collections of biographies of Englishmen 920.042

► 920.1–928 Biography of specific classes of persons

(Optional; prefer standard subdivision **092**)

920.1   *Bibliographers

.2   *Librarians and book collectors

.3   *Encyclopedists

.4   *Publishers and booksellers

.5   *Journalists and news commentators

.7   *Persons by sex

.71   *Men

.72   *Women

.9   *Persons associated with other subjects

Not provided for in **920.1–920.5, 921–928**

921   *Philosophers and psychologists

922   *Religious leaders, thinkers, workers

Including collected biographies of communicants of specific religions and sects

923   *Persons in social sciences

Heads of state, nobility, public administrators, politicians, statesmen, military persons, philanthropists, social reformers, educators, explorers, geographers, pioneers; persons in economics (including labor leaders), law (including criminals), commerce, communication, transportation

924   *Philologists and lexicographers

925   *Scientists

926   *Persons in technology

927   *Persons in the arts

928   *Persons in literature

Including historians

* Optional; prefer standard subdivision **092**

929	Genealogy, names, insignia
.1	Genealogy

For sources, see **929.3**; *family histories,* **929.2**

.2	Family histories

For royal houses, peerage, gentry, see **929.7**

.3	Genealogical sources

Registers, wills, tax lists, census records, court records compiled for genealogical purposes

For epitaphs, see **929.5**

.4	Personal names
.5	Epitaphs
.6	Heraldry

For armorial bearings, see **929.8**

.7	Royal houses, peerage, landed gentry

Rank, precedence, titles of honor

.8	Armorial bearings

Coats of arms, crests, seals

.9	Flags

National, state, ship, ownership flags

Class military use in **355.1**

► **930–990 Geographical treatment of general history**

History of specific continents, countries, localities

(Optional: geography of specific places; prefer **913–919**)

Add area notations 3–9 to 9, e.g., general history of British Isles **942**; then, unless otherwise specified, add further as follows:

001–008	Standard subdivisions
01–09	Historical periods
	As shown in the schedules that follow

930 **The ancient world to ca. 500 A.D.**

> Use **930.01–930.08** for standard subdivisions

931   *China to 420 A.D.

932   *Egypt to 640 A.D.

933   *Palestine to 70 A.D.

934   *India to 647 A.D.

935   *Mesopotamia and Iranian Plateau to 642 A.D.

936   *Europe north and west of Italian peninsula

937   *Italian peninsula and adjacent territories to 476 A.D.

938   *Greece to 323 A.D.

939   Other parts of ancient world to ca. 640 A.D.

► **940–990 The modern world**

940 **Europe**

> From fall of Rome, 476, to present
>
> Use **940.01–940.08** for standard subdivisions

.1   Middle Ages, 476–1453

.2   Modern period, 1453–

> *For World War I, see* **940.3**; *20th century, 1918–*   , **940.5**

.3   World War I, 1914–1918

> Social, political, economic, diplomatic history, causes, results
>
> Including participation of specific countries and groups of countries
>
> *For military history, see* **940.4**

.4   Military history of World War I (Conduct of the war)

> Including celebrations, commemorations, memorials, prisons, health, social services, secret service and spies, propaganda
>
> Use **940.400 1 – 940.400 8** for standard subdivisions

* Add as instructed under **930–990**

940.5	20th century, 1918–
.53	World War II, 1939–1945

For military history, see **940.54**

.531	Social, political, economic history

Including diplomatic causes and results

For diplomatic history, see **940.532**

.532	Diplomatic history
.533	Participation of specific groups of countries

United Nations, Axis Powers, neutrals, occupied
countries

For participation of specific countries, see
940.534–940.539; *a specific activity, the subject,*
e.g., diplomatic history **940.532**

.534–.539	Participation of specific countries

Scope: governments in exile, underground movements,
anti-Axis and pro-Axis national groups, mobilization

Add area notations **4–9** to **940.53**

For a specific activity, see the subject, e.g.,
diplomatic history **940.532**

.54	Military history of World War II (Conduct of the war)

Including strategy, mobilization, racial minorities as
troops, repressive measures and atrocities, military
participation of specific countries

Use **940.540 01 – 940.540 08** for standard subdivisions

.541	Operations

For specific campaigns and battles, see **940.542;** *aerial*
operations, **940.544;** *naval operations,* **940.545**

.542	Specific campaigns and battles
.544	Aerial operations
.545	Naval operations
.546	Celebrations, commemorations, memorials

940.547	Prisons, health, social services
.548	Other topics

> Military life and customs, intelligence, subversion, sabotage, infiltration, psychological warfare (propaganda)

.55	Later 20th century, 1945–

► **941–949 Specific parts of Europe**

941	*Scotland and Ireland

> Do not use standard subdivisions

.001–.008	Standard subdivisions of Scotland
.5	*Ireland

> Use **941.501–941.508** for standard subdivisions

942	*British Isles
.01	Early history to 1066
.02	Norman period, 1066–1154
.03	House of Plantagenet, 1154–1399
.04	Houses of Lancaster and York, 1399–1485
.05	Tudor period, 1485–1603
.06	Stuart period, 1603–1714
.07	House of Hanover, 1714–1837
.08	Victoria and House of Windsor, 1837–
.081	Victoria, 1837–1901
.082	20th century, 1901–

> *For George V, see* **942.083**; *period of World War II,* **942.084**; *later 20th century,* **942.085**

.083	George V, 1910–1936
.084	Period of World War II, 1936–1945

> Reigns of Edward VIII, 1936 and George VI, 1936–1952

.085	Later 20th century, 1945–

> Reign of Elizabeth II, 1952–

* Add as instructed under **930–990**

943   ***Central Europe**

        Do not use standard subdivisions

  .001–.008   Standard subdivisions of Germany

  .08   Germany since 1866

  .085   Weimar Republic, 1918–1933

  .086   Third Reich, 1933–1945

  .087   Later 20th century, 1945–

944   ***France**

  .04   Revolution, 1789–1804

  .05   First Empire, 1804–1815

  .06   Restoration, 1815–1848

  .07   Second Republic and Second Empire, 1848–1870

  .08   Third, Fourth, Fifth Republics, 1870–

  .081   Third Republic, 1870–1945

  .082   Fourth Republic, 1945–1958

  .083   Fifth Republic, 1958–

945   ***Italy and adjacent territories**

  .09   Italy since 1870

  .091   Fascist regime, 1918–1946

  .092   Republic, 1946–

946   ***Iberian Peninsula and adjacent islands**

        Do not use standard subdivisions

  .001–.008   Standard subdivisions of Spain

  .08   Spain since 1868

  .081   Second Republic, 1931–1939

  .082   Regime of Francisco Franco, 1939–

* Add as instructed under **930–990**

947   *Eastern Europe
            Do not use standard subdivisions

.001–.008   Standard subdivisions of Russia

.08   Russia since 1855

.084   Communist regime, 1917–   (Union of Soviet
               Socialist Republics, 1923–   )
                    For later 20th century, see **947.085**

.085   Later 20th century, 1953–

948   *Scandinavia

949   *Other parts of Europe

950   Asia
            Use **950.01–950.08** for standard subdivisions

.4   20th century, 1905–

.41   Early 20th century, 1905–1945

.42   Later 20th century, 1945–

951   *China and adjacent areas
            Do not use standard subdivisions

.001–.008   Standard subdivisions of China

►   951.04–951.05 China since 1912

.04   Early 20th century, 1912–1949

.05   People's Republic, 1949–

952   *Japan and adjacent islands
            Do not use standard subdivisions

.001–.008   Standard subdivisions of Japan

►   952.03–952.04 Japan since 1868

.03   Re-establishment of imperial power, 1868–1945

.04   Postwar period, 1945–

* Add as instructed under **930–990**

953	*Arabian Peninsula and adjacent areas
954	*South Asia
.03	British rule, 1774–1947
.04	Independence and partition, 1947–
955	*Iran (Persia)
956	*Middle East
957	*Siberia (Asiatic Russia)
958	*Central Asia
959	*Southeast Asia

960 Africa

Use 960.01–960.08 for standard subdivisions

961	*North Africa
962	*Egypt and Sudan

Do not use standard subdivisions

.001–.008	Standard subdivisions of Egypt
963	*Ethiopia
964	*Northwest African coast and offshore islands

Do not use standard subdivisions

.001–.008	Standard subdivisions of Morocco
965	*Algeria
966	*West Africa and offshore islands
967	*Central Africa and offshore islands
968	*South Africa
969	*South Indian Ocean islands

* Add as instructed under 930–990

970   **North America**

> (Optional: discovery and exploration to ca. 1600; prefer **973.1**)

> Use 970.001–970.008 for standard subdivisions

  .1   Indians of North America

> History and civilization

>> *For specific tribes, see* **970.3**; *Indians in specific places,* **970.4**; *government relations,* **970.5**

  [.2]   Biography of Indians

> Class biographies of persons associated with a specific subject in standard subdivision **092**, of persons not so related in **920**

  .3   Specific Indian tribes

> *For government relations, see* **970.5**

  .4   Indians in specific places

> *For specific tribes, see* **970.3**; *government relations,* **970.5**

  .5   Government relations with Indians

> History and policy

> Class Indian wars of a specific place and period with history of the appropriate place and period

  [.6]   Specific subjects in relation to Indians

> Class with the subject

971   *****Canada**

  .01   Early history to 1763

  .02   Early British rule, 1763–1791

  .03   Period of the separate colonies, 1791–1841

  .04   Growth of responsible government, 1841–1867

  .05   Dominion of Canada during period 1867–1914

  .06   20th century, 1914–

***** Add as instructed under **930–990**

972   *Middle America

>   Use 972.000 1 – 972.000 8 for standard subdivisions

.001–.008   Standard subdivisions of Mexico

.08   Mexico since 1867

973   United States

>   Use 973.01–973.08 for standard subdivisions

.1   Discovery and exploration to 1607

>   Scope: discovery and exploration of America; if preferred, class in 970
>
>   Class discoveries and explorations in a specific country with history of the country

.2   Colonial period, 1607–1775

>   Class local history in 974–975

.3   Revolution and confederation, 1775–1789

.31   Social, political, economic history

>   *For diplomatic history, see 973.32*

.32   Diplomatic history

>   Relations of United States with other nations

.33   Operations

>   *For naval operations, see 973.35*

.35   Naval operations

>   Including ships, privateering

.38   Treason, secret service, spies, propaganda

.4   Constitutional period, 1789–1809

>   Administrations of Washington, John Adams, Jefferson

* Add as instructed under 930–990

973.5	Early 19th century, 1809–1845

> Administrations of Madison, Monroe, John Quincy Adams, Jackson, Van Buren, William Henry Harrison, Tyler
>
> Including War of 1812

.6	Middle 19th century, 1845–1861

> Administrations of Polk, Taylor, Fillmore, Pierce, Buchanan
>
> Including Mexican War

.7	Administration of Lincoln, 1861–1865 (Civil War)
.71	Social, political, economic history

> *For diplomatic history, see* **973.72**

.72	Diplomatic history
.73	Operations

> *For naval operations, see* **973.75**

.75	Naval operations

> Including ships, privateering, blockade running

.77	Prisons, health, social services
.78	Military life and customs, secret service and spies
.8	Later 19th century, 1865–1901 (Period of reconstruction)

> Administrations of Andrew Johnson, Grant, Hayes, Garfield, Arthur, Cleveland, Benjamin Harrison, McKinley
>
> Including Spanish-American War

.9	20th century, 1901–
.91	Early 20th century, 1901–1953

> Including administrations of Theodore Roosevelt, Taft, Wilson, Harding, Coolidge, Hoover

.917	Administration of Franklin D. Roosevelt, 1933–1945
.918	Administration of Truman, 1945–1953

973.92	Later 20th century, 1953–
.921	Administration of Eisenhower, 1953–1961
.922	Administration of Kennedy, 1961–1963
.923	Administration of Lyndon B. Johnson, 1963–

▶ 974–979 Specific states of United States

974 *Northeastern states

975 *Southeastern (South Atlantic) states

976 *South central states

977 *North central states

978 *Western states

979 *States of Great Basin and Pacific Slope

980 South America

Use **980.001–980.008** for standard subdivisions

.1–.5 Indians of South America

Divide like **970.1–970.5**, e.g., specific tribes **980.3**

Class biographies of persons associated with a specific subject in standard subdivision **092**, of persons not so related in **920** [*both formerly* **980.2**]

[.6] Specific subjects in relation to Indians

Class with the subject

981 *Brazil

982 *Argentina

983 *Chile

984 *Bolivia

985 *Peru

* Add as instructed under **930–990**

986   *Northwestern South America and Panama

987   *Venezuela

988   *Guiana

989   *Other parts of South America

990   **Other parts of world**

     Do not use standard subdivisions

▶   991–996 Pacific Ocean islands (Oceania)

▶   991–995 Southwest Pacific

991   *Malay Archipelago

     Use **991.000 1 – 991.000 8** for standard subdivisions

.001–.008   Standard subdivisions of Indonesia

992   *Sunda Islands

993   *New Zealand and Melanesia

994   *Australia

995   *New Guinea (Papua)

996   *Other parts of Pacific

     Do not use standard subdivisions

997   *Atlantic Ocean islands

998   *Arctic islands

999   *Antarctica

* Add as instructed under **930–990**

Table of Standard Subdivisions

As fully explained in the introduction, section 3.37, and as shown by the dashes that precede them, the following standard subdivisions (formerly known as form divisions) are never used alone, but may be used as required with any number from the general tables, e.g., classification (01 in this table) of modern Indic languages (491.4): 491.401.

—01   Philosophy and theory

> Classification, value, linguistic and scientific aspects, indexes, research methodology, psychological aspects
>
> (Optional: techniques of writing, prefer **808.06**; bibliographies and catalogs, prefer **016**; professional and occupational ethics, prefer **174**)
>
> *For dictionaries, see standard subdivision* **03**

—02   Miscellany

> Including synopses, outlines, manuals, humorous and audio-visual treatment, commercial miscellany

—021   Tabulated and related materials

> Tables, formulas [*both formerly* standard subdivision **083**], specifications, lists, inventories, catalogs of articles
>
> *For catalogs of museums and exhibits, see standard subdivision* **074**

—022   Illustrations [*formerly* standard subdivision 084]

> Pictures, charts, designs, plans

—023   The subject as a profession, occupation, hobby

> If preferred, class the subject as a profession or occupation in **331.7**

—024   Works for specific types of users

—025   Directories [*formerly* standard subdivision 058]

—026   Law

> (Optional; prefer **340**)

—027   Inventions and identification marks

> Patents, trademarks, service marks, ownership marks, artists'
> and craftsmen's marks

—028   Techniques, apparatus, equipment

—03   Dictionaries, encyclopedias, concordances

—[04]   Collected essays and lectures

> Class in standard subdivision **08**

—05   Serial publications

> Class administrative reports and proceedings of organizations
> in standard subdivision **06**

—[058]   Directories

> Class in standard subdivision **025**

—06   Organizations

> History, charters, regulations, membership lists, administrative
> reports and proceedings

▶   —061–063 Professional

> International, national, state, provincial, local organizations
> not engaged in profit-motive activities

—061   Permanent government organizations

—062   Permanent nongovernment organizations

—063   Temporary organizations

—065   Business organizations

> Individual proprietorships, partnerships, companies,
> corporations, combinations

—[069]   Professional and occupational ethics

> Class in **174**

—07   Study and teaching
—071   Schools and courses
—072   Research
                 Historical, descriptive, experimental

—074   Museums and exhibits
                 Collections, guidebooks, catalogs

—075   Collecting and collections of objects
                 For museums and exhibits, see standard subdivision 074

—076   Review and exercise
                 Workbooks with problems, questions, answers
                 Including civil service examinations [*formerly* 351.3]

—077   Programed teaching and learning
—078   Use of apparatus and equipment
                 Including use of teaching machines

—079   Competitions and awards
                 Prizes, scholarships, fellowships, honorary titles

—08   Collections and anthologies
                 Collections not planned as composite works
                 Including collected essays and lectures [*both formerly* standard subdivision 04]

—[081]   Critical appraisal of a person's work
                 Class in standard subdivision 092

—[083]   Tables and formulas
                 Class in standard subdivision 021

—[084]   Illustrations
                 Class in standard subdivision 022

—09   Historical and geographical treatment

—091   Regional treatment

> History and description by region, area, place, group in general, not limited by continent, country, locality
>
> Add area notation **1** to **09**, e.g., the subject in Torrid Zone **091 3**

—092   Persons

> Critical appraisal [*formerly* standard subdivision **081**] and description of work, biography of persons associated with the subject
>
> Scope: Indians of North America [*formerly* **970.2**], of South America [*formerly* **980.2**], slaves [*formerly* **326**]
>
> If preferred, class biography in **920.1–928**
>
> Class biography not clearly related to any specific subject in **920**
>
> Observe exceptions under **180–190, 750, 809, 810–890**

—092 2   Collected

—092 4   Individual

> If preferred, class in **92** or **B**

—093–099   Geographical treatment

> History and description by continent, country, locality, specific instance of the subject
>
> Add area notations **3–9** to **09**, e.g., the subject in United States **097 3**
>
> Class persons associated with the subject in standard subdivision **092**

Area Table

As fully explained in the introduction, section 3.353 1, and as shown by the dashes that precede them, the following area notations are never used alone, but may be used as required (either directly when so noted or thru the interposition of standard subdivision 09) with any number from the general tables, e.g., cultural processes (301.29) in Japan (52 in this table):   301.295 2.

SUMMARY

—1   Regions, areas, places, groups in general
—2   Persons
—3   The ancient world
       —4–9 The modern world
—4   Europe
—5   Asia
—6   Africa
—7   North America
—8   South America
—9   Other parts of world

—1   Regions, areas, places, groups in general
Not limited by continent, country, locality

──────────
► —11–13 Zonal regions

—11   Frigid Zones
—12   Temperate Zones (Middle Latitude Zones)
—13   Torrid Zone (Tropics)

──────────
► —14–16 Physiographic regions

—14   Land and land forms

Islands [*formerly* area 9], continents, mountains, caves, plains, coastal regions, soil

—15   Types of vegetation

         Forests, grasslands, deserts

—16   Air and water

         Including ocean and sea waters, fresh and brackish waters

—161   Atmosphere

—17   Socioeconomic regions and groups

—171   Political orientation

         Empires and political unions [*both formerly* areas 3–9], blocs, nonself-governing territories

—172   Degree of economic development

         Regions of high, medium, low development

—173   Concentration of population

         Urban, suburban, rural regions

—174   Ethnic groups

         Including ancient European tribes [*formerly* area 36], Arabs [*formerly* area 53], Jews [*formerly* area 569 3], Negroes [*formerly* area 67], Gipsies [*formerly* 397]

—175   Lingual regions

—176   Religious culture groups

—18   Other kinds of terrestrial regions

         Including Western [*formerly* area 7], Eastern, Northern, Southern hemispheres; Mediterranean [*formerly* area 4], Atlantic, Pacific, Indian Ocean basins

         Class here the Occident

—19   Space

—2   Persons

—22   Collected

—24   Individual

►   —3–9 Specific continents, countries, localities

Class regions, areas, places, groups not limited by continent, country, locality in area **1**

Class empires and political unions [*formerly* areas **3–9**] in area **171**

—3   The ancient world

If preferred, class in areas **4–9**

—31   China

—32   Egypt

—33   Palestine [*formerly also* area **39**]

Including Judea

—34   India

—35   Mesopotamia and Iranian Plateau

Class region east of Caspian Sea in area **39**

—36   Europe north and west of Italian peninsula

Class ancient European tribes [*formerly* area **36**] in area **174**

—37   Italian peninsula and adjacent territories

—38   Greece

For Aegean Sea islands, see area **39**

—39   Other parts of ancient world

Aegean Sea islands, Asia Minor, Cyprus, Syria, Arabia, Black Sea and Caucasus regions, central Asia, north Africa, southeastern Europe

Class Palestine [*formerly* area **39**] in area **33**

► ## —4–9 The modern world

(Optional: the ancient world; prefer area **3**)

—4   Europe

Class Mediterranean region [*formerly* area **4**] in area **18**

SUMMARY

—41	Scotland and Ireland
—42	British Isles
—43	Central Europe
—44	France
—45	Italy and adjacent territories
—46	Iberian Peninsula and adjacent islands
—47	Eastern Europe
—48	Scandinavia
—49	Other parts of Europe

—41   Scotland and Ireland

► ## —411–414 Divisions of Scotland

—411   Northern Scotland

Shetland and Orkney Islands, Caithness, Sutherland, Ross and Cromarty

—412   North central Scotland

Inverness, Nairn, Moray, Banff, Aberdeen, Kincardine

—413   Central Scottish Lowlands

Angus, Perth, Fife, Kinross, Clackmannan, Stirling, Dunbarton, Argyll, Bute

—414   Southern Scotland

Renfrew, Ayr, Lanark, the Lothians, Berwick, Peebles, Selkirk, Roxburgh, Dumfries, Kirkcudbright, Wigtown

—415   Ireland

For divisions of Ireland, see areas **416–419**

▶ —416–419 Divisions of Ireland

—416   Ulster

           Class here Northern Ireland

—417   Connacht (Connaught)

—418   Leinster

—419   Munster

—42   British Isles

           Class here Great Britain, United Kingdom

           For Scotland and Ireland, see area 41

▶ —421–428 England

—421   Greater London

           Including Outer Ring, Middlesex

               For a specific part of Outer Ring, see the county in which located, e.g., Surrey area 422

—422   Southeastern England

           Surrey, Kent, Sussex, Hampshire, Berkshire, Isle of Wight

               For Greater London, see area 421

—423   Southwestern England and Channel Islands

           Wiltshire, Dorset, Devon, Cornwall, Somerset

—424   Midlands of England

           Gloucester, Monmouth, Hereford, Shropshire, Stafford, Worcester, Warwick

               For East Midlands, see area 425

—425   East Midlands of England

           Derby, Nottingham, Lincoln, Leicester, Rutland, Northampton, Huntingdon, Bedford, Oxford, Buckingham, Hertford, Cambridge, Soke of Peterborough, Isle of Ely; the Fens

—426   Eastern England

         Norfolk, Suffolk, Essex

—427   North central England

         Cheshire, Lancashire, York

—428   Northern England and Isle of Man

         Durham, Northumberland, Cumberland, Westmorland;
         Lake District

—429   Wales

         For Monmouth, see area 424

—43   Central Europe

         Class here Germany

—436   Austria and Liechtenstein

         Class Trieste in area 45, Slovenia and Dalmatia in area
         497 [*all formerly* area 436]

—437   Czechoslovakia

         Class Galicia in area 438, Bukovina in area 498 [*both*
         formerly area 437]

—438   Poland

         Including Galicia [*formerly* area 437]

—439   Hungary

         Class Transylvania in area 498, Slavonia, Croatia, Bosnia
         and Herzegovina in area 497 [*all formerly* area 439]

—44   France

         For Corsica, see area 459; *a specific department outside*
         Metropolitan France, the subject, e.g., Martinique area 729 8

—443   Paris metropolitan area
—449   Riviera

         Including Monaco

—45	**Italy and adjacent territories**

Including Trieste [*formerly* area **436**], independent state of San Marino

—453	**Venice**
—455	**Florence**
—456	**Rome and Vatican City**
—458	**Sicily and Malta**
—459	**Sardinia and Corsica**
—46	**Iberian Peninsula and adjacent islands**

Including Spain (with Balearic Islands), Andorra, Gibraltar

*For Canary Islands, see area **64***

—469	**Portugal**

Including Madeira and Azores

—47	**Eastern Europe**

Class here Union of Soviet Socialist Republics (Soviet Union)

*For Asiatic Russia, see area **57**; Soviet Republics of central Asia, area **58**; Balkan Peninsula, area **496***

—471	**Finland**
—473	**Moscow**
—477	**Moldavian [*formerly* area 498 5] and Ukrainian Soviet Socialist Republics**
—479	**Caucasus**

Including Armenian Soviet Socialist Republic [*formerly* area **566 4**]

—48	**Scandinavia**

Class here northern Europe

*For Finland, see area **471**; Iceland, area **491***

—481	**Norway**

*For divisions of Norway, see areas **482–484***

►   —482–484 Divisions of Norway

—482   Southeastern Norway

        Vest-Agder, Aust-Agder, Telemark, Vestfold, Ostfold, Oslo, Akershus, Buskerud, Opland, Hedmark counties

—483   Southwestern Norway

        Rogaland, Hordaland, Bergen, Sogn og Fjordane, More og Romsdal counties

—484   Central and northern Norway

        Sor-Trondelag, Nord-Trondelag, Nordland, Troms, Finnmark counties

—485   Sweden

        For divisions of Sweden, see areas **486–488**

►   —486–488 Divisions of Sweden

—486   Southern Sweden (Gotaland)

        Malmohus, Kristianstad, Blekinge, Kalmar, Kronoberg, Halland, Jonkoping, Alvsborg, Goteborg och Bohus, Skaraborg, Ostergotland, Gotland counties

—487   Central Sweden (Svealand)

        Sodermanland, Stockholm, Uppsala, Vastmanland, Orebro, Varmland, Kopparberg, Gavleborg counties; Stockholm city

—488   Northern Sweden (Norrland)

        Jamtland, Vasternorrland, Vasterbotten, Norrbotten counties

        For Gavleborg, see area **487**

—489   Denmark

        For Faeroes, see area **491**; *Greenland, area* **98**

—49   Other parts of Europe

—491   Iceland and Faeroes

—492   Netherlands (Holland)

—493   Belgium and Luxembourg

—494   Switzerland

—495   Greece

For Aegean Sea islands, see area **499**

—496   Balkan Peninsula

Including Turkey in Europe, Albania

If preferred, class Turkey in Europe in area **563**

Class here Ottoman Empire

For a specific country of Balkan Peninsula, of Ottoman Empire, see the subject, e.g., Greece area **495**

—497   Yugoslavia and Bulgaria

Including Slovenia and Dalmatia [*both formerly* area **436**]; Slavonia, Croatia, Bosnia and Herzegovina [*all formerly* area **439**]

—498   Romania

Including Bukovina [*formerly* area **437**], Transylvania [*formerly* area **439**]

—[498 5]   Moldavian Soviet Socialist Republic

Class in area **477**

—499   Aegean Sea islands

—5   Asia

Class here the Orient, Eurasia

▶   —51–52 Far East

For Siberia, see area 57; *Southeast Asia, area* 59

SUMMARY

    —51   China and adjacent areas
    —52   Japan and adjacent islands
    —53   Arabian Peninsula and adjacent areas
    —54   South Asia
    —55   Iran (Persia)
    —56   Middle East
    —57   Siberia (Asiatic Russia)
    —58   Central Asia
    —59   Southeast Asia

—51   China and adjacent areas

—512   Taiwan (Formosa), and Hong Kong and Macao
        colonies

—515   Tibet

—517   Outer Mongolia (Mongolian People's Republic)

—519   Korea

—52   Japan and adjacent islands

Class southern Sakhalin, Kurile Islands [*both formerly* area
52] in area 57

—521   Tokyo

—528   Ryukyu and Bonin Islands

—53   Arabian Peninsula and adjacent areas

Including Sinai Peninsula, Bahrein

Class Arabs [*formerly* area 53] in area 174

—54   South Asia

      Class here India

       For Southeast Asia, see area 59

—[547]   Pakistan

      Class in area 549

—[548 9]   Ceylon and Maldive Islands

       Class Ceylon in area 549 3, Maldive Islands in area
       549

—549   Pakistan [*formerly* area 547] and other jurisdictions

      Including eastern Baluchistan [*formerly* area 588],
      Maldive Islands [*formerly* area 548 9], Nepal, Sikkim,
      Bhutan

—549 3   Ceylon [*formerly* area 548 9]

—55   Iran (Persia)

      Including western Baluchistan [*formerly* area 588]

—56   Middle East

      Class here Near East

       For a specific country of Middle or of Near East, see the
       subject, e.g., Iran area 55

—561   Asia Minor and adjacent islands

      Class here Turkey

       For divisions of Asia Minor and adjacent islands, see
       areas 562–566; *Aegean Sea islands, area* 499

▶   —562–566 Divisions of Asia Minor and adjacent
islands

—562   Western Asia Minor

      Canakkale, Balikesir, Manisa, Kutahya, Usak, Afyon,
      Denizli, Burdur, Mugla, Aydin, Izmir (Smyrna)
      provinces of Turkey

—563   North central Asia Minor

      Bursa, Bilecik, Kocaeli, Bolu, Eskisehir, Ankara, Cankiri, Zonguldak, Kastamonu, Sinop, Samsun, Amasya, Corum, Yozgat, Sakarya provinces of Turkey

      (Optional: Turkey in Europe; prefer area 496)

—564   South central Asia Minor and Cyprus

      Including Antakya, Isparta, Konya, Kirsehir, Kayseri, Nevsehir, Nygde, Icel, Seyhan (Adana), Hatay, Gaziantep provinces of Turkey

—564 5   Island of Cyprus

—565   East central Asia Minor

      Trebizond (Trabzon), Gumusane, Giresun, Ordu, Tokat, Sivas, Maras, Malatya, Adiyaman, Urfa provinces of Turkey

—566   Eastern Asia Minor

      Armenia (Rize, Coruh, Erzurum, Kars, Agri, Van, Hakari provinces of Turkey), Kurdistan (Erzincan, Elazig, Tunceli, Diyarbakir, Mus, Bingol, Bitlis, Sürt, Mardin provinces of Turkey)

—[566 4] Armenian Soviet Socialist Republic

      Class in area 479

—567   Iraq

—569   Eastern Mediterranean

—569 1   Syria

—569 2   Lebanon

—[569 3] Jews after dispersion

      Class in area 174

—569 4   Israel

      Class here Palestine

      For Jordan, see area 569 5

—569 5   Jordan

—57	Siberia (Asiatic Russia)

Including southern Sakhalin, Kurile Islands [*both formerly area* 52]

Class here Soviet Union in Asia

For Soviet Republics of central Asia, see area 58

—58	Central Asia

Including Kirghiz, Kazakh, Turkmen, Tadzhik, Uzbek Soviet Socialist Republics

—581	Afghanistan
—[588]	Baluchistan

Class eastern Baluchistan in area 549, western Baluchistan in area 55

—59	Southeast Asia

For Malay Archipelago, see area 91

—591	Burma
—593	Thailand (Siam)
—594	Laos
—595	Malaysia

Class Malaysian Borneo in area 911

—596	Cambodia
—597	Vietnam
—6	Africa
—61	North Africa

Including Libya, Tunisia

For a specific part of North Africa, see the subject, e.g., Algeria area 65

—62　　　　Egypt and Sudan
　　　　　　For Sinai Peninsula, see area **53**

—624　　　Sudan
　　　　　　For provinces of Sudan, see areas **625–629**

▶　　　　　　　　　—625–629 Provinces of Sudan

—625　　　Northern Province
　　　　　　Class here Nubian Desert

—626　　　Central provinces
　　　　　　Khartoum, Blue Nile

—627　　　Darfur Province
—628　　　Kordofan Province
—629　　　Eastern and southern provinces
　　　　　　Kassala, Upper Nile, Bahr el Ghazal, Equatoria

—63　　　　Ethiopia

—64　　　　Northwest African coast and offshore islands
　　　　　　Morocco, Spanish West Africa, Canary Islands

—65　　　　Algeria

—66　　　　West Africa and offshore islands
　　　　　　Including Mauritania, Mali, Upper Volta, Niger, Senegal,
　　　　　　Sierra Leone, the Gambia, Guinea republic, Portuguese
　　　　　　Guinea, Cape Verde Islands, Liberia, Ivory Coast,
　　　　　　Dahomey, Togo, islands of the Gulf of Guinea
　　　　　　Class here Sahara Desert

—667　　　Ghana
—669　　　Nigeria

—67	**Central Africa and offshore islands**

Including Cameroun, Rio Muni, Gabon, Congo (Brazzaville), Angola, Central African Republic, Chad, Rwanda, Burundi, French Somaliland, Socotra, Somalia, Mozambique

Class here Negro Africa, Africa south of the Sahara

Class Negroes not limited by continent [*formerly* area **67**] in area **174**

> *For a specific country of Negro Africa, of Africa south of the Sahara, see the subject, e.g., Nigeria area* **669**

—675	**Congo (Leopoldville)**

Former Belgian Congo

—676	**Uganda and Kenya**

—678	**Tanganyika and Zanzibar (Tanzania)**

—68	**South Africa**

Including Republic of South Africa, Bechuanaland Protectorate, Swaziland, Basutoland (Basotho)

—689	**Rhodesia, Zambia, Malawi**

Formerly Southern Rhodesia, Northern Rhodesia, Nyasaland

—69	**South Indian Ocean islands**

Including Madagascar (Malagasy Republic), Seychelles, Réunion, Mauritius

—7	**North America**

Class Western Hemisphere [*formerly* area **7**] in area **18**

—701	**Indians of North America**

Class North American Indians not limited by continent in area **174**

SUMMARY

—71 Canada
—72 Middle America
—73 United States
—74 Northeastern states
—75 Southeastern (South Atlantic) states
—76 South central states
—77 North central states
—78 Western states
—79 States of Great Basin and Pacific Slope

—71 Canada

—711 British Columbia

—712 Northern territories and prairie provinces

Including Yukon and Northwest Territories

—712 3 Alberta

—712 4 Saskatchewan

—712 7 Manitoba

—713 Ontario

—714 Quebec

Class here Saint Lawrence River and Seaway

—715 New Brunswick

Class here Maritime Provinces

For Nova Scotia, see area 716; Prince Edward Island, area 717

—716 Nova Scotia

—717 Prince Edward Island

—718 Newfoundland, and Saint Pierre and Miquelon

For Labrador territory, see area 719

—719 Labrador territory of province of Newfoundland

—72	Middle America
	Class here Mexico
—725	Valley of Mexico
	Including Mexico City
—728	Central America
	For Panama, see area **862**
—728 1	Guatemala
—728 2	British Honduras (Belize)
—728 3	Honduras
—728 4	El Salvador
—728 5	Nicaragua
—728 6	Costa Rica
—729	West Indies (Antilles)

►   —729 1 – 729 5 Greater Antilles

—729 1	Cuba and Isle of Pines
—729 2	Jamaica and Cayman Islands

►   —729 3 – 729 4 Hispaniola and adjacent islands

—729 3	Dominican Republic
—729 4	Haiti
—729 5	Puerto Rico
—729 6	Bahama, Turks, Caicos Islands

►   —729 7 – 729 8 Lesser Antilles (Caribbees)

—729 7	Leeward Islands

Virgin Islands, Saint Christopher, Nevis, Anguilla, Sombrero, Antigua, Barbuda, Montserrat, Guadeloupe, Saint Martin, Saint Eustatius, Saba

—729 8	Windward and other southern islands

Barbados, Martinique, Trinidad and Tobago, Dominica, Saint Lucia, Saint Vincent, Grenadines, Grenada, Carriacou, Curaçao, Aruba, Bonaire

—729 9	Bermuda
—73	United States

For specific states, see areas 74–79

▶   —74–79 Specific states of United States

For Hawaii, see area 969

—74	Northeastern states

Class here Appalachian Mountains, Connecticut River

▶   —741–746 New England

—741	Maine
—742	New Hampshire
—743	Vermont
—744	Massachusetts
—745	Rhode Island
—746	Connecticut

▶   —747–749 Middle Atlantic states

—747	New York
—747 1	New York City
—748	Pennsylvania
—749	New Jersey
—75	Southeastern (South Atlantic) states

Class here Southern states, Piedmont, Atlantic Coastal Plain

—751	Delaware
—752	Maryland

Class here Potomac River

—753	District of Columbia (Washington)
—754	West Virginia
—755	Virginia

        Class here Blue Ridge, Chesapeake Bay

—756	North Carolina
—757	South Carolina
—758	Georgia
—759	Florida

—76   South central states

        Class here Old Southwest, lower Mississippi River and Valley

▶   **—761–764 Gulf Coast states**

                For Florida, see area 759

—761	Alabama
—762	Mississippi
—763	Louisiana
—764	Texas

        Class here Rio Grande

—766	Oklahoma
—767	Arkansas
—768	Tennessee

        Class here Tennessee River and Valley

—769   Kentucky

        Class here Ohio River

        Class Ohio Valley in area 77

—77   North central states

        Class here Middle West, Mississippi River and Valley, Ohio Valley, Great Lakes

        Class Ohio River in area 769

► —771–776 Lake states

For New York, see area 747; Pennsylvania, area 748

—771   Ohio

—772   Indiana

—773   Illinois

—774   Michigan

—775   Wisconsin

—776   Minnesota

—777   Iowa

—778   Missouri

—78   Western states

Class here the West, Missouri River, Rocky Mountains

For states of Great Basin and Pacific Slope, see area 79

—781   Kansas

—782   Nebraska

—783   South Dakota

—784   North Dakota

► —786–789 Rocky Mountains states

For Idaho, see area 796

—786   Montana

—787   Wyoming

—788   Colorado

—789   New Mexico

—79   States of Great Basin and Pacific Slope

Class here Pacific Coast states

—791   Arizona

Class here New Southwest

—792	Utah
—793	Nevada
—794	California
—795	Oregon

> Class here Pacific Northwest, Cascade and Coast Ranges

—796	Idaho
—797	Washington
—798	Alaska
—8	**South America**

> Class here Latin America, Spanish America, the Andes
>
> *For Middle America, see area* 72

—801	Indians of South America

> Class South American Indians not limited by continent in area 174

—81	Brazil
—82	Argentina
—83	Chile
—84	Bolivia
—85	Peru
—86	Northwestern South America and Panama
—861	Colombia
—862	Panama
—863	Panama Canal Zone
—866	Ecuador
—87	Venezuela
—88	Guiana

> British, Dutch (Surinam), French

—89	Other parts of South America
—892	Paraguay
—895	Uruguay

—9   Other parts of world

Class islands of the world [*formerly* area **9**] in area **14**

———————

►   —91–96 Pacific Ocean islands (Oceania)

For a specific island or group of islands, see the subject, e.g., Japan area **52**

———————

►   —91–95 Southwest Pacific

—91   Malay Archipelago

Including Indonesian Borneo, Celebes, Moluccas (Spice Islands)

Class here Indonesia

For Sunda Islands, see area **92**; *New Guinea, area* **95**

—911   North Borneo

Malaysian Borneo and Brunei

—914   Philippine Islands

—92   Sunda Islands

Sumatra, Java, Madura, Bali, Timor, lesser islands

Class Borneo and Celebes in area **91**

—93   New Zealand and Melanesia

Including New Caledonia territory, New Hebrides, Bismarck Archipelago; Loyalty, Solomon, Admiralty Islands

For Louisiade Archipelago, D'Entrecasteaux Islands, see area **95**; *Fiji Islands, area* **96**

—931   New Zealand

—94   Australia

—95   New Guinea (Papua)

Including Louisiade Archipelago, D'Entrecasteaux Islands

—96   Other parts of Pacific

Including Fiji, Easter, Pitcairn, Henderson, Ducie, Oeno, Society, Tubuai (Austral), Gambier, Rapa, Cook, Manihiki, Marquesas, Tuamotu, Line, Caroline, Marianas (Ladrone), Gilbert, Ellice, Phoenix, Marshall Islands; Tonga, Samoa, Tokelau, Nauru, Palmyra, Midway

Class here Polynesia, Micronesia

—969   **Hawaii**

—97   Atlantic Ocean islands

Bouvet Island, Falklands, Saint Helena, their dependencies

For a specific island or group of islands, see the subject, e.g., Azores area 469

—98   Arctic islands

Svalbard (Spitsbergen), Greenland, Jan Mayen Island, Franz Josef Land, Novaya Zemlya (New Land), Severnaya Zemlya (Northern Land)

For a specific Arctic island or group of islands, see the subject, e.g., Northwest Territories of Canada area 712

—99   Antarctica

Synthesis of Notation

The following numbers and sequences of numbers are used as the basis for synthesis of other sequences. Here, arranged by the secondary number or sequence, are enumerated all the "divide-like" notes that appear in the tables. The procedure for number synthesis thru division is described in the introduction, section 3.353 2.

In this list, numbers or spans of numbers preceded by asterisks are numbers whose starred subdivisions are to be divided as instructed at the place indicated.

Since every number in the tables may be built upon by the addition of the numbers of the area table, either direct (where the tables say "Add area notation . . .") or thru the use of standard subdivision 09, the "add" notes are not enumerated. Observe also that any standard subdivision may be added to *any* class number.

Like 001–999
016

Like 001–899
910.1

Like 220.1–.9
221.1–.9
225.1–.9

Like 281–289
230.1–.9
252.01–.09
264.01–.09
266.1–.9

Like 291
292

Like 351.1–.9
353.001–.009

Like 355
358.41

Like 355.1–.2
359.1–.2

Like 355.4–.8
359.4–.8

Like 420–490
572.8

Like 421–428
*430–490

Like 421–426
*430–490

Like 423
*430–490

Like 428
*430–490

Like 430–490
220.53–.59
423.3–.9

Like 439
839

Like 491
891

Like 492
892

Like 510–590
630.21–.29

Like 574
576.1

Like 574.1–.9
581.1–.9
591.1–.9

Like 574.9
560.9

Like 583–589
635.933–.939

Like 597.2–.5
799.17

Like 708.1–.9
747.21–.29
749.21–.29

Like 725–728
690.5–.8

Like 747.201–.204
749.201–.204

Like 808.1–.7
808.81–.87
809.1–.7

Like 811–817
869.1–.7

Like 970.1–.5
980.1–.5

Like area 42–48
708.2–.8
759.2–.8

Like area 73–79
708.13–.19

Like area 74–79
759.14–.19

Relative Index

Use of the Relative Index

Full instructions on use appear in the introduction, section 3.6.

A dagger (†) preceding a number means that one or more topics, not necessarily including the one named, have been relocated to this number from another number in Abridged edition 8.

An entry and number in **boldface** means that this subject and number are subdivided in the tables.

A number preceded by *"area"* may be found in the Area Table, and indicates geographical specification; a number preceded by *"s.s."* may be found in the Table of Standard Subdivisions, and indicates a form of presentation or a mode of treatment. Neither area nor standard subdivision numbers are used alone, but both may be used as required with any number from the general tables.

Abbreviations Used in the Index

ASSR	Autonomous Soviet Socialist Republic	Ia.	Iowa
admin.	administration(s)	Ida.	Idaho
Ala.	Alabama	Ill.	Illinois
anal.	analytic(al), analysis	Ind.	Indiana
arch.	architectural, architecture	ind.	industrial, industries, industry
Ariz.	Arizona	internat.	international
Ark.	Arkansas	isl(s).	island(s)
bus.	business(es)	Kan.	Kansas
bus. tech.	business technology	Ky.	Kentucky
Calif.	California	La.	Louisiana
chem. tech.	chemical technology	lit.	literary, literature(s)
co.	county	Mass.	Massachusetts
Colo.	Colorado	Md.	Maryland
comp.	comparative	Me.	Maine
Conn.	Connecticut	meas.	measures
Del.	Delaware	med.	medical, medicine
dept(s).	department(s)	med. sci.	medical sciences
econ.	economic(s)	Mich.	Michigan
econ. geol.	economic geology	mil.	military
ed.	education(al)	mil. sci.	military science
elect.	electric(al), electricity	Minn.	Minnesota
Eng.	England	Miss.	Mississippi
eng.	engineering, engineers	Mo.	Missouri
equip.	equipment	Mont.	Montana
Fla.	Florida	mt(s).	mountain(s)
Ga.	Georgia	N.C.	North Carolina
gen.	general	N.D.	North Dakota
gen. wks.	general works	N.H.	New Hampshire
geol.	geological, geology	N.J.	New Jersey
govt.	government(s), governmental	N.M.	New Mexico
		N.T.	New Testament
hist.	historical, history	N.Y.	New York
		N.Z.	New Zealand

nat.	national, natural	rel.	religion(s)
Neb.	Nebraska	res.	reservoir
Nev.	Nevada	S.C.	South Carolina
O.	Ohio	S.D.	South Dakota
O.T.	Old Testament	SSR	Soviet Socialist
Okla.	Oklahoma		Republic
Ore.	Oregon	sci.	science(s), scientific
P.E.I.	Prince Edward Island	spec.	specific
Pa.	Pennsylvania	St.	Saint
par.	parish	subj.	subject(s)
pol.	political, politics	Tenn.	Tennessee
pol. sci.	political science	Ter.	Territory
prac.	practical, practice	Tex.	Texas
prod.	producing, production, products	U.S.	United States
		USSR	Union of Soviet Socialist Republics
psych.	psychological, psychology	Va.	Virginia
pub.	public	vet.	veterinary
qual.	qualitative, quality	vet. sci.	veterinary science
quan.	quantitative, quantity	Vt.	Vermont
R.I.	Rhode Island	W.Va.	West Virginia
RSFSR	Russian Soviet Federated Socialist Republic	Wash.	Washington
		Wis.	Wisconsin
		Wyo.	Wyoming
reg.	regulation(s), regulatory		

Relative Index

A

Aardwolves
  culture   636.9
  see also Proteles
Abandoned
  children *see* Children
Abbey
  schools *see* Monastic schools
Abbeys
  buildings *see* Monastic
      buildings
  religion *see* Religious
      congregations
Abbreviations
  linguistics
    English   421
    see also other spec.
      languages
  see also   *s.s.*–01
Abdias (O.T.) *see* Prophetic
    books
Abduction *see* Offenses
Aberdeen Scotland   *area* –412
Abnormal
  children *see* Exceptional
      children
  psychology
    animals   †156
    gen. wks.   157
    pedology   †155.45
Abnormalities *see* Teratology
Abolition
  slavery *see* Slavery
Aborigines *see* Ethnology
Abortion
  criminal *see* Offenses
  spontaneous
    animals
      vet. sci.   636.089
      zoology   591.2
      see also spec. animals
    man   618.3
    see also Miscarriage

Abortionists *see* Offenders
Absentee
  ownership
    economics
      industries   338
      land   333.4
    see also other spec. subj.
Absolute
  democracy *see* Pure
      democracy
  geometries
    gen. wks.   513
    see also   *s.s.*–01
  monarchy *see* Monarchical
      absolutism
  temperature *see* Cryogenics
Absolution
  penance *see* Sacraments
  see also other spec. rites
Absolutism
  monarchical *see* Monarchical
      absolutism
  religion *see* Predestination
Abstinence
  ethics   178
  religion *see* Religious
      experience
Abstract
  art
    gen. wks.   704.945
    see also spec. art forms
  thought
    philosophy   128
    psychology   153.2
Abstractions *see* Abstract
Abutments *see* Columns
Abyssinia *see* Ethiopia
Abyssinian
  Church
    religion   281
    see also Church buildings
  see also Ethiopic

Academic
  high schools *see* Secondary
    schools
  robes *see* Garments
Academies (organizations) *see*
  Organizations
Academies (schools) *see*
  Secondary schools
Acari
  paleozoology   565
  zoology   595
Acceleration
  motion *see* Kinematics
  particles *see* Particle
    acceleration
Accelerators *see* Particle
  acceleration
Accessioning
  library functions   025.2
  museum functions   069
  see also other institutions
Accident
  insurance
    govt.-sponsored   368.4
    voluntary   368.3
    see also Financial
      institutions
Accidents
  catastrophic *see* Disasters
  prevention *see* Safety
    measures
  psychology   †155.9
  statistics *see* Demography
Acclimation
  ecology *see* Ecology
  hygiene
    animals
      gen. wks.   636.089
      see also spec. animals
    man   613.1
Accomplished
  redemption *see* Atonement
Accordions
  manufacture
    economics   338.4
    technology   681
  music   786.9
Accountability
  government *see* Governmental
    accountability

Accountability (continued)
  religion
    Christian   233
    gen. wks.   291.2
    see also other spec. rel.
    see also other spec. aspects
Accounting (activity)
  economics   338.4
  technology   **657**
Accounting
  finance *see* Financial
    administration
  wealth *see* National
    accounting
Acculturation *see* Culture
Accumulators
  engineering
    electric *see* Batteries
    hydraulic   621.2
  see also spec. applications
Achievement
  tests *see* Mental tests
Acids *see* Chemistry
Acoustics
  architecture   729
  biophysics *see* Biophysics
  engineering   †620.2
  music   781.2
  physics   **534**
Acquisitions
  library functions   025.2
  museum functions   069
  see also other institutions
Acrobatics
  circuses *see* Circuses
  gymnastics *see* Gymnastics
Acronyms
  English language
    abbreviations   421
    lexicology   **†422–423**
    usage   **†428**
  see also other spec. languages
Acrostics *see* Puzzles
Actinopterygii
  paleozoology   567
  zoology   597.4
Action
  games
    indoor
      customs   394
      gen. wks.   793.4

Aircraft (continued)
  insurance *see* Transportation
      insurance
Air-cushion
  vehicles
    architecture   725
    construction
      economics   338.4
    technology
      gen. wks.   629.3
      military   623.7
    see also Transportation
        services
Airedales *see* Terriers
Airmail *see* Postal
    communication
Airplanes *see* Heavier-than-air
    aircraft
Airports
  eng. & construction
    economics   338.4
  technology
    gen. wks.   629.136
    military   623.6
  see also Transportation
      services
Air-raid
  shelters *see* Blastproof
      structures
  warning
    systems *see* Alarm systems
Airships *see* Lighter-than-air
    aircraft
Akershus Norway   *area* –482
Akkadian
  ethnic groups   *area* –174
  languages   492
  lingual groups   *area* –175
  see also other spec. subj.
Alabama (state)   *area* –761
Alarm
  systems
    civil defense *see* Civil
        defense
    communication *see*
        Telecommunication
    engineering
      economics   338.4
    technology
      gen. wks.   621.389
      military   623.7
  see also Communication

Alaska (state)   *area* –798
Alaskan
  malamutes *see* Working dogs
Alaudidae *see* Passeriformes
Albania (ancient country) *area* –39
Albania (modern country) *area* –496
Albanian
  ethnic groups   *area* –174
  language   491.9
  lingual groups   *area* –175
  see also other spec. subj.
Albatrosses *see* Pelagic birds
Alberta   *area* –712 3
Albigensian
  Church   284
  see also Heresies
Alcae *see* Charadriiformes
Alcantarines *see* Religious
    congregations
Alcedines *see* Coraciiformes
Alchemy
  chemistry   540.1
  occultism   133.4
  philosophy   117
Alcoholic
  beverages *see spec. kinds*
Alcoholism *see* Addictions
Alcohols
  chemistry   547
  manufacture
    economics   338.4
    technology   661
  see also spec. products
Ale *see* Beers
Aleutian (subject) *see* Eskimo-
    Aleut
Algebra
  gen. wks.   **512**
  see also   *s.s.* –01
Algebraic
  geometry *see* Analytical
      geometry
Algeria   *area* –65
Algicides *see* Pesticides
Algonkian-Mosan
  ethnic groups   *area* –174
  languages   497
  lingual groups   *area* –175
  see also other spec. subj.
Algonkin *see* Algonkian-Mosan
Algonquin *see* Algonkian-Mosan

Ammunition (continued)
  mil. sci.
    gen. wks.   355.8
    tech. forces *see* Technical
      forces
    see also spec. mil. branches
Ammunition-ships *see*
  Government vessels
Amos (O.T.) *see* Prophetic
  books
Amphibian
  planes *see* Heavier-than-air
    aircraft
Amphibians
  culture   639
  paleozoology   567
  zoology   597
  see also spec. animals
Amphibious
  landing craft *see* Warships
  warfare
    gen. wks.   †359.9
    see also hist. of spec. wars
Amphitheaters *see* Recreation
  buildings
Amulets *see* Talismans
Amusement
  park buildings *see* Park
    buildings
  parks *see* Recreational land
Amusements *see* Recreational
  activities
Amvets *see* Military societies
Ana *see* Collected writings
Anabaptists
  religion   284
  see also Church buildings
Anagrams *see* Puzzles
Analog
  instruments
    engineering   621.381 9
    managerial use   658.5
    mathematics   510.78
    office equipment   651
    see also   *s.s.*–01
Analogy
  logic   169
  psychology   †153.4
  religion
    gen. wks.   219
    see also spec. rel.

Analysis
  chemistry *see* Analytical
    chemistry
  mathematics
    calculus   **517**
    geometry   **516**
    see also   *s.s.*–01
  physics
    sound waves   534
    see also Vibrations
  see also Reasoning
Analysis situs *see* Topology
Analytic *see* Analytical
Analytical
  chemistry
    gen. wks.   543–545
    organic   547
    pharmacy
      med. sci.   615
      vet. sci.
        gen. wks.   636.089
        see also spec. animals
  geometry
    gen. wks.   **516**
    see also   *s.s.*–01
Anamnia
  paleozoology   567
  zoology   **597**
Anarchism *see* Ideal states
Anatolian
  ethnic groups   *area* –174
  language   491.9
  lingual groups   *area* –175
  see also other spec. subj.
Anatomy
  biology
    animals   591.4
    gen. wks.   574.4
    plants   581.4
    see also spec. organisms
  cells *see* Cytology
  med. sci.
    animals
      gen. wks.   636.089
      see also spec. animals
    man   611
Ancestry *see* Genealogy
Anchors *see* Nautical equipment
Ancient
  civilization *see* Ancient world

Antarctic
 waters
  geography
   gen. wks.   910.09
   physical   †910.02
  geology   551.4
  regional subj.
   treatment   *area* –16
Antarctica   *area* –99
Anteaters *see* Edentates
Antelopes
 conservation   639
 culture   636.2
 hunting
  industries   639
  sports   799.27
 see also Bovoidea
Antennas
 engineering
  economics   338.4
  technology
   radio   621.384 1
   television   621.388 3
 see also spec. applications
Anthems *see* Choral music
Anthologies *see* Collected
  writings
Anthropogeography
 biology   **572.9**
 psychology   †155.8
 sociology   301.453
Anthropoidea *see* Primates
Anthropology
 criminal *see* Criminal
  anthropology
 cultural *see* Culture
 physical *see* Physical
  anthropology
 social *see* Culture
Anthropometry
 anthropology   573
 crime detection   364.12
 medicine   616
Anthroposophy *see* Mysticism
Antiaircraft
 artillery
  forces *see* Artillery forces
  pieces *see* Artillery
   (pieces)
 cruisers *see* Warships
Antichrist *see* Demonology

Antigua West Indies   *area* –729 7
Antilles *see* West Indies
Antimissile
 missiles *see* Guided missiles
Antimony *see* Metals
Antinomianism *see* Heresies
Antiphonal
 readings *see* Responsive
  readings
Antiques
 gen. wks.   745.1
 see also spec. art forms
Antiquities
 gen. wks. *see* Ancient world
 law   †340
Anti-Semitism
 pol. sci.   323.1
 psychology   155.9
 sociology   301.451
Antisocial
 compulsions *see* Personality-
  disorders
Antitank
 artillery
  forces *see* Artillery forces
  pieces *see* Artillery
   (pieces)
Anti-Trinitarianism *see*
  Unitarianism
Antonyms
 English language
  lexicology   †422–423
  usage   †428
 see also other spec. languages
Ants
 agricultural pests   632
 culture   638
 see also Hymenoptera
Apachean *see* Na-Dene
Apartment
 buildings *see* Residential
  buildings
 house
  districts *see* Residential
   areas
 houses *see* Public
  accommodations
Apes
 conservation   639
 culture   636.9
 see also Primates

Artificial (continued)

insemination

animals	636.08
man	618.1

see also Sexual ethics

islands

engineering

economics	338.4
technology	627

see also spec. applications

languages

gen. wks.	†499.9
literature	†899.9

see also other spec. subj.

precipitation

physical geology	†551.6

see also spec. applications

satellites

engineering

economics	338.4

technology

crafts	629.46
flights	629.43
weather prediction	†551.6

see also other spec.
applications

stones

construction indus.

economics	338.4
technology	693.5

manufacture

economics	338.4
technology	666

materials

construction	691
engineering	620.1

see also spec. applications

weather control

physical geology	†551.6

see also spec. applications

Artigue

process see Special-process
photography

Artillery (pieces)

art metalwork	739.7
customs	399

industries

economics	338.4
technology	623.4

mil. sci.

gen. wks.	355.8

Artillery (pieces)

mil. sci. (continued)

tech. forces see Technical
forces

see also spec. mil.
branches

Artillery

ammunition see Ammunition

forces

mil. sci.	358

see also spec. kinds of
warfare

Artiodactyla

paleozoology	569
zoology	599.7

Arts

creative see Creative arts

industrial see Industrial arts

manual see Manual arts

mil. recreation see Special
services

religion

Christian	246–247
gen. wks.	291.3

see also other spec. rel.

Aruba West Indies	area –729 8

Aryan see Indo-Iranian

Asbestos

geology

gen. wks.	553

mineralogy

gen. wks.	549.6

see also spec. minerals

industries

extractive see Mining

manufacturing see spec.
products

properties

construction	691
engineering	620.1

see also Refractory materials

Ascension

Thursday see Holy days

Asceticism see Religious
experience

Ash

Wednesday see Holy days

Ashuanipi Ter.	area –719
Asia	**area –5**

Baby-sitting *see* Child care
Backgammon *see* Dice games
Bacon *see* Red meats
Bacteria *see* Schizomycetes
Bacteriological
    warfare *see* Biological
        warfare
Bacteriology *see* Schizomycetes
Badgers *see* Mustelines
Badminton *see* Racket games
Baffin Bay *see* Arctic Ocean
Bagpipes *see* Wind instruments
        (musical)
Bahai faith *see* Bahaism
Bahaism
    culture groups
        geography   910.09
        history   909
        subject treatment   *area* –176
    philosophy   181
    religion   297
Bahama Isls.   *area* –729 6
Bahr el Ghazal Sudan   *area* –629
Bahrein   *area* –53
Bakery
    products
        manufacture
            economics   338.4
            technology
                commercial   664
                home   641.8
        marketing   658.8
Baking
    ceramics *see* Ceramics
    food *see* Cooking processes
Balalaikas *see* Guitars
Bali   *area* –92
Balikesir Turkey   *area* –562
Balinese *see* Austronesian
Balkan Peninsula   *area* –496
Ball
    bearings *see* Bearings
    games
        customs   394
        ethics   175
        gen. wks.   **796.3**
Ballades *see* Choral music
Ballads
    folklore *see* Rhymes
    literature *see* Poetry
    music *see* Choral music

Ballet
    ethics   175
    music
        gen. wks.   782.9
        see also spec. mediums
    performances   **792.8**
Ballistic
    missiles *see* Guided missiles
Ballistics
    engineering   623.5
    mechanics
        solids   531
        see also spec. branches
    see also spec. applications
Ballot
    systems
        laws   †340
        pol. sci.   324
Balls (dances) *see* Dancing
Balls (sporting goods) *see*
        Recreational
        equipment
Baltic Sea *see* Atlantic Ocean
Baltic
    ethnic groups   *area* –174
    languages   491.9
    lingual groups   *area* –175
    see also other spec. subj.
Balto-Slavic *see* Slavic
Baluchi *see* Iranian
Baluchistan   *area* –†549
Bamboowork *see* Basketry
Banat   *area* –†498
Band
    music *see* Bands
    saws *see* Tools
Bandicoots *see* Marsupials
Bands
    music   785.1
    performance   785.06
    recreation
        military *see* Special
            services
        students
            gen. wks.   †371.89
            see also spec. levels
            of ed.
Banjos *see* String instruments
Bank
    buildings *see* Commercial
        buildings

Basketry
  crafts   746.4
  industry
    economics   338.4
    technology   677
  study & teaching
    elementary ed.   372.5
    see also   *s.s.–07*
Basotho *see* Basutoland
Basque
  ethnic groups   *area* –174
  language   499
  lingual groups   *area* –175
  see also other spec. subj.
Bass
  fiddles *see* String instruments
Basset
  horn *see* Wind instruments
        (musical)
  hounds *see* Hounds
Bassoons *see* Wind instruments
        (musical)
Basutoland   *area* –68
Bat
  games
    customs   394
    gen. wks.   **796.35**
Bath mitzvah *see* Rites
Bathing
  customs   391
  hygiene   613.4
  techniques
    children *see* Child care
    gen. wks.   646.7
Bathing-beaches
  civic art   711
  pub. health   614
  recreation
    gen. wks.   796.5
    see also Swimming
        activities
  see also Safety measures
Bathing-suits *see* Garments
Bathrooms *see* Lavatories
Baths *see* Bathing
Batik *see* Resist-dyeing
Bats (animals)
  agricultural aids   632
  culture   636.9
  hunting   †639
  see also Chiroptera

Bats (sporting goods) *see*
      Recreational
      equipment
Battalions *see* Organizational
      units
Batteries
  elect. eng.   621.35
  see also spec. applications
Battle
  cries *see* War customs
  songs *see* National songs
  tactics
    mil. sci.
      gen. wks.   **355.4**
      see also spec. mil.
         branches
    see also hist. of spec. wars
Battledore & shuttlecock *see*
      Racket games
Battles
  history
    gen. wks.   904
    see also spec. wars
  mil. sci.
    analysis
      gen. wks.   355.4
      see also spec. mil.
        branches
Battleships *see* Warships
Beach
  formation *see* Marine waters
  protection *see* Shore
      reclamation
Beaches
  gen. wks. *see* Coasts
  recreational *see* Bathing-
      beaches
Beadwork
  crafts   746.5
  industry
    economics   338.4
    technology   677
Beagles *see* Hounds
Bearbaiting *see* Animal
      performances
Bearings
  engineering
    economics   338.4
    technology
      gen. wks.   621.8
      see also spec. branches
  see also spec. applications

Bengal (bay) *see* Indian
     Ocean
Bengali *see* Prakrits
Berber
  ethnic groups   *area* –174
  languages   493
  lingual groups   *area* –175
  see also other spec. subj.
Bergen Norway   *area* –483
Bering
  Sea *see* Pacific Ocean
Berith milah *see* Rites
Berkshire Eng.   *area* –422
Bermuda   *area* –729 9
Bernardines *see* Religious
     congregations
Berths
  docks *see* Docks
  shipyards *see* Shipyards
Berwick Scotland   *area* –414
Beryllium *see* Metals
Bessarabia   *area* –†477
Betatrons *see* Particle
    acceleration
Betting *see* Gambling
Beverages
  manufacture
    economics   .338.4
    technology
      commercial   663
      domestic   641.8
  marketing
    technology   658.8
    see also Liquor traffic
  pub. health meas.   614
Bhagavad Gita
  literature   891.2
  religion   294.5
Bhutan   *area* –†549
Bible
  literature   †809.9
  religion
    gen. wks.   **220**
    theology   **230**
    see also Scripture readings
Biblical
  Sabbath *see* Holy days
Bibliographical
  centers
    management   658

Bibliographical
  centers (continued)
    planning
      civic art   711
      sociology   301.3
      services   †021.6
Bibliographies
  books   **010**
  music scores   781.9
Bicameral
  legislatures *see* Legislative
     bodies
Bicycles *see* Cycles (vehicles)
Bicycling *see* Cycling
Bids *see* Procurement
Biennials
  botany   **582.1**
  floriculture   635.93
  landscaping   712
  see also spec. plants
Big
  businesses
    economics   338.6
    management   658
  game
    hunting *see* Hunting
      (activity)
Bigamists *see* Offenders
Bigamy *see* Offenses
Bigotry *see* Evils
Bihari *see* Prakrits
Bill
  of Rights *see* Constitutional
    law
Billeting *see* Quarters
Billiards *see* Indoor ball games
Billing-machines *see* Digital
    machines
Bills (legislation)
  gen. wks.   328.3
  spec. localities   **328.4–.9**
Bills
  of credit *see* Credit
    instruments
Bindery *see* Bookbinding
Binding
  books *see* Bookbinding
Bio-astronautics *see* Biophysics

Bison
  conservation   639
  culture   636.2
  see also Bovoidea
Bithynia   *area* –39
Bitlis Turkey   *area* –566
Bitterns
  conservation   639
  culture   636.6
  see also Ciconiiformes
Bituminous
  coal *see* Coals
  materials
    construction   691
    engineering
      gen. wks.   620.1
      see also spec. branches
      see also spec. applications
Black
  Sea *see* Atlantic Ocean
Black
  art *see* Witchcraft
  Friars *see* Religious
      congregations
Muslims
  religion   297
  soc. groups   301.451
  see also other aspects
Blackmail *see* Defrauding
Blackmailers *see* Offenders
Blackouts *see* Camouflage
Blacksmithing *see* Small forge
      work
Blank
  verse *see* Poetry
Blasphemy
  ethics   179
  religion
    Christian   241.3
    comp. rel.   291.5
    see also other spec. rel.
Blasting
  operations
    hydraulic eng.   627
    mining eng.   622
    see also other spec.
      applications
Blastproof
  structures
    civil defense *see* Civil
      defense

Blastproof
  structures (continued)
    engineering
      economics   338.4
      technology   623
Bleaching
  hair *see* Hairdressing
  textiles
    commercial   667
    domestic   648
Bleach-out
  process *see* Special-process
      photography
Blind
  children *see* Exceptional
      children
  people
    library services
      gen. wks.   027.6
      see also spec. functions
    service institutions   362.4
Blindness *see* Ocular disorders
Blizzards *see* Storms
Block Isl.   *area* –745
Block
  books
    gen. wks.   092
    library treatment   025.17
  printing *see* Printing
      processes
Blockades
  international law
    peace time   341.6
    war time   341.3
  mil. sci. *see* Siege warfare
Bloodhounds *see* Hounds
Blowers
  engineering
    economics   338.4
    technology
      gen. wks.   621.6
      see also spec. branches
    see also spec. applications
Blue
  Nile Province Sudan   *area* –626
Blue
  jays *see* Jays
Blueprinting
  process *see* Special-process
      photography

Book
  trade (continued)
    technology   †658.8
    see also Communication
Bookbinding
  economics   338.4
  library services   025.7
  technology   655.7
Bookkeepers *see* Office
        personnel
Bookkeeping
  economics   338.4
  technology   657.2
Bookmaking (gambling) *see*
    Gambling
Bookmobiles *see* Motor vehicles
Books
  marketing *see* Book trade
  publishing *see* Publishing
Booksellers' catalogs   017–019
Bookselling *see* Book trade
Boolean
  algebra *see* Universal algebra
Boosters
  detonators *see* Detonators
  elect. *see* Direct-current
    machinery
Bootlegging *see* Offenses
Boots *see* Footwear
Boring-machinery *see* Tools
Borneo   *area* –91
Boroughs *see* Communities
Borrowing
  public *see* Public debts
Borzois *see* Hounds
Boston
  terriers *see* Nonsporting dogs
Botanical
  sciences
    agriculture   **631–632**
    botany   **581**
    paleobotany   561
    see also   *s.s.*–01
Botany *see* Botanical sciences
Boundary
  surveying
    gen. wks.   526.9
    see also spec. applications
Bourses *see* Investment
    institutions
Bouvet Isl.   *area* –97

Bovoidea
  paleozoology   569
  zoology   599.7
Bowed
  instruments *see* String
    instruments
Bowling
  activity *see* Indoor ball
    games
  alleys *see* Recreation
    buildings
Boxers (dogs) *see* Working
    dogs
Boxes
  gen. wks. *see* Containers
  wooden *see* Sawmill
    products
Boxing
  ethics   175
  sports
    management   658
    performance   796.8
Boy Scouts *see* Young people
    organizations
Boycotts
  labor *see* Union-
    management disputes
  sociology *see* Group behavior
Boys (children) *see* Children
Boys'
  clothing *see* Garments
  clubs *see* Young people
    organizations
  Town *see* Junior republics
Bozcaada Turkey *see* Tenedos
Braces *see* Fastenings
Brackish
  water *see* Salt-water
Brahmanism
  culture groups
    geography   910.09
    history   909
    subject treatment   *area* –176
  philosophy   181
  religion   **294**
Braiding
  crafts   746.4
  industry
    economics   338.4
    technology   677

Canada	*area* –71
Canakkale Turkey	*area* –562
Canalboats *see* Towed craft	
Canals	
drainage *see* Drainage	
structures	
engineering	
economics	338.4
technology	627
irrigation *see* Irrigation	
transportation	386
Canapés *see* Auxiliary foods	
Canaries *see* Finches	
Canary Isls.	*area* –64
Candies	
marketing	658.8
production	
economics	338.4
technology	
commercial	664
domestic	641.8
Candlemas *see* Holy days	
Canework *see* Basketry	
Canidae	
paleozoology	569
zoology	599.7
Canine	
corps	
services	363.2
training	636.7
Canines *see* Dogs	
Cankiri Turkey	*area* –563
Canning	
food *see* Food technology	
Cannons *see* Artillery (pieces)	
Canoeing *see* Boating	
Canoes *see* Hand-propelled	
craft	
Canon	
law *see* Religious law	
music	
gen. wks.	781.4
see also spec. mediums	
Canonical	
hours *see* Divine Office	
Cantatas	
sacred	783.4
secular	782.8

Canteens	
military *see* Military	
buildings	
public *see* Public	
accommodations	
Canticle of Canticles *see* Poetic	
books	
Canticles *see* Songs	
Canzonets *see* Choral music	
Cape	
Verde Isls.	*area* –66
Capital	
goods	
gen. wks.	339
see also Finance	
punishment	
ethics	179
see also Punishment	
Capitalism *see* Economic	
systems	
Capitalization	
finance *see* Financial	
administration	
Capital-surplus	
accounting *see* Financial	
accounting	
Capitol	
buildings *see* Government	
buildings	
Capitulations *see* Diplomacy	
Cappadocia	*area* –39
Caps *see* Garments	
Captains *see* Personnel	
Captured	
soldiers *see* War prisoners	
Capuchins *see* Religious	
congregations	
Carabao *see* Water buffaloes	
Caravels *see* Historic ships	
Carbines *see* Small arms	
Carbon	
compounds	
inorganic *see* Inorganic	
chemistry	
organic *see* Organic	
chemistry	
Carbonated	
drinks *see* Soft drinks	
water *see* Mineralized	
waters	

Cascades *see* Water bodies
Case
  studies
    gen. wks. †001.4
    see also s.s.–01
Cases
  internal law
    Anglo-U.S. 345–346
    other **349**
Casks
  wooden *see* Sawmill products
Casserole
  foods *see* Entrees
Cassowaries *see* Emus
Castanets *see* Percussion
      instruments
Caste
  system
    ethics 177
    sociology 301.44
    see also Discriminatory
      practices
Castes *see* Social classes
Casting
  metals
    arts
      metalwork 739
      sculpture 731.4
    technology
      gen. wks. 671.2
      see also spec. *metals*
Castles *see* Residential
    buildings
Castrametation
  tactics *see* Logistics
  training *see* Training
    maneuvers
Casual-migratory
  workers *see* Seasonal workers
Casualty
  insurance
    gen. wks. 368
    see also Financial
      institutions
  prevention *see* Safety
    measures
Casuariiformes *see* Palaeog-
    nathae
Casuistry *see* Conscience

Catalan
  ethnic groups *area* –174
  language 449
  lingual groups *area* –175
  see also other spec. subj.
Cataloging
  books 025.3
  museum pieces 069
Catalogs
  books **010**
  music scores 781.9
  recordings 789.9
  see also s.s.–†021
Cataracts (water) *see* Water
    bodies
Catastrophes *see* Disasters
Catboats *see* Sailing craft
Catechisms
  religion
    Christian 238
    gen. wks. 291.2
    see also other spec. rel.
  see also s.s.–076
Catering
  services
    management 658
    technology 642
Caterpillars
  agricultural pests 632
  culture 638
  see also Lepidoptera
Cathedral
  buildings
    architecture 726
    construction 690.6
    religion *see* Sacred places
  schools
    education *see* Church-
      supported schools
    rel. training *see* Religious
      training
  systems *see* Episcopal system
Catholic
  epistles
    liturgy 264
    N.T.
      gen. wks. 227
      see also Pseudepigrapha
  socialism *see* Socialistic states

Cemeteries
  burial customs   393
  folklore   398.3
  landscaping   718
  mil. admin.
    gen. wks.   355.6
    see also spec. mil.
        branches
  public health meas.
    animals
      gen. wks.   636.089
      see also spec. animals
    man   614
  war memorials *see spec. wars*
Censored
  books *see* Prohibited books
Censuses *see* National statistics
Centipedes
  agricultural pests   632
  culture   †639
  see also Opisthogoneata
Central
  African Republic   *area* −67
  America   *area* −728
  Asia
    ancient   *area* −39
    modern   *area* −58
Central
  administration *see* Top
      management
  banks *see* Financial
      institutions
  governments
    administration
      gen. wks.   351
      spec. governments   353–354
    see also other spec. subj.
  heating *see* Heating-systems
  stations
    engineering
      electricity   621.312
      gen. wks.   621.4
      steam   621.1
    see also other spec. subj.
  Treaty Organization
    defense   355.03
    organization   341.18
    see also spec. services
Ceramics
  arts   738

Ceramics (continued)
  industries
    economics   338.4
    technology   666
Ceremonials *see* Official
      ceremonies
Ceremonies
  official *see* Official
      ceremonies
  religious *see* Public worship
Certified
  public accountant practice
        see Public accounting
Certitude *see* Belief
Cervoidea
  paleozoology   569
  zoology   599.7
Cesium *see* Metals
Cesspools *see* Unsewered
      structures
Cetacea
  paleozoology   569
  zoology   599.5
Ceylon   *area* −†549 3
Chad (country)   *area* −67
Chad
  ethnic groups   *area* −174
  languages   493
  lingual groups   *area* −175
  see also other spec. subj.
Chafing
  dish cookery *see* Cookery
Chagos Isls. Indian
      Ocean   *area* −69
Chain
  banking *see* Financial
      institutions
  gangs *see* Convict labor
  gearing *see* Gears
  hoists *see* Materials-handling
      equipment
  power transmission *see*
        Flexible connections
  stores *see* Retail marketing
Chains
  manufacture
    economics   338.4
    technology
      gen. wks.   671.8
      see also spec. materials
  see also Structural forms

Chattels
law *see* Private law
Cheating *see* Evils
Chechen *see* Caucasian
Checkers
  ethics   175
  customs   394
  gen. wks.   794.2
Checks
  financial *see* Credit
    instruments
Cheerfulness *see* Virtues
Cheese
  food   641.3
  industry
    economics   338.1
    technology   637
  see also Dairy products
Cheetahs *see* Cats
Chelonia
  paleozoology   568
  zoology   598.13
Chemical
  analysis *see* Analytical
    chemistry
  engineering *see* Chemical
    technology
  jurisprudence *see* Forensic
    chemistry
  metallurgy
    gen. wks.   669.9
    see also spec. applications
  technology
    economics   338.4
    manufactures   **660**
  warfare
    defenses
      mil. eng.   623
      welfare services †363.35
    forces
      gen. wks.   358
      see also spec. kinds of
        warfare
Chemicals
  industrial *see* Industrial
    chemicals
Chemistry
  applied *see* Chemical
    technology
  gen. wks.   **540**
  soils *see* Soil chemistry

Chemurgy *see* Chemical
  technology
Cheremiss *see* Finno-Ugric
Cherokee (subject) *see*
    Hokan-Siouan
Cherubim *see* Angelology
Chesapeake Bay
  gen. wks.   *area* –755
  Md.   *area* –752
Cheshire Eng.   *area* –427
Chess
  customs   394
  ethics   175
  gen. wks.   **794.1**
Chesterfield
  Isls. *see* New Caledonia
Cheviot Hills Eng.   *area* –428
Chevon *see* Red meats
Chevrotains
  conservation   †639
  culture   636.9
  see also Tragulida
Chewing
  tobacco
    addiction *see* Addictions
    customs
      private   392
      public   394
Chewing-tobacco *see* Tobacco
    products
Chicken
  eggs *see* Eggs
Chickens
  culture   636.5
  disease carriers *see* Disease
    carriers
  food *see* Poultry
  see also Galliformes
Chief
  executives
    government
      gen. wks.   †350
      see also spec. levels of
        govt.
Chiggers
  agricultural pests   632
  culture   †639
  disease carriers *see* Disease
    carriers
  see also Acari
Chihuahuas *see* Miniature dogs

Church (continued)
  libraries *see* Religious
      organizations
  music *see* Sacred music
  of Christ, Scientist
    religion   289.5
    see also Church buildings
  of England *see* Anglican
      churches
  of God *see* Adventists
  of God in Christ *see*
      Mennonites
  of Jesus Christ of Latter-
      Day Saints *see*
      Latter-Day Saints
  of Scotland *see* Presbyterian
      churches
  of the Brethren *see* Baptist
      churches
  of the Nazarene *see* Recent
      Christian sects
  of the New Jerusalem
    religion   289.4
    see also Church buildings
  polity *see* Ecclesiology
  precepts
    gen. wks.   241.5
    see also spec. applications
  schools
    education *see* Church-
        supported schools
    rel. training *see* Religious
        training
  Slavonic *see* Bulgarian
  suppers *see* Hospitality
  year *see* Liturgical year
Churches of God *see* Recent
    Christian sects
Church-supported
  schools
    gen. wks.   377
    see also spec. levels of ed.
Cicadas *see* Insects
Ciconiiformes
  paleozoology   568
  zoology   598.3
Cigarettes *see* Tobacco
    products
Cigars *see* Tobacco products
Cilicia
  ancient   *area* –39
  modern   *area* –564

Cinder
  blocks *see* Artificial stones
Circassian *see* Caucasian
Circuitry
  engineering
    electronics
      gen. wks.   621.381
      see also spec. branches
    power transmission   621.319
  physics
    electricity   537.6
    electronics   537.5
    see also spec. applications
Circulation-services
  libraries   025.6
  museums   069
Circumnavigation *see* Travels
Circus
  animals *see* Stunt animals
Circuses
  gen. wks.   791.3
  management   658
  see also Recreational
      activities
Cirripedia
  culture   †639
  paleozoology   565
  zoology   595
Cistercians *see* Religious
    congregations
Cities *see* Communities
Citizenship
  ethics   172
  pol. sci.   323.6
  training
    prisons   365
    schools
      elementary   372.8
      see also   *s.s.*–07
City
  governments *see* Local
      governments
  halls *see* Government
      buildings
  libraries *see* Public libraries
  managers *see* Chief
      executives
  parks *see* Recreational land
  planning *see* Planning
      communities
Civets *see* Viverrines

Civic
  art *see* Planning
      communities
  centers
    planning
      civic art   711
      sociology   301.3
Civics *see* Citizenship
Civil
  defense
    administration
      government
        gen. wks.   †350
        see also spec. levels
          of govt.
      private   658
    services   †363.35
  engineering
    gen. wks.   624
    see also spec. branches
  government
    church relations
      pol. sci.   322
      religion
        Christian   261.7
        gen. wks.   291
        see also other spec.
          rel.
    see also Government
      (state)
  rights
    law   **342**
    pol. sci.   **323.4**
  service
    gen. wks.   †350
    see also spec. levels of
      govt.
  war
    international law   341.3
    mil. sci.   355
    societies *see* Hereditary
      societies
  wars
    crime *see* Offenses
    ethics   172
    history
      U.S.   **973.7**
      see also other spec.
        countries

Civilization
  gen. wks.   **901.9**
  see also spec. places
Clackmannan Scotland   *area* –413
Clairaudience *see* Extrasensory
    perception
Clairvoyance *see* Extrasensory
    perception
Clams
  fisheries
    economics   338.3
    technology   †639
  food *see* Seafood
  see also Mollusca
Clans
  biology *see* Ecology
  sociology *see* Kinship
Clare Co.
  Ireland   *area* –419
Clarinet *see* Wind instruments
    (musical)
Classical
  high schools *see* Secondary
    schools
  languages
    gen. wks.   **†480**
    see also spec. languages
  religions
    culture groups
      geography   910.09
      history   909
      subject treatment   *area* –176
    gen. wks.   292
Classical-language
  literature
    gen. wks.   **880**
    see also spec. literatures
Classification
  systems
    knowledge   112
    library services   025.4
    see also   *s.s.*–01
Classified
  catalogs
    books   017
    see also   *s.s.*–†021
Clavichords *see* Keyboard
    string instruments
Clay
  industries *see* Ceramics

Concerti
  grossi *see* Orchestras
Concertinas *see* Accordions
Concertos *see* Orchestras
Concerts
  gen. wks.   780.73
  see also spec. mediums
Conchology *see* Mollusca
Conciliation
  practices
    ind. relations   331.15
    international relations
      law   341.6
      pol. sci.   **327**
    management *see*
        Employer-employee
        relationships
Concourses *see* Trafficways
Concrete
  blocks *see* Artificial stones
  masonry *see* Masonry
      (construction)
  music *see* Musique concrète
Condemned
  books *see* Prohibited books
Conditioned
  reflexes *see* Reflex actions
Conduct
  of life *see* Ethics
  of war *see* Warfare
Conduits
  drainage *see* Drainage
      structures
  irrigation *see* Irrigation
Confectionery *see* Candies
Conferences
  organizations *see*
        Organizations
  teaching *see* Discussion
      methods
Confession
  penance *see* Sacraments
Confessions
  of faith *see* Creeds
Configuration
  psychology *see* Gestalt
        psychology
Confinement
  childbirth *see* Parturition
Confirmation *see* Sacraments

Conformity
  psychology   †153.8
  sociology   301.15
Confucianism
  culture groups
    geography   910.09
    history   909
    subject treatment   *area* −176
  philosophy   181
  religion   299
Congo (Brazzaville)   *area* −67
Congo (Leopoldville)   *area* −675
Congregational
  Christian Churches *see*
        Congregationalism
  Methodist Church *see*
        Methodist churches
  singing *see* Hymnology
  system   262
Congregationalism
  religion   285
  see also Church buildings
Congregations
  denominational *see* Parishes
  religious *see* Religious
        congregations
Congresses
  legislative *see* Legislative
        bodies
  organizations *see*
        Organizations
Congressional
  immunity *see* Political
        immunity
Conies *see* Hyracoideans
Conjuring *see* Magic arts
Connacht Ireland   *area* −417
Connaught Ireland *see*
        Connacht
Connecticut (state)   *area* −746
Consanguinity
  gen. wks. *see* Kinship
  law *see* Family (institution)
Conscience
  ethics   171
  religion
    Christian   241
    gen. wks.   291.5
    see also other spec. rel.

Cork
  products
    manufacture
      economics 338.4
      technology 674
    see also spec. applications
Cornets *see* Wind instruments
      (musical)
Cornetts *see* Wind instruments
      (musical)
Cornish *see* Celtic
Cornwall Eng. *area* –423
Coronations *see* Official
      ceremonies
Corporal
  punishment
    ethics 179
    see also Punishments
Corporations
  economics 338.7
  government
    gen. wks. †350
    *see also spec. levels of
      govt.*
  management 658
  see also s.s.–065
Corporative
  state *see* Fascist states
Corps
  military *see* Organizational
      units
Correctional
  institutions *see* Reformatories
Correspondence (letters) *see*
      Letters
Correspondence (reasoning)
      see Analogy
Corrosion *see* Deterioration
Corsages
  customs 391
  see also Floral arts
Corse *see* Corsica
Corsica
  ancient *area* –37
  modern *area* –459
Corvidae *see* Passeriformes
Cosmetics
  chem. analysis *see*
      Analytical chemistry

Cosmetics (continued)
  manufacture
    economics 338.4
    technology 668
  marketing 658.8
  use
    customs 391
    hygiene 613.4
    technology 646.7
Cosmetology *see* Cosmetics
Cosmic
  rays *see* Ionizing radiation
Cosmogony
  astronomy 523.1
  philosophy 113
  religion
    gen. wks. 213
    see also spec. rel.
Cosmoledo Isls. *area* –69
Cosmology
  astronomy 523.1
  philosophy 113–119
  religion
    gen. wks. 213
    see also spec. rel.
Cost
  control *see* Financial
      administration
  of living
    economics
      gen. wks. 339.42
      see also spec. elements
    see also spec. applications
Costa Rica *area* –728 6
Costs
  economics **338**
  see also spec. products
Costume
  art †746.9
  customs
    gen. wks. 391
  military
    gen. wks. 355.1
    see also spec. services
  jewelry *see* Jewelry
  see also Personal
      appearance
Cottage
  industries
    economics
      gen. wks. 338.4

Crafts (continued)
  mil. recreation *see* Special
    services
  see also spec. crafts
Craftsmen
  economics
    labor   331.7
    production   338.1–.4
  see also spec. subj.
Cranes (birds)
  culture   636.6
  see also Gruiformes
Cranes (mechanical)
  engineering
    economics   338.4
    technology
      gen. wks.   621.8
      see also spec. branches
    see also spec. applications
Craniology
  anthropometry   573
  phrenology   139
Crates
  wooden *see* Sawmill products
Crayfish
  fisheries
    economics   338.3
    technology   †639
  food *see* Seafood
  see also Macrura
Creation
  of man *see* Cosmology
Creative
  activities
    children *see* Child play
  arts
    gen. wks.   **700–800**
    study & teaching
      elementary schools   372.5
      see also   *s.s.*–07
Creativity *see* Imagination
Credit
  administration
    gen. wks.   †350
    see also spec. levels of
      govt.
  bonds *see* Public securities
  economics
    gen. wks.   332.7
    public   336.3

Credit (continued)
  institutions *see* Financial
    institutions
  instruments
    economics   332.7
    see also spec. applications
  management   658.88
  unions *see* Financial
    institutions
Credos *see* Creeds
Cree *see* Algonkian-Mosan
Creeds
  religion
    dogmatics
      Christian   238
      gen. wks.   291.2
      see also other spec. rel.
    liturgy
      Christian   264
      gen. wks.   291.3
      see also other spec. rel.
Creek (subject) *see* Hokan-
    Siouan
Creeks *see* Water bodies
Cremation
  rites *see* Funeral rites
Crests
  heraldic *see* Heraldic design
Crete
  ancient   *area* –39
  modern   *area* –499
Cricket *see* Bat games
Crickets *see* Grasshoppers
Crimea   *area* –477
Crimes *see* Offenses
Criminal
  abortion *see* Offenses
  anthropology
    gen. wks.   364.2
    see also Abnormal
      psychology
  anthropometry *see*
    Anthropometry
  law
    internal   343
    international   341.4
  libel *see* Offenses
Criminals *see* Offenders
Criminology
  gen. wks.   **364**
  see also Personality disorders

Cuitlatec *see* Miskito-
    Matagalpan
Culinary
  arts *see* Cookery
Cultivation
  techniques
    gen. wks.   631.5
    see also spec. crops
Cultural
  anthropology *see* Culture
  areas
    geography *see spec. areas*
    landscaping   712
    planning
      civic art   711
      sociology   301.3
Culture
  anthropology   †390
  govt. control
    gen. wks.   †350
    see also spec. levels of
      govt.
  sociology   301.2
  see also Civilization
Culverts *see* Drainage
    structures
Cumberland Eng.   *area* –428
Curates *see* Clergy
Curb
  exchanges *see* Investment
    institutions
Curbs (pavements) *see*
    Auxiliary pavements
Curlews
  culture   636.6
  see also Charadriiformes
Curling (sport) *see* Ice sports
Curling
  hair *see* Hairdressing
Currents
  oceanic *see* Marine waters
Curriculums
  gen. wks.   375
  see also spec. levels of ed.
Curses
  folklore *see* Superstitions
Cursing *see* Profanity
Curtains
  interior decoration
    art   747
    home economics   645

Curtains (continued)
  manufacture
    economics   338.4
    technology   684.3
Cushitic
  ethnic groups   *area* –174
  languages   493
  lingual groups   *area* –175
  see also other spec. subj.
Customhouses *see*
    Government
    buildings
Customs (conventions)
  military
    gen. wks.   355.1
    see also spec. services
  social *see* Social customs
Customs (taxes)
  economics   336.2
  gen. wks.   †382
  govt. control
    gen. wks.   †350
    see also spec. levels of
      govt.
Cut
  flowers
    arrangement   †745.92
    culture
      gen. wks.   635.96
      see also spec. plants
  stock *see* Sawmill products
Cutlery
  manufacture
    economics   338.4
    technology   683
  table decor *see* Table decor
Cutters
  revenue *see* Government
    vessels
  sailing ships *see* Sailing craft
Cutting
  hair
    men *see* Barbering
    women *see* Hairdressing
  metals
    arts   739
    technology
      gen. wks.   671.5
      see also spec. metals
Cutting-machinery *see* Tools

Dancing
  recreational programs (cont.)
    student life
      gen. wks.   †371.89
      see also spec. levels
        of ed.
  see also Dance music
Dancing-games *see* Child
    play
Daniel (O.T.) *see* Prophetic
    books
Danish *see* Germanic
Danube River
  gen. wks.   *area* –496
  see also spec. areas
Dard *see* Prakrits
Darwinism *see* Organic
    evolution
Dassies *see* Hyracoideans
Data
  processing
    equipment *see* Computers
    lib. sci.   025.3–.4
    office services   †651.8
    see also Documentation
  treatment *see* Statistics
Day
  nurseries
    management   658
    services   362.7
  of Atonement *see* Holy days
  schools *see* Secondary
    schools
Dead Sea
  Scrolls
    Biblical   221
    gen. wks.   091
Deaf
  children *see* Exceptional
    children
  people
    psychology   †155.9
    welfare institutions   362.4
Deaf-mute
  children *see* Exceptional
    children
  people *see* Deaf people
Deafness *see* Audiology
Death
  biology
    gen. wks.   577

Death
  biology (continued)
    see also spec. causes
  customs *see* Funeral rites
  metaphysics   128
  religion
    Christian   236
    gen. wks.   291.2
    see also other spec. rel.
  statistics *see* Demography
  see also Life cycle
Debates *see* Speeches
Debts
  private *see* Credit
  public *see* Public debts
Debuts *see* Puberty rites
Decalcomania
  crafts
    gen. wks.   745.7
    interior decoration   747
Decalog *see* Ten
    Commandments
Deception
  tactics *see* Camouflage
Deciphering
  codes *see* Cryptography
Decision
  making
    management *see*
      Administration
    psychology   †153.8
Decoding
  ciphers *see* Cryptography
Decoration
  arts
    gen. wks.   701.8
    see also spec. art forms
  table decor *see* Table decor
Decoration Day *see* Holidays
Decorative
  arts *see* Minor arts
Decoy
  construction *see* Camouflage
Dedication (Feast of) *see*
    Holy days
Deer
  conservation   †639
  culture   636.2
  disease carriers *see* Disease
    carriers

Denominational (continued)
 societies *see* Religious
  organizations
Denominations
 Christian religion   280
 gen. wks.   291.9
 see also other spec. rel.
Dentistry
 economics   338.4
 technology
  animals
   gen. wks.   636.089
   see also spec. animals
  man   617
D'Entrecasteaux Isls.   *area* –95
Denumerative
 geometry   513
 see also   *s.s.*–01
Department
 stores
  gen. wks. *see* Commercial
   buildings
  marketing *see* Retail
   marketing
Dependent
 states
  geography   910.09
  history   909
  pol. sci.   321
  subj. treatment   *area* –171
  see also spec. states
Deposit
 banks *see* Financial
  institutions
 insurance *see* Bank deposits
 transfer instruments *see*
  Credit instruments
Depressions
 economic *see* Business cycles
Depth
 psychology
  animals   †156
  gen. wks.   **†154**
  see also Psychoanalysis
Derby Eng.   *area* –425
Derricks *see* Materials-
  handling equipment
Derry Ireland *see*
  Londonderry

Descriptive
 astronomy
  earth   525
  gen. wks.   **523**
 geometry
  gen. wks.   515
  see also   *s.s.*–01
Desert
 plants *see* Xerophytes
Desertion *see* Offenses
Deserts
 geography
  gen. wks.   910.09
  physical   †910.02
 history   909
 reclamation *see* Land
  reclamation
 subj. treatment   *area* –15
 see also spec. areas
Design
 arts
  gen. wks.   745.4
 study & teaching
  elementary ed.   372.5
  see also   *s.s.*–07
 see also spec. art forms
 see also Operations research
Designing
 arts
  gen. wks.   701.8
  see also spec. art forms
 see also Operations research
Desmans *see* Insectivores
Despotic
 states
  pol. sci.   321.1
  see also spec. areas
Desserts
 cookery   641.8
 food tech. *see spec. foods*
Deterioration
 materials
  construction   691
  engineering
   gen. wks.   620.1
   see also spec. kinds
  see also spec. products
Determinism
 metaphysics   123
 religion *see* Predestination

Dikes (structures) *see* Flood
    control
Dining
  places *see* Public
    accommodations
  service *see* Meals
Dinners *see* Meals
Diocesan
  schools *see* Church-
    supported schools
Dioceses *see* Episcopal system
Diplomacy
  administration   †350
  law   341.7
  pol. sci.   327
Diplomatic
  conduct *see* Diplomacy
  immunity *see* Political
    immunity
Diplomatics *see* Paleography
Diptera
  paleozoology   565
  zoology   595.77
Direct-current
  machinery
    economics   338.4
    engineering   621.313
    manufacture   681
    see also spec. applications
  motors
    generators *see* Direct-
      current machinery
    prime movers   621.4
  transmission
    engineering
      economics   338.4
      technology   621.319
Direction
  finders
    engineering
      economics   338.4
      technology
        radar   621.384 8
        radio   621.384 19
    navigation
      aircraft   629.132
      ships   623.89
    see also Magnetic
      compasses
  finding *see* Navigation

Direct-mail
  advertising
    economics   338.4
    technology   659.13
  marketing *see* Retail
    marketing
Dirigibles *see* Lighter-than-air
  aircraft
Dirks *see* Side arms
Disability
  insurance
    govt. sponsored   368.4
    voluntary   368.3
    see also Financial
      institutions
  pensions *see* Pension systems
Disabled
  children *see* Exceptional
    children
  people
    labor economics   331.5
    service institutions   362.4
  veterans
    benefits *see* Postmilitary
      benefits
    gen. wks. *see* Disabled
      people
Disarmament *see* Armament
  limitation
Disasters
  history   †904
  psych. effects   †155.9
  relief
    administration
      government
        gen. wks.   †350
        see also spec. levels
          of govt.
        private   658
    police planning   363.3
    services   361.5
    technology   **614.8**
Disciples
  of Christ
    churches
      religion   286
      see also Church
        buildings
Discography *see* Catalogs

Diving
  aerodynamics *see*
      Aerodynamics
  hydraulic eng. *see*
      Underwater
      operations
  sports
      hygiene   †613.7
      performance   797.2
Divinities *see* Deities
Divinity *see* God
Divorce
  ethics
      philosophy   173
      religion
          Christian   241
          see also other spec. rel.
  laws   347.6
  psychology   †155.6
  sociology   301.42
  statistics *see* Demography
Diyarbakir Turkey   *area* –566
Doberman
  pinschers *see* Working dogs
Docks
  eng. & construction
      economics   338.4
      technology
          gen. wks.   627
          military   623.6
      see also Transportation
          services
Doctrinal
  theology *see* Dogmatism
Documentation
  equipment *see* Computers
  library sci.   †029.7
  see also Records
      management
Documents
  collections
      general   †080
      see also   *s.s.*–08
  library treatment   025.17
Dodecanese Greece
  ancient   *area* –39
  modern   *area* –499
Dogmas *see* Dogmatism

Dogmatism
  philosophy   148
  religion
      Christian   230
      comp. rel.   291.2
      see also other spec. rel.
Dogs
  culture   636.7
  disease carriers *see* Disease
      carriers
  see also Canidae
Dolls *see* Toys
Dolphins (mammals) *see*
      Odontocetes
Dolphins (mooring structures)
      see Port installations
Domestic
  animals *see* Livestock
  art *see* Folk art
  arts
      customs   392
      technology   **640**
  cats *see* Cats
  commerce *see* Trade
      (activity)
  fowls *see* Poultry
  science *see* Domestic arts
  see also Family
Dominica West Indies   *area* –729 8
Dominican Republic   *area* –729 3
Dominicans *see* Religious
      congregations
Dominion
  Day *see* Holidays
Dominoes *see* Counter games
Donegal Ireland   *area* –416
Donkeys *see* Asses
Dorset Eng.   *area* –423
Double
  basses *see* String instruments
Double-reed
  instruments *see* Wind
      instruments
      (musical)
Doubt *see* Skepticism
Doves *see* Pigeons
Down Ireland   *area* –416
Dowry *see* Marriage

Edentates
conservation †639
culture 636.9
see also Edentata
Edible
plants
agriculture *see* Agriculture
(activity)
botany *see* Economic
biology
Editing
gen. wks. †808.02
journalism 070.4
Edom *area –39*
Education
govt.
control
gen. wks. †350
*see also spec. levels of
govt.*
supervision 379
of veterans *see* Postmilitary
benefits
religious *see* Religious
training
science 370
see also *s.s.–07*
Educational
functions
libraries 021.2
museums 069
guidance *see* Counseling
programs
personnel management
business 658.3
government
gen. wks. †350
*see also spec. levels
of govt.*
see also spec. institutions
psychology *see* Learning
sociology
gen. wks. 370.19
see also spec. levels of ed.
tests *see* Mental tests
Education-departments *see*
Executive
departments
Edward Nyanza
gen. wks. *area –675*
see also other areas

Eggs
food
cookery 641.6
gen. wks. 641.3
marketing 658.8
production
economics 338.1
technology 637
zoology *see spec. animals*
Egoism
philosophy
ethics 171
metaphysics 126
see also Subconscious
Egrets
conservation †639
culture 636.6
see also Ciconiiformes
Egypt
ancient *area –32*
modern *area –62*
Egyptian
modern *see* Arabic
old *see* Old Egyptian
Elamitic
ethnic groups *area –174*
language 499
lingual groups *area –175*
see also other spec. subj.
Elands *see* Antelopes
Elasig Turkey *area –566*
Elasticity
engineering
materials 620.1
structures 624
mechanics
gases 533
liquids 532
solids 531
Elastomers
manufacture
economics 338.4
technology 678
materials
arts 702.8
engineering 620.1
see also spec. products
Elderly
people *see* Aged people
Elders *see* Clergy

Embryology
  biology
    animals   591.3
    gen. wks.   574.3
    plants   581.3
    see also spec. organisms
  med. sci.
    animals
      gen. wks.   636.089
      see also spec. animals
    man
      anatomy   611
      physiology   612.64
    see also Pregnancy
Emeralds *see* Precious stones
Emergency
  labor *see* Drafted labor
  money *see* Noncommodity
    money
Emicons *see* Electronic
    musical instruments
Emigration *see* Population
    movement
Eminent
  domain *see* Expropriation
Emotionally
  disturbed
    children *see* Exceptional
      children
    people
      psychology *see*
        Abnormal
        psychology
      treatment *see*
        Psychoneuroses
      welfare service   362.2
Emotions
  psychology
    animals   †156
    gen. wks.   †152.4
  religion   200.1
Empire
  Day *see* Holidays
Empires
  geography   910.09
  history   909
  pol. sci.   321
  subj. treatment   *area* –171
  see also spec. areas
Empiricism *see* Positivism

Employees
  labor economics   331.1
  management *see* Personnel
    management
Employer-employee
  relationships
    business   658.31
    government
      gen. wks.   †350
      *see also spec. levels of
        govt.*
    labor   **331.1**
Employment
  labor economics   331.1
  management
    gen. wks.   658.31
    see also Civil service
  see also Postmilitary
    benefits
Emus
  conservation   †639
  culture   636.6
  see also Palaeognathae
Enamels
  arts
    ceramics   738.4
    metals   739
  manufacture
    economics   338.4
    technology
      ceramics   666
      metals *see* Surface
        finishing
Encyclicals *see* Religious law
Encyclopedias
  gen. wks.   **030**
  see also   *s.s.*–03
Endowment
  education
    schools   379
    students   **378.3**
  research   †001.4
Energism
  philosophy   146
  psychology *see*
    Reductionism
Engineer
  forces
    mil. sci.
      gen. wks.   358
      *see also spec. kinds of
        warfare*

412

Equestrian	
sports	
customs	394
ethics	175
performance	798
see also Horses	
Equidae	
paleozoology	569
zoology	599.7
Equinoxes *see* Seasons	
Equipment	*s.s.*–028
Equity	
law	
internal	347
international	341.5
see also Capital goods	
Erie (lake)	
gen. wks.	*area* –771
Ont.	*area* –713
see also other areas	
Eritrea	*area* –63
Erosion	
soils *see* Soil erosion	
Erse *see* Celtic	
Erzincan Turkey	*area* –566
Escalators *see* Materials-	
handling equipment	
Escape	
velocity	
astronautics	†629.4
biophysics *see* Biophysics	
physics	531
Eschatology	
Christian religion	†236
gen. wks.	291.2
see also other spec. rel.	
Esdras	
apocrypha	229
O.T. *see* Historical books	
(O.T.)	
Eskimo	
dogs *see* Working dogs	
Eskimo-Aleut	
ethnic groups	*area* –174
languages	497
lingual groups	*area* –175
see also other spec. subj.	
Eskimos	
history	970.1
see also Eskimo-Aleut	
Eskisehir Turkey	*area* –563

Esoteric	
associations	
gen. wks.	366
see also	*s.s.*–06
philosophy *see* Mysticism	
traditions *see* Mystic	
traditions	
Esperanto *see* Artificial	
languages	
Espionage	
administration	355.3
criminology	364.13
law	
internal	343
international	341.3
Essays	
literature	
collections	808.84
criticism	809.4
rhetoric	808.4
see also spec. lit.	
see also Collected writings	
Essential	
oils	
agriculture	
economics	338.1
technology	633
manufacture	
economics	338.4
technology	661
see also spec. products	
Essex Eng.	*area* –426
Esther	
deuterocanonical wks.	229
O.T. *see* Historical books	
(O.T.)	
Esthetics	
arts	
gen. wks.	701.17
literature	801
see also other spec. art	
forms	
metaphysics	111.8
Estonia	*area* –47
Estonian *see* Finnic	
Estuaries *see* Water bodies	
Etching	
glass *see* Glass	
graphic arts	767
see also other spec. subj.	

Eyeglasses (continued)
manufacture
  economics   338.4
  technology   681
marketing   658.8
optometry *see* Optometry
Ezechiel (O.T.) *see* Prophetic
  books
Ezekiel (O.T.) *see* Prophetic
  books
Ezra (O.T.) *see* Historical
  books (O.T.)

F

Fables *see* Mythology
Fabrication *see* Manufactures
Fabrics *see* Textiles
Facsimile
  production *see*
    Photoduplication
  telegraphy *see*
    Telecommunication
Factory
  buildings *see* Industrial
    buildings
  management *see* Production
    management
  operations
    economics   338.4
    technology
      gen. wks.   621.7
      see also spec. branches
  ships *see* Merchant ships
  systems *see* Big businesses
Faculty (schools) *see* School
  organization
Faculty psychology
  gen. wks.   150.19
  see also spec. aspects
Fads *see* Group behavior
Faeroes   *area* –491
Fair
  buildings *see* Public
    buildings
Fairies *see* Supernatural beings
Fairs
  business *see* Distribution
    channels
  description   **914–919**
  soc. customs   394
  see also   *s.s.*–074

Fairy
  tales *see* Mythology
Faith
  metaphysics   121
  religion
    Christian   234
    gen. wks.   291.2
    see also other spec. rel.
Falangist
  state *see* Fascist states
Falconiformes
  paleozoology   568
  zoology   598.9
Falcons *see* Hawks
Falkland Isls.   *area* –97
Falling
  bodies *see* Gravity
Family (institution)
  customs   392
  ethics   173
  law   347.6
  sociology
    gen. wks.   301.42
    welfare services   †362.8
Family
  counseling *see* Counseling
  histories *see* Genealogy
  libraries
    gen. wks.   027
    see also spec. functions
  prayer
    Christian religion   249
    gen. wks.   291.4
    see also other spec. rel.
Famines *see* Disasters
Fancywork *see* Embroidery
Fan-jet
  engines *see* Internal-
    combustion engines
Fans
  mechanical *see* Blowers
  ornamental
    arts   736
    customs   391
Far East   *area* –5
Farce *see* Drama
Farm
  animals *see* Livestock
  buildings
    architecture   728

418

Feeble-minded
  children *see* Exceptional
    children
Feeblemindedness *see* Mental
    deficiency
Feedback
  electronics *see* Circuitry
  systems *see* Automatic control
Feeding
  boilers *see* Boiler-house
    practices
  children
    gen. wks.   649.3
    see also Cookery
  invalids
    cookery *see* Cookery
    gen. wks. *see* Nursing
  livestock
    gen. wks.   636.08
    see also spec. animals
Feelings
  psychology
    animals   †156
    gen. wks.   †152.4
  religion   200.1
Fees
  compensation *see* Wages
  revenue *see* Taxation
Felidae
  paleozoology   569
  zoology   599.7
Fellowships
  education   378.33
  gen. wks.   †001.4
  see also   *s.s.*–079
Felonies *see* Offenses
Femininity *see* Sex differences
Feminism *see* Women
Fencing
  ethics   175
  mil. sci. *see* Training
    maneuvers
  sports   796.8
Fens Eng.   *area* –425
Fermanagh Ireland   *area* –416
Ferroconcrete
  blocks *see* Artificial stones
Ferroprussiate
  process *see* Special-process
    photography

Ferrotype
  process *see* Special-process
    photography
Ferryboats *see* Small craft
Fertilizers
  agriculture
    gen. wks.   631.8
    see also spec. crops
  manufacture
    economics   338.4
    technology   668
  marketing   658.8
Festivals
  gen. wks. *see* Pageants
  religion *see* Holy days
Fêtes *see* Pageants
Feudal
  states
    pol. sci.   321.3
    see also spec. areas
  tenure *see* Private land
Fezzan   *area* –61
Fiction
  collections   **808.83**
  criticism   **809.3**
  rhetoric   **808.3**
  see also spec. lits.
Field
  athletics *see* Track athletics
  crops
    agriculture
      economics   338.1
      technology   633
    processing *see spec.*
      products
  hockey *see* Mallet games
  service
    mil. sci.
      gen. wks.   355.4
      see also spec. services
      see also hist. of spec. wars
  work *see* Laboratory
    methods
Fife Scotland   *area* –413
Fifes *see* Wind instruments
    (musical)
Fighters (aircraft) *see*
    Heavier-than-air
    aircraft
Fighting
  sports *see* Boxing

Floors (continued)
  construction
    carpentry   694.2
    economics   338.4
  painting   698.1
  see also spec. structures
Floral
  arts
    arrangements   †745.92
    landscape design   715–716
Floriculture
  economics   338.1
  technology   635.9
Florida (state)   *area* –759
Flower
  arrangement
    gen. wks. *see* Floral arts
    table decor *see* Table
      decor
  gardening *see* Floriculture
Flowering
  plants
    floriculture   635.93
    landscaping   715–716
    see also Angiospermae
Flow-of-funds
  accounts *see* National
    accounting
Flues
  heating eng.   697.8
  see also spec. applications
Fluid-power
  engineering
    gen. wks.   621.1–.2
    see also spec. branches
Fluids
  physics
    mechanics   532
    see also spec. branches
  see also spec. applications
Fluorescent
  lighting *see* Electric lighting
Fluoridation
  water supply
    engineering
      economics   338.4
      technology   628
    pub. health   614.5
Fluorination *see* Fluoridation
Fluoroscopy *see* Radiography
Flutes *see* Wind instruments
    (musical)

Flying
  aircraft
    gen. wks. *see* Flight
      engineering
    sports *see* Air sports
Foliage-plants
  botany   581
  culture   635.97
  landscaping   712–716
  see also spec. plants
Folk
  art
    gen. wks.   745.5–.9
    see also spec. art forms
  music *see* Ethnic music
  songs
    customs   394
    folklore   398.8
    music   784.4
    singing   784.9
  tales *see* Mythology
Folklore *see* Mythology
Food
  analysis
    pub. health *see* Food-&-
      drug control
  animals
    culture   636.08
    zoology   591.6
    see also spec. animals
  cookery *see* Cookery
  customs *see* Eating-customs
  folklore
    hist. & criticism   398.3
    legends   398.2
  microbiology
    gen. wks.   576.16
    see also   *s.s.*–01
  preservation *see* Food
      technology
  salts
    nutrition   641.1
    see also spec. uses
  supply
    economics   †338.1
    mil. sci.
      administration   355.6
      gen. wks.   355.8
      *see also spec. mil.
        branches*
    see also Agriculture
      (activity)

427

Fuel
  cells
    engineering
      economics   338.4
      technology   621.35
    see also spec. applications
  oils *see* Petroleum products
  ships
    commercial *see* Merchant
      ships
    govt. *see* Government
      vessels
  systems
    engineering
      gen. wks.   621.43
      see also spec. applications
    heating *see* Heating-
      systems
Fuels
  gaseous *see* Industrial gases
  processing
    economics   338.4
    technology   662
  see also spec. applications
Fugues (music)
  gen. wks.   781.4
  see also spec. mediums
Fulah *see* Chari-Nile
Fulmars *see* Pelagic birds
Functionalism
  philosophy   144
  psychologies
    gen. wks.   150.19
    see also spec. aspects
Fund
  raising *see* Financial
    administration
Fundamental
  education
    gen. wks.   370.19
    see also spec. subj.
Funded
  debts *see* Public securities
Funeral
  rites
    etiquette   395
    gen. wks.   393
    mil. sci. *see* Official
      ceremonies

Funeral
  rites (continued)
    religion
      Christian   265
      gen. wks.   291.3
      see also other spec. rel.
Funicular
  railways *see* Railroads
Fur
  animals
    culture
      economics   †338.1
      technology
        gen. wks.   †636.08
        see also spec. animals
      see also Mammals
  coats *see* Fur garments
  farming *see* Fur animals
  garments
    manufacture
      economics   338.4
      technology   685
    marketing   658.8
    see also spec. applications
  processing
    economics   338.4
    technology   675
  seals *see* Eared seals
Fur-bearing
  animals *see* Fur animals
Furcrafts
  art   745.53
  industry
    economics   338.4
    technology   685
Furnishings
  households *see* Household
    furnishings
Furniture
  arts   **749**
  home economics   645
  manufacture
    economics   338.4
    technology   684.1
  ships *see* Nautical equipment
  specific kinds
    churches *see* Sacred
      furniture
    libraries   022
    museums   069

Garden
- crops
  - agriculture
    - economics — 338.1
    - **technology** — **635**
  - sculpture
    - arts — 731.7
  - landscaping
    - fountains — 714
    - gen. wks. — 717

Gardens
- **horticulture** — **635**
- landscaping — 712
- *see also* Garden crops

Gargoyles
- architecture — 729
- sculpture — 731.5

Garmentmaking *see* Garments

Garments
- customs — 391
- fur *see* Fur garments
- home sewing — 646.2–.6
- hygiene — 613.4
- leather *see* Leather goods
- manufacture
  - economics — 338.4
  - technology — 687
- marketing — 658.8

Garnishes
- food *see* Auxiliary foods

Gas (utility)
- economics
  - manufactured — 338.4
  - natural — 338.2
- govt. control
  - gen. wks. — †350
  - services — 363.6
- *see also spec. levels of govt.*

Gas
- lighting
  - engineering
    - economics — 338.4
    - technology — 621.32
  - home econ. — 644
- mains *see* Utility lines
- warfare *see* Chemical warfare
- *see also* Natural gas

Gaseous
- fuels *see* Industrial gases
- illuminants *see* Industrial gases

Gases
- industrial *see* Industrial gases
- physics
  - gen. wks. — 530.4
  - **mechanics** — **533**
  - sound transmission — 534

Gasolines *see* Petroleum products

Gastropoda *see* Mollusks

Gas-turbine
- engines *see* Internal-combustion engines

Gaul — *area* –36

Gauntlets *see* Handwear

Gaviiformes
- paleozoology — 568
- zoology — 598.4

Gavleborg Sweden — *area* –487

Gazelles *see* Antelopes

Gazetteers
- geography — 910.3
- *see also* — *s.s.* –03

Gaziantep Turkey — *area* –564

Gears
- engineering
  - economics — 338.4
  - technology
    - gen. wks. — 621.8
  - *see also spec. branches*
- *see also spec. applications*

Geckos *see* Lizards

Geese
- culture — 636.59
- food *see* Poultry
- hunting
  - sports — 799.24
- *see also* Anseriformes

Geez *see* Ethiopic

Gelatin
- desserts *see* Puddings

Gelatins
- manufacture
  - economics — 338.4
  - technology
    - crude — 668
    - edible — 664
- *see also spec. applications*

Gemara *see* Talmud

Gems
- natural *see* Precious stones
- synthetic *see* Synthetic minerals

Gestalt
  psychology
    gen. wks.   †150.19
    see also spec. aspects
Geysers
  geography
    gen. wks.   †910.02
    see also spec. places
  geology   551.2
Ghana   *area* –667
Ghosts
  folklore
    hist. & criticism   398.4
    legends   398.2
  occultism   133.1
Giants
  natural
    phys. anthropology   573
  supernatural *see* Supernatural
    beings
Gibbons *see* Apes
Gibraltar   *area* –46
Gifted
  children *see* Exceptional
    children
Gifts
  books
    library functions   025.2
    state aid   021.8
  see also Procurement
Gila
  monsters *see* Lizards
Gilbert Isls.   *area* –96
Gilyak *see* Paleosiberian
Gipsy
  ethnic groups   *area* –174
  languages   491.4
  lingual groups   *area* –175
  see also other spec. subj.
Giraffes
  conservation   †639
  culture   636.2
  see also Cervoidea
Giresun Turkey   *area* –565
Girl
  Guides *see* Young people
    organizations
  Scouts *see* Young people
    organizations
Girls (children) *see* Children

Girls'
  clothing *see* Garments
  clubs *see* Young people
    organizations
Glaciology
  geography
    gen. wks.   †910.02
    see also spec. places
  geology   551.3
Glass
  arts
    arch. decoration   729
    gen. wks.   **748**
  manufacture
    economics   338.4
    technology   666
  properties
    construction   691
    engineering   620.1
Glassware
  production *see* Glass
  table decor *see* Table decor
Glees *see* Choral music
Gliders *see* Heavier-than-air
    aircraft
Gliding
  eng. *see* Aerodynamics
  sports *see* Air sports
Glires
  paleozoology   569
  zoology   599.3
Glockenspiel *see* Percussion
    instruments
Gloucester Eng.   *area* –424
Gloves *see* Handwear
Glues
  manufacture
    economics   338.4
    technology   668
  materials
    engineering   620.1
    see also spec. applications
Gluttony
  ethics   178
  religion
    Christian   241.3
    see also other spec. rel.
Glyptics
  arts   736
  industry   688

Grade-school
  children *see* Children
  libraries *see* School libraries
Graduate
  schools *see* Universities
Graft *see* Offenses
Grail
  legends *see* Mythology
Grammar
  gen. wks. — 415
  study & teaching
    elementary ed. — 372.6
    see also — *s.s.–07*
  see also spec. languages
Grammar-school
  children *see* Children
  libraries *see* School libraries
Grammar-schools *see*
      Elementary schools
Grampian Mts. Scotland — *area –412*
Grand
  Army of the Republic *see*
    Patriotic societies
  juries *see* Judicial system
  Old Party *see* Political parties
Granite
  geology
    deposits — 553
    petrology — 552
    see also spec. minerals
  industries
    construction
      economics — 338.4
      technology — 693.1
    extractive
      economics — 338.2
      technology — 622
  properties
    construction — 691
    engineering — 620.1
Graphic
  arts
    creative — **760**
    industrial
      economics — 338.4
      technology — 655.1–.3
  expressions
    psychology
      animals — †156
      gen. wks. — †152.3
    see also spec. forms

Graphic (continued)
  illustrations
    geography — **912**
    see also — *s.s.–†022*
  statics *see* Statics
Graphology
  crime detection — 364.12
  diagnostic — †155.28
  divinatory — 137
Grasshoppers *see* Insects
Grasslands
  economics
    gen. wks. — 333.7
    see also Real-estate
  geography
    gen. wks. — 910.09
    physical — †910.02
  history — 909
  subj. treatment — *area –15*
  see also spec. areas
Graves *see* Cemeteries
Graveyards *see* Cemeteries
Gravies *see* Auxiliary foods
Gravitation
  astronomy — 521
  physics — 531
Gravity
  determinations
    geodesy — 526
    physics — 531
  railways *see* Railroads
Gravure
  printing *see* Metal engraving
Gray
  Friars *see* Religious
      congregations
Grazing
  land *see* Grasslands
Greasing *see* Lubrication
Great
  Basin U.S. — *area –79*
  Britain — *area –42*
  Lakes
    Canada — *area –713*
    gen. wks. — *area –77*
    see also spec. lakes
Great
  Danes *see* Working dogs
  Pyrenees
    dogs *see* Working dogs

Guarani *see* Amerindians
Guard
  animals *see* Working animals
  duty *see* Logistics
Guardhouses *see* Quarters
Guatemala   area –728 1
Guerrilla
  warfare
    international law   341.3
    mil. sci.   355.4
    see also hist. of spec. wars
Guessing
  games
    entertainment   793.5–.7
    folklore   398.8
Guiana   area –88
Guidance
  counsel *see* Counseling
  systems *see* Command systems
Guided
  aircraft *see* Heavier-than-air
      aircraft
  missiles
    manufacture
      economics   338.4
      technology   623.4
    mil. sci.
      gen. wks.   355.8
      see also spec. mil. forces
Guinea
  coast
    lower   area –67
    upper   area –66
  gulf *see* Atlantic Ocean
  isls.   area –66
Guinea
  fowl
    culture   636.59
    food *see* Poultry
    see also Galliformes
  pigs *see* Hystricomorphs
Guitars *see* String instruments
Gujarati-Rajasthani *see* Prakrits
Gulf Coast states U.S.   area –76
Gulfs *see* Marine waters
Gulls
  culture   636.6
  see also Charadriiformes
Gum-bichromate
  process *see* Special-process
      photography

Gumusane Turkey   area –565
Gun
  carriages *see* Gun mounts
  dogs
    culture   636.75
    use
      hunting   799.2
      see also other purposes
    see also Canidae
  mounts
    art metalwork   739.7
    industries
      economics   338.4
      technology   623.4
    mil. sci.
      gen. wks.   355.8
      see also spec. mil.
        branches
Gunboats *see* Warships
Gunnery
  engineering   623.5
  training
    gen. wks.   355.5
    see also spec. mil. branches
Guns *see* Artillery (pieces)
Gunsmithing *see* Small arms
Gymnasiums
  gen. wks. *see* Recreation
      buildings
  school equipment *see* School
      buildings
Gymnastics
  customs   394
  gen. wks.   796.4
  hygiene   †613.7
  see also Circuses
Gymnospermae
  botany   585
  floriculture   635.935
  paleobotany   561
Gymnosperms
  forestry   634.9
  see also Gymnospermae
Gynecology
  medicine   618.1
  vet. sci.
    gen. wks.   636.089
    see also spec. animals
  see also Obstetrics
Gypsy *see* Gipsy

Housing-renewal *see* Slums
    redevelopment
Howland Isl.   *area* –96
Hudson
  Bay *see* Arctic Ocean
  Strait *see* Arctic Ocean
Huguenots *see* Reformed
    churches
Hull
  construction
    ships
      economics   338.4
      technology   623.84
Human
  ecology *see* Adaptability
  figure
    arts
      gen. wks.   704.94
      see also spec. art forms
    see also Anatomy
  races *see* Ethnology
  relations
    psychology   †158
    sociology   **301.1**
Humanism
  philosophy   144
  religion
    gen. wks.   211
    see also spec. rel.
Humanitarian
  philosophy *see* Humanism
  socialism *see* Ideal states
Humanities
  gen. wks.   001.3
  see also spec. branches
Hummingbirds *see* Apodiformes
Humor
  literature
    collections   808.87
    criticism   809.7
    rhetoric   808.7
    see also spec. lit.
  see also Collected writings
Humpback
  whales *see* Mysticetes
Hungarian *see* Finno-Ugric
Hungary   *area* –439
Hunting (activity)
  industries
    technology   639
    see also Primary industries
  sports   **799.2**

Hunting-animals *see* Working
    animals
Hunting-dogs *see* Sporting dogs
Huntingdon Eng.   *area* –425
Hunting-guns *see* Small arms
Hunting-songs *see* Folk songs
Huon Isls. *see* New Caledonia
Hurdy-gurdies *see* Mechanical
    musical instruments
Huron (lake)
  gen. wks.   *area* –774
  Ont.   *area* –713
Huron (subject) *see* Hokan-
    Siouan
Hurricanes
  disasters *see* Disasters
  meteorology *see* Storms
Hurricane-warning
  systems *see* Alarm systems
Hussites
  religion   284
  see also Church buildings
Hutterian
  Brethren *see* Mennonites
Hyaenidae
  paleozoology   569
  zoology   599.7
Hydraulic
  engineering
    economics   338.4
    technology   627
    see also Fluids
Hydraulic-power
  engineering
    gen. wks.   621.2
    see also spec. operations
Hydraulics *see* Fluids
Hydrodynamics
  engineering
    gen. wks.   627
    see also spec. branches
  mechanics   532
  see also spec. applications
Hydrogenated
  oils *see* Fats
Hydrographic
  biology
    animals   **591.92**
    gen. wks.   **574.92**
    plants   **581.92**
    see also spec. organisms

Inns *see* Public
    accommodations
Inorganic
  chemistry
    applied   661
    pure   546
Input-output
  accounts *see* National
    accounting
Insecta
  paleozoology   565
  zoology   **595.7**
Insecticides *see* Pesticides
Insectivora
  paleozoology   569
  zoology   599.3
Insectivores
  agricultural pests   632
  culture   636.9
  hunting   †639
  see also Insectivora
Insectivorous
  plants *see* Carnivorous
    plants
Insects
  agricultural pests   632
  culture   638
  disease carriers *see* Disease
    carriers
  see also Insecta
Insignias
  religious
    Christian   247
    gen. wks.   291.3
    see also other spec. rel.
  secular
    gen. wks.   **929**
    military
      gen. wks.   355.1
      see also spec. branches
Inspiration
  art   701.15
  Bible   220.1
  psychology   †153.2
  see also   s.s.–01
Installment
  plans *see* Credit
Institutes (education) *see*
    Extension

Institutional
  cookery *see* Cookery
  household *see* Public
    accommodations
Instrumentalism
  philosophy   144
  see also   s.s.–01
Instruments
  manufacture
    economics   338.4
    technology   681
  see also spec. applications
Insulated
  construction *see* Resistant
    construction
Insulating
  materials
    construction   691
    engineering
      gen. wks.   620.1
      see also spec. branches
    see also spec. applications
Insulation
  electric conductors   621.319
  see also Thermology
Insurance
  gen. wks.   **†368**
  see also Financial institutions
Intaglio
  processes
    arts   765–767
    industry   655.3
    see also Carving-
      techniques
Intaglios
  gems *see* Carvings
  prints *see* Prints
Integration
  racial *see* Racial integration
Intellectual
  guidance *see* Counseling
  occupations *see* Professional
    occupations
  processes
    animals   †156
    children   †155.41
    gen. wks.   **†153**
  see also Intellectualism
Intellectualism
  gen. wks.   001.2
  philosophy   149

Interplanetary
  flights *see* Space
      (extraterrestrial)
      flights
Interscholastic
  athletics *see* Sports
      (recreation)
Interstate
  commerce *see* Trade
      (activity)
  planning *see* Planning
Interviewing
  personnel management
    gen. wks.   **658.3**
    pub. admin.
      gen. wks.   †350
      see also spec. levels of
        govt.
  psychology   †158
Intonation *see* Phonology
Intracoastal
  waterways *see* Inland
      waterways
Intramural
  athletics *see* Sports
      (recreation)
Intuition *see* Intuitionism
Intuitionism
  philosophy
    ethics   171
    gen. wks.   143
  psychology   †153.4
Invasion
  warfare
    international law   341.3
    mil. sci.   355.4
  see also history of spec. wars
Inventions
  sociological effects   301.2
  technology
    gen. wks.   **608.7**
    see also spec. inventions
Inventory
  control *see* Financial
      administration
  economics   338.4
  management
    materials control   658.7
    production   658.5
Inverness Co. Scotland   *area* –412

Invertebrates
  culture   †638–639
  paleozoology   562
  zoology   592
Investment
  companies *see* Combinations
  institutions
    economics   332.6
    govt. control
      gen. wks.   †350
      see also spec. levels of
        govt.
    management   658
Investments
  control *see* Financial
      administration
  economics   **332.6**
  insurance   368
Ionia (ancient region)   *area* –39
Ionian Isls. Greece
  ancient   *area* –38
  modern   *area* –495
Ionization
  electrolytic *see* Physical
      chemistry
  electronic *see* Electronics
  nuclear *see* Nuclear energy
Ionizing
  radiation
    biophysics
      gen. wks.   574.1
      see also spec. organisms
    chemistry *see* Physical
      chemistry
    engineering *see* Nuclear
      engineering
    meteorology   551.5
    physics   539.7
    see also spec. applications
Ionosphere
  magnetism   538
  meteorology
    gen. wks.   551.5
    see also spec. phenomena
  regional subj.
    treatment   *area* –161
Iowa (state)   *area* –777
Iran
  ancient   *area* –35
  modern   *area* –55

Italy	
ancient	*area* –37
modern	**area –45**
Ivory Coast	*area* –66
Ivory	
carvings	736
products	
manufacture	
economics	338.4
technology	679
see also spec. applications	
Izmir Turkey	*area* –562

J

Jacamars *see* Piciformes	
Jacanas *see* Charadriiformes	
Jackasses *see* Asses	
Jacobite	
Church *see* Monophysite churches	
Jade	
mineralogy	549.6
see also Semiprecious stones	
Jaguars *see* Cats	
Jai alai *see* Racket games	
Jail	
buildings *see* Prison buildings	
Jails *see* Prisons	
Jainism	
culture groups	
geography	910.09
history	909
subject treatment	*area* –176
philosophy	181
religion	294.4
Jamaica (West Indian island)	*area* –729 2
James (N.T.) *see* Catholic epistles	
Jams	
cookery	641.6
production	
commercial	†664
home	641.8
Jamtland Sweden	*area* –488
Jan Mayen Isl.	*area* –98
Jansenist	
Church *see* Schismatic churches	
religion *see* Heresies	

Japan (country)	**area –52**
Japan (sea) *see* Pacific Ocean	
Japanese	
ethnic groups	*area* –174
language	495.6
lingual groups	*area* –175
wrestling *see* Unarmed combat	
see also other spec. subj.	
Japanning *see* Lackering	
Japans	
manufacture	
economics	338.4
technology	667
see also spec. applications	
Java	*area* –92
Javanese *see* Austronesian	
Javelin	
throwing *see* Track athletics	
Jays	
agricultural pests	632
see also Passeriformes	
Jazz	
gen. wks.	781.5
see also spec. mediums	
Jehovah *see* God	
Jehovah's Witnesses *see* Recent Christian sects	
Jellies	
cookery	641.6
production	
commercial	664
home	641.8
Jeremiah (O.T.) *see* Prophetic books	
Jeremias (O.T.) *see* Prophetic books	
Jeremy (Apocrypha) *see* Epistle of Jeremy	
Jesuits *see* Religious congregations	
Jesus	
Christianity *see* Christology	
Islam *see* Koran	
Jet	
aircraft *see* Heavier-than-air aircraft	
engines *see* Internal-combustion engines	
streams *see* Winds	

Judith
  Apocrypha   229
  liturgy
    Christianity   264
    Judaism   296.4
Judo *see* Unarmed combat
Jugatae *see* Lepidoptera
Juggling *see* Magic arts
Jujitsus *see* Unarmed combat
Jumping *see* Track athletics
June
  beetles
    agricultural pests   632
    culture   638
    see also Coleoptera
Jungle
  warfare *see* Battle tactics
Junior
  college
    libraries *see* College
        libraries
    colleges *see* Colleges
    high school
      libraries *see* School
          libraries
    high schools *see* Secondary
        schools
    misses' clothing *see*
        Garments
  republics
    management   658
    services   362.7
Juries *see* Judicial system
Jurisprudence *see* Law
Jury
  trials
    civil cases   347.9
    criminal cases   343
Justice
  departments *see* Executive
      departments
  govt. control
    gen. wks.   †350
    *see also spec. levels of
        govt.*
  law *see* Law
Juvenile
  delinquents
    criminology *see* Offenders
    gen. wks. *see* Exceptional
        children
Juveniles *see* Young people

K

Kabyle *see* Berber
Kallitype
  process *see* Special-process
      photography
Kalmar Sweden   *area* –486
Kalmyk (subject) *see*
    Mongolic
Kanarese *see* Dravidian
Kandh *see* Dravidian
Kangaroos *see* Marsupials
Kannada *see* Dravidian
Kansas   *area* –781
Kantianism
  gen. wks.   †142
  see also spec. philosophers
Kanuri *see* Chad
Karate *see* Unarmed combat
Karelian *see* Finnic
Karpathos Greece
  ancient   *area* –39
  modern   *area* –499
Kars Turkey   *area* –566
Karting *see* Motoring
Kartvelian *see* Caucasian
Kashubian *see* Polish
Kastamonu Turkey   *area* –563
Katharevusa *see* Greek
Katydids *see* Insects
Kayseri Turkey   *area* –564
Kazakhstan USSR   *area* –584
Kechua *see* Amerindians
Keeshonden *see* Nonsporting
      dogs
Keewatin   *area* –712
Kennels *see* Shelters
Keno *see* Counter games
Kent Eng.   *area* –422
Kentucky   *area* –769
Kenya   *area* –676
Kerguelen Isls. Indian
      Ocean   *area* –69
Kerosenes *see* Petroleum
      products
Ket *see* Paleosiberian
Kettledrums *see* Percussion
      instruments
Key
  bugles *see* Horns (musical
      instruments)

Larceny
  criminal *see* Offenses
  psychopathic *see* Personality
      disorders
Lard *see* Fats
Larks *see* Passeriformes
Lasers
  engineering
    economics   338.4
    technology   621.32
  physics   535.5
  see also spec. applications
Lasethi Greece   *area* –499
Last
  judgment *see* Judgment
  Supper
    of Jesus Christ   232.95
    see also Sacraments
  things *see* Eschatology
Latexes *see* Elastomers
Lathwork
  economics   338.4
  technology   693.6
Latin America   *area* **–8**
Latin
  ethnic groups   *area* –174
  language   **471–478**
  lingual groups   *area* –175
  see also other spec. subj.
Latin grammar schools *see*
      Secondary schools
Latter-Day Saints
  Church
    religion   289.3
    see also Church buildings
Latvia   *area* –47
Latvian
  ethnic groups   *area* –174
  language   491.9
  lingual groups   *area* –175
  see also other spec. subj.
Launches *see* Small craft
Laundering
  commercial   667
  domestic   648
Lavatories
  equipment
    homes   643
    schools *see* School
      buildings
    see also other spec.
      structures

Lavatories (continued)
  public *see* Sanitation
Law
  Biblical   220.8
  gen. wks.   **†340**
  military
    gen. wks.   355.1
    see also spec. services
Law enforcement *see* Police
    services
Law of nations *see*
    International
    relations
Lawlessness *see* Offenses
Lawmaking *see* Legislation
Lawn
  billiards *see* Mallet games
  bowling *see* Simple ball
    games
  tennis *see* Racket games
Laws *see* Statutes
Laz *see* Caucasian
Lazarists *see* Religious
    congregations
Lead *see* Metals
Leadership
  psychology   †158
  sociology   301.15
Leaf
  beetles
    agricultural pests   632
    culture   638
    see also Coleoptera
  hoppers
    agricultural pests   632
    culture   638
    see also Insecta
League
  of Nations
    gen. wks.   341.12
    see also spec. services
Learned
  societies
    gen. wks.   **060**
    library services
      gen. wks.   †027.6
      see also spec. functions
Learning
  education
    gen. wks.   370.15
    techniques   **371.3**

Lotteries
  advertising *see* Contest
      advertising
  games *see* Gambling
  investments *see* Interest
      lotteries
  revenue *see* Nontax
      revenues
Lotto *see* Counter games
Louisiade Archipelago   *area* –95
Louisiana   *area* –763
Louth Ireland   *area* –418
Love
  psychology *see* Emotions
  sexual *see* Courtship
Low Archipelago *see* Tuamotu
      Isls.
Low
  German *see* Germanic
Loyalty Isls.   *area* –93
Loyalty
  employee *see* Employer-
      employee
      relationships
  ethics   179
  military
    gen. wks.   355.1
    see also spec. branches
  social   301.15
Lubricants
  gen. *see* Fixed oils
  petroleum *see* Petroleum
      products
Lubrication
  engineering
    economics   338.4
    technology
      gen. wks.   621.8
      see also spec. branches
    see also spec. applications
Luchu *see* Ryukyu Isls.
Lucrative
  capital *see* Finance
Ludo *see* Dice games
Luggage
  manufacture
    economics   338.4
    technology   685
  see also spec. applications

Luke (N.T.) *see* Gospels
Lullabies *see* Folk songs
Lumber
  industries
    logging *see* Logging
      (trees)
    processing
      economics   338.4
      technology   674
  see also Woods (substance)
Lunar
  astronomy *see* Moon
  flights *see* Space
      (extraterrestrial)
      flights
Lunchroom
  meals
    cookery *see* Cookery
    service   642
Lunchrooms
  public *see* Public
      accommodations
  school equipment *see*
      School buildings
Luorawetlin *see* Paleosiberian
Lusitania   *area* –36
Lutes *see* String instruments
Lutheran
  churches
    religion   **284**
    see also Church buildings
Lutheranism *see* Lutheran
      churches
Luxembourg (grand
      duchy)   *area* –493
Lycia   *area* –39
Lydia   *area* –39
Lying
  ethics   177
  psychopathology *see*
      Personality-disorders
  religion
    Christian   241.3
    see also other spec. rel.
Lynching
  ethics   179
  see also Offenses
Lynx *see* Cats
Lyres *see* String instruments

M

Magicians
 religion
  gen. wks.   291.6
  see also spec. *rel.*
 see also Magic arts
Magna Carta *see*
   Constitutional law
Magnetic
 compasses
  physics   538
  see also Direction finders
Magnetism
 chemistry *see* Physical
   chemistry
 physics   **538**
Magnetochemistry *see* Physical
   chemistry
Magyar *see* Finno-Ugric
Mahabharata
 literature   891.2
 religion   294.5
Mahayana *see* Buddhism
Mah-jongg *see* Counter games
Mahomet *see* Prophets
Mahri   *area* –53
Mahri-Sokotri *see* South Arabic
Mail
 services *see* Postal
   communication
Mail-order
 catalogs *see* Direct-mail
   advertising
 houses *see* Retail marketing
Maine (state)   *area* –741
Malachi (O.T.) *see* Prophetic
   books
Malachias (O.T.) *see* Prophetic
   books
Maladjusted
 children *see* Exceptional
   children
Maladjustments
 prod. economics
  gen. wks.   338.54
  see also spec. *industries*
 psychology *see* Abnormal
   psychology
Malagasy Republic *see*
   Madagascar
Malatya Turkey   *area* –565
Malawi *see* Nyasaland

Malay Archipelago   *area* –91
Malaya   *area* –595
Malayalam *see* Dravidian
Malayan *see* Austronesian
Malay-Javanese *see*
   Austronesian
Malayo-Polynesian *see*
   Austronesian
Malaysia (archipelago) *see*
   Malay Archipelago
Malaysia (country)   *area* –595
Maldive Isls.   *area* –†549
Malfeasance *see* Offenses
Malformations *see* Teratology
Mali   *area* –66
Mallet
 games
  customs   394
  gen. wks.   796.35
Malmohus Sweden   *area* –486
Malpractice *see* Quackery
Malta
 ancient   *area* –37
 modern   *area* –458
Malted
 beverages
  alcoholic *see* Beers
  nonalcoholic *see* Soft
   drinks
Maltese
 dogs *see* Miniature dogs
Mammalia
 paleozoology   569
 zoology   **599**
Mammals
 conservation practices †639
 hunting
  industries   †639
  sports   799.27
 husbandry   **636**
 see also Mammalia
Mammoths *see* Proboscidea
Man (isle) Eng.   *area* –428
Man
 biology *see* Hominidae
 metaphysics   128
 religious doctrines
  Christian   233
  gen. wks.   291.2
  see also other spec. *rel.*
 see also Men

Marble
  industries (continued)
    extractive
      economics   338.2
      technology   622
    properties
      construction   691
      engineering   620.1
March
  tactics *see* Logistics
Mardi gras *see* Pageants
Mardin Turkey   *area* –566
Margarines *see* Fats
Margays *see* Cats
Margiana   *area* –39
Marginal
  land
    economics
      gen. wks.   333.7
    see also Real-estate
    reclamation *see* Land
      reclamation
Mari (subject) *see* Finno-Ugric
Marianas Isls.   *area* –96
Marimbas *see* Percussion
      instruments
Marinas *see* Docks
Marine
  biology *see* Hydrographic
      biology
  carnivores *see* Pinnipedia
  engineering
    economics   338.4
    technology   623.87
  engines *see* Marine
      engineering
  forces
    gen. wks.   359.9
    see also spec. kinds of
      warfare
  law *see* Commercial law
  plants *see* Hydrophytes
  salvage see Underwater
      operations
  surveying *see* Hydrographic
      surveying
  warfare *see* Sea warfare
  waters
    economics
      production   338.2
      resources   333.9

Marine
  waters (continued)
    geography
      gen. wks.   910.09
      physical   †910.02
    geology
      activities   551.3
      morphology   551.4
    regional subj.
      treatment   *area* –16
    see also spec. places
Mariology
  gen. wks.   †232.91
  see also spec. aspects
Marionette
  plays *see* Miniature theater
Mariotype
  process *see* Special-process
      photography
Marital
  relations *see* Sex relations
Maritime Provinces Can.   *area* –715
Maritime
  law *see* Commercial law
  surveying *see* Hydrographic
      surveying
  warfare *see* Sea warfare
Mark (N.T.) *see* Gospels
Market
  research & analysis
    advertising   659.11
    management
      marketing   658.83
      production   658.5
Marketing
  gen. wks.   †380.1
  govt. control
    gen. wks.   †350
    see also spec. levels of
      govt.
  management   †**658.8**
Markets *see* Distribution
      channels
Marmalades *see* Jams
Marmarica   *area* –39
Marmosets *see* Monkeys
Marquesas Isls.   *area* –96
Marriage
  counseling *see* Counseling
  ethics
    philosophy   173

Meditation (continued)
  religion
    Christian   †248.3
    gen. wks.   291.4
    see also other spec. rel.
Meditations
  religion
    Christian   †242
    gen. wks.   291.4
    see also other spec. rel.
    see also other spec. subj.
Mediterranean
  region
    geography   910.09
    history   909
    subj. treatment   *area* –†18
    see also spec. areas
  Sea *see* Atlantic Ocean
Melanesia   *area* –93
Melanesian *see* Austronesian
Meliorism
  philosophy   149
  see also spec. philosophers
Melodeons *see* Wind
      instruments (musical)
Melodrama *see* Drama
Melody *see* Composition
Membranophones *see*
      Percussion
      instruments
Memel   *area* –47
Memoirs *see* Biographies
Memorial
  Day *see* Holidays
Memory
  aids *see* Mnemonics
  games   793.7
  processes
    education   370.15
    psychology   †153.1
Men
  psychology   †155.6
  sociology   †301.4
  see also other spec. aspects
Mende *see* Niger-Congo
Mending
  books   025.7
  clothes   646.2
Mennonites
  religion
    gen. wks.   289.7

Mennonites
  religion (continued)
    see also Church buildings
    see also Social classes
Menstruation
  disorders   618.1
  physiology   612.66
Mensuration
  arithmetic *see* Business
    arithmetic
  weights & measures *see*
    Metrology
Mental
  deficiency
    welfare services   362.3
    see also Abnormal
      psychology
  diseases
    medicine *see* Psychiatry
    psychology *see* Abnormal
      psychology
  health *see* Mental hygiene
  hospitals
    management   658
    services   362.2
  hygiene
    gen. wks.   †614.58
    hospital services   362.2
  illness
    medicine *see* Psychiatry
    psychology *see* Abnormal
      psychology
    physiology *see* Physiological
      psychology
  retardation *see* Mental
    deficiency
  tests
    education   371.26
    psychology   †153.9
Mentally
  deficient
    children *see* Exceptional
      children
  people
    med. treatment *see*
      spec. diseases
    welfare services   362.3
  ill
    children *see* Exceptional
      children

Meters
  engineering (continued)
    see also other spec.
      branches
    see also spec. applications
Methodist
  churches
    religion   287
    see also Church buildings
Methodology
  gen. wks.   †001.4
  philosophy   112
  see also   *s.s.–01*
Metrology
  gen. wks.   389
  govt. control
    gen. wks.   †350
    see also spec. levels of
      govt.
  science   502
  see also spec. applications
Metropolitan
  areas *see* Communities
  governments *see* Local
    governments
Mexican
  hairless
    dogs *see* Miniature dogs
Mexico (country) *area –72*
Mexico (gulf) *see* Atlantic
    Ocean
Mezzotinting
  arts   766
  industry   655.3
Mezzotints *see* Prints
Micah (O.T.) *see* Prophetic
    books
Mice *see* Myomorphs
Micheas (O.T.) *see* Prophetic
    books
Michigan (lake)
  gen. wks.   *area –774*
  see also other areas
Michigan (state)   *area –774*
Microbiology
  gen. wks.   **576**
  see also   *s.s.–01*
Microcards *see* Micro-
    reproductions
Microfilms *see*
    Microreproductions

Microminiaturization *see*
    Miniaturization
Micronesia   *area –96*
Micronesian *see* Austronesian
Microorganisms
  gen. wks. *see* Microbiology
  pathogenic *see* Pathogenic
    microorganisms
Microphotography
  gen. wks.   778.3
  see also Duplication
Microprints *see*
    Microreproductions
Microreproductions
  business records   651
  communication   †001.5
  library treatment 025.17
  production *see*
    Microphotography
Microscopes
  biology   578
  physics   535
  see also spec. applications
Microscopic
  books *see* Miniature editions
Microwaves
  engineering
    economics   338.4
    technology
      gen. wks.   621.381
      see also Radar
  physics   537.5
Middle
  America   *area –72*
  Atlantic states U.S. *area –74*
  Congo *see* Congo
    (Brazzaville)
  East
    ancient   *area –39*
    modern   *area –56*
  West U.S.   *area –77*
Middle
  Ages
    church hist.   270.2–.5
    gen. hist.   940.1
  Low
    German *see* Germanic
  management
    business   658.43
    military
      gen. wks.   355
      see also spec. branches

Mineral
  oils
    industries (continued)
      manufacturing
        economics   338.4
        technology   665
    resources
      economics   333.8
      geology   553
    surveys
      geology   553
    mining
      economics   338.2
      technology   622
  waxes *see* Mineral oils
Mineralized
  waters
    extraction
      economics   338.2
      technology   622
      geology   553
    treatment
      economics   338.4
      technology
        chem. tech.   661
        water-supply eng.   628
    see also Soft drinks
Mineralogy
  gen. wks.   **549**
  see also   *s.s.–01*
Minerals
  folklore
    hist. & criticism   398.3
    legends   398.2
  geology
    deposits   553
    mineralogy   **549**
Minesweepers *see* Government
      vessels
Minesweeping *see* Defense
      operations
Mingrelian *see* Caucasian
Miniature
  dogs
    culture   636.76
    use *see spec. purposes*
    see also Canidae
  editions
    book rarities   099
    library treatment   025.17
  golf *see* Mallet games

Miniature (continued)
  theater
    plays *see* Drama
    programs
      ethics   175
      production
        gen. wks.   791.5
        management   658
Miniaturization
  electronics
    economics   338.4
    technology   621.381 7
  see also Models
Mining
  engineering   622
  see also Primary industries
Ministerial
  authority
    government *see* Executive
      departments
    religion
      Christian   262
      gen. wks.   291.6
      see also other spec. rel.
Ministers (religion) *see*
      Clergy
Ministries *see* Executive
      departments
Ministry (religion) *see* Clergy
Minks *see* Mustelines
Minnesota (state)   *area* –776
Minoan
  Linear A *see* Canaanite-
      Phoenician
  Linear B *see* Classical
      languages
Minor
  arts
    gen. wks.   **745–749**
    see also spec. art forms
  prophets (O.T.) *see*
      Prophetic books
Minority
  groups
    labor economics
      gen. wks.   331.6
      see also spec.
        occupations
    pol. status   323.1
    sociology   **301.45**
    welfare services   †362.8
    see also Social classes

Models
manufacture
economics   338.4
technology   688
see also Operations research
Moesia   *area* –39
Mohammed *see* Prophets
Mohammedanism *see* Islam
Molding
metals
arts
metalwork   739
sculpture   731.4
technology
gen. wks.   671.2
see also spec. metals
see also other spec. materials
Moldlofts *see* Shipyards
Molecular
compounds *see* Salts
structure *see* Molecules
Molecules
chemistry   541
physics   539
Moles (animals) *see*
Insectivores
Molinism *see* Heresies
Mollusca
culture   639
paleozoology   564
zoology   594
Mollusks
fisheries
economics   338.3
technology   †639
see also Mollusca
Moluccas   *area* –91
Mon *see* Austroasian
Monaco   *area* –449
Monaghan Ireland   *area* –416
Monarchical
absolutism
pol. sci.   321.6
see also spec. areas
Monarchies
absolute *see* Monarchical
absolutism
limited *see* Constitutional
monarchies

Monasteries
buildings *see* Monastic
buildings
religion *see* Religious
congregations
Monastic
buildings
architecture   726
construction
economics   338.4
technology   690.6
life
Christian religion   †248.8
gen. wks.   291.4
see also other spec. rel.
orders *see* Religious
congregations
schools
education   377
see also Church-
supported schools
Money
economics   332.4–.5
govt. control
gen. wks.   †350
see also spec. levels of
govt.
numismatics *see*
Numismatics
see also Financial
administration
Mongolia   *area* –51
Mongolic
ethnic groups   *area* –174
languages   494
lingual groups   *area* –175
see also other spec. subj.
Mongooses *see* Viverrines
Monism
philosophy   147
science   501
Monkeys
conservation   †639
culture   636.9
experimental med.
animals   636.089
man   619
see also Primates
Mon-Khmer *see* Austroasian
Monmouth Eng.   *area* –424

Municipalities *see*
    Communities
Munitions
  equipment *see* Firearms
  limitations *see* Armament
    limitation
Munster Ireland   *area* –419
Muong *see* Austroasian
Mural
  painting *see* Paintings arts
  paintings *see* Paintings
Murals
  arch. decoration   729
  paintings *see* Paintings
Murder
  ethics   179
  see also Offenses
Murderers *see* Offenders
Mus Turkey   *area* –566
Muscat & Oman   *area* –53
Museum
  buildings
    architecture   727
    construction
      economics   338.4
      technology   690.7
    description   069
Museums
  art
    gen. wks.   **708**
    see also spec. art forms
  gen. wks.   069
  see also   *s.s.*–074
Music
  arts   **780**
  boxes *see* Mechanical
    musical instruments
  halls *see* Recreation
    buildings
  publications
    economics   338.4
    technology
      printing   655.3
      publishing   655.5
  religion
    Christian
      gen. wks.   246
      pub. worship   264
    gen. wks.   291
    see also other spec. rel.

Music (continued)
  reproduction *see* Electro-
    acoustical devices
  scores
    bibliographies   781.9
    library treatment   025.17
    see also spec. mediums
  study & teaching
    elementary ed.   372.8
    see also   *s.s.*–07
Musical
  comedies *see* Musical shows
  drama
    music   **782**
    see also spec. literatures
  glasses *see* Percussion
    instruments
  instruments
    gen. wks.   781.9
    manufacture
      economics   338.4
      technology   681
    see also spec. instruments
  performance
    gen. wks.   781.6
    see also spec. mediums
  psychology
    music   781.1
    psychology   152.1
  shows
    music   782.8
    see also Drama
Music-hall
  shows *see* Drama
Musicology *see* Music
Musique
  concrète
    gen. wks.   789.9
    see also spec. mediums
Musk
  oxen
    culture   636.2
    see also Bovoidea
Mustangs *see* Ponies
Mustelidae
  paleozoology   569
  zoology   599.7
Mustelines
  conservation   †639
  culture   636.9
  see also Mustelidae

Nuclear
  accidents *see* Disasters
  energy
    engineering   621.48
    physics   **539.7**
    see also spec. applications
  engineering
    economics   338.4
    technology
      gen. wks.   621.48
      see also spec.
        applications
  engines *see* Nuclear reactors
  fission *see* Nuclear energy
  fusion *see* Thermonuclear
      fusion
  heating
    gen. wks.   697.7
    see also spec. applications
  physics
    gen. wks.   **539.7**
    see also spec. applications
  reactors *see* Nuclear
      engineering
  war *see* Strategy
  warfare
    defenses
      mil. eng.   623
      welfare services   †363.35
    forces
      gen. wks.   358
      see also spec. kinds of
        warfare
Nudes *see* Human figure
Number
  metaphysics   119
  see also spec. philosophers
Numbers (O.T.) *see* Historical
      books (O.T.)
Numbers (symbols)
  algebra *see* Algebra
  occultism *see* Divination
Numbers-game *see* Gambling
Numeration
  systems *see* Arithmetic
Numerology *see* Divination
Numidia   *area* –39
Numismatics
  gen. wks.   **†737**
  see also Paper money

Nunneries *see* Religious
      congregations
Nurseries (children) *see*
      Rooms
Nurseries (plants)
  agriculture
    gen. wks.   635.9
    see also spec. plants
  management
    economics   338.4
    technology   658
  see also Nursery stock
Nursery
  rhymes *see* Rhymes
  schools *see* Elementary
      schools
  stock
    gen. wks.   631.5
    see also spec. crops
Nurses *see* Nursing
Nursing
  home economics   649.8
  med. sci.   610.73
  mil. sci. *see* Special services
Nursing-homes *see*
      Convalescent homes
Nuthatches *see* Passeriformes
Nutrition
  biology
    animals   591.1
    gen. wks.   574.1
    plants   581.1
    see also spec. organisms
  practices
    animals
      gen. wks.   636.089
      see also spec. animals
    man
      home econ.   **641**
      hygiene   613.2
Nuts (mechanics) *see*
      Fastenings
Nyasaland   *area* –689
Nygde Turkey   *area* –564

O

Oases
  geography
    gen. wks.   910.09
    physical   †910.02

Offaly Ireland   *area* –418
Offenders
  criminology   †364.3
  law *see* Criminal law
  see also Personality-disorders
Offenses
  criminology   †364.3
  govt. control
    gen. wks.   †350
    see also spec. levels of govt.
  law *see* Criminal law
  military   355.1
  protective services   363.2–.4
Office
  buildings *see* Commercial
        buildings
  equipment
    gen. wks.   651
    manufacture *see spec.*
        items
  personnel
    gen. wks.   651
    labor economics   331.7
    management   †658.3
  services
    economics   338.4
    technology   651
Official
  ceremonies
    customs   394
    history *see history of spec.*
        areas
  mil. sci.
    gen. wks.   355.1
    see also spec. branches
Offset
  lithography *see* Planographic
        processes
  printing
    economics   338.4
    technology   655.3
Ogres *see* Supernatural beings
Ohio (state)   *area* –771
Ohio
  River
    gen. wks.   *area* –769
    see also other areas
  Valley
    gen. wks.   *area* –77
    see also other areas

Oil
  gas *see* Industrial gases
  painting *see* Painting arts
  paintings *see* Paintings
  varnishes *see* Japans
Oils
  cooking *see* Fixed oils
  edible *see* Fixed oils
  essential *see* Essential oils
  fixed *see* Fixed oils
  industrial *see* Fixed oils
  mineral *see* Mineral oils
  nonvolatile *see* Fixed oils
  petroleum *see* Petroleum oils
  saponifying *see* Fixed oils
  vegetable *see* Fixed oils
  volatile *see* Essential oils
Oil-transfer
  photography *see* Special-
        process photography
Ojibway *see* Algonkian-Mosan
Okapis
  conservation   †639
  culture   636.2
  hunting
    sports   799.27
  see also Cervoidea
Okhotsk Sea *see* Pacific Ocean
Oklahoma (state)   *area* –766
Old
  age *see* Old-age
  Catholic Church *see*
        Schismatic churches
  Egyptian
    ethnic groups   *area* –174
    language   493
    lingual groups   *area* –175
    see also other spec. subj.
  English *see* Anglo-Saxon
  Frisian *see* Germanic
  Icelandic *see* Germanic
  Low
    Franconian *see* Germanic
    German *see* Germanic
  Norse *see* Germanic
  Prussian
    ethnic groups   *area* –174
    language   491.9
    lingual groups   *area* –175
    see also other spec. subj.
  Saxon *see* Germanic

Orange
  Free State South
      Africa   *area* –68
Orangutans *see* Apes
Orâon *see* Dravidian
Orations *see* Speeches
Oratories *see* Chapels
Oratorios
  sacred   783.3
  secular   782.8
Oratory *see* Speeches
Orbits
  astronautics   629.4
  astronomy
    descriptive   **523**
    theoretical   521
Orchards
  agriculture
    economics   338.1
    technology   634
Orchestras
  music   785.1–.8
  performance   785.06
Orchestrions *see* Mechanical
      musical instruments
Order
  work
    library functions   025.2
    museum functions   069
    see also other spec.
        organizations
Ordnance (firearms) *see*
      Firearms
Ordu Turkey   *area* –565
Orebro Sweden   *area* –487
Oregon (state)   *area* –795
Ores
  geology
    gen. wks.   553
    see also spec. minerals
  industries
    extractive
      economics   338.2
      technology
        metallurgy   **669**
        mining   622
Organic
  chemistry
    applied   †661
    pure   547
    see also spec. products

Organic (continued)
  evolution
    animals   591.3
    gen. wks.   **575**
    man   573.2
    plants   581.3
    see also other spec.
        organisms
  fertilizers *see* Fertilizers
Organization
  of American States
    gen. wks.   341.18
    see also spec. services
Organizational
  units
    mil. sci.
      gen. wks.   355.3
      see also spec. mil.
          branches
      see also Combat units
Organizations
  employee *see* Employer-
      employee
      relationships
  gen. wks.   **060**
  international peace   **341.1**
  religion *see* Religious
      organizations
  social & welfare   **366–369**
  sociology *see* Behavior-
      groups
  students
    gen. wks.   **371**
    see also spec. levels of ed.
  see also   *s.s.*–06
Organs (instruments)
  manufacture
    economics   338.4
    technology   681
  music   786.6
Orient   *area* –5
Oriental
  churches
    religion   281
    see also Church buildings
Origami *see* Paper sculpture
Orinoco River
  gen. wks.   *area* –87
  see also other areas
Oriya *see* Prakrits
Orkney Isls.   *area* –411

Pathology (continued)
  man
    gen. wks.   616.07
    psych. effects   †155.9
  plants
    agriculture   632
    botany   581.2
Patience (virtue) *see* Virtues
Patio
  furniture *see* Furniture
  lighting *see* Illumination
Patriotic
  holidays *see* Holidays
  societies
    gen. wks.   369
    see also spec. activities
  songs *see* National songs
Patternmaking
  foundries
    gen. wks.   671.2
    see also spec. metals
  garment industries
    commercial   687
    domestic   646.4
Pauline
  epistles
    liturgy   264
    N.T.
      gen. wks.   227
      see also Pseudepigrapha
Paupers *see* Poor people
Pavements
  engineering
    economics   338.4
    technology   625.8
  see also Trafficways
Pawnshops *see* Financial
    institutions
Pay
  plans *see* Wages
Paymaster's
  department *see* Payroll
    administration
Payroll
  administration
    business   †658.32
    government
      gen. wks.   †350
      see also spec. levels of
        govt.

Peace
  corps
    soc. planning *see* Planning
    spec. operations *see spec.*
        subj.
  movements
    international law   **341.1**
    religion
      Christian   †261.8
      see also other spec. rel.
Peacocks *see* Peafowl
Peafowl
  conservation   †639
  culture   636.59
  food *see* Poultry
  see also Galliformes
Peahens *see* Peafowl
Peasant
  art *see* Folk art
Peasants *see* Social classes
Peccaries
  conservation   †639
  culture   636.9
  see also Suiformes
Pederasty
  crime *see* Offenses
  sex *see* Sexual disorders
Pediatrics
  hygiene   613.97
  medicine
    gen. wks.   618.92
    surgery   617
Pedigrees
  stockbreeding
    gen. wks.   636.08
    see also spec. animals
  see also Genealogy
Pedology (child study) *see*
    Children
Pedology (soils) *see* Soils
Peebles Scotland   *area* –414
Pekingese
  dogs *see* Miniature dogs
Pelagianism *see* Heresies
Pelagic
  birds
    conservation   †639
    culture   636.6
    see also Procellariiformes

Poverty
  economics *see*
      Underconsumption
  people *see* Poor people
Powder
  magazines *see* Military
      buildings
  metallurgy *see* Metallurgy
Powder-process
  photography *see* Special-
      process photography
Power (control)
  metaphysics   118
  pol. sci. *see* State (The)
Power
  craft *see* Power-driven ships
  lines
    electric transmission   621.319
    installation
      design   711
      technology   625.7
  mechanics *see* Mechanical
      engineering
  plants
    engineering
      gen. wks.   621.4
      see also spec. branches
    see also Central stations
  politics *see* International
      relations
  shears *see* Tools
  stations *see* Central stations
  transmission
    electricity *see* Power lines
    machinery
      engineering
        economics   338.4
      technology
        gen. wks.   621.8
        see also spec.
          branches
      see also spec.
        applications
Power-driven
  ships
    engineering   623.82
    see also Transportation
Practical
  astronomy
    gen. wks.   522
    see also spec. applications

Practical (continued)
  geology *see* Economic
    geology
  nurses *see* Nursing
  politics
    gen. wks.   **329**
    law   **†340**
    see also Government
      (state)
  psychology *see* Applied
    psychology
Pragmatism
  philosophy   144
  see also spec. philosophers
Prairie
  plants *see* Mesophytes
Prairies
  gen. wks. *see* Plains
  reclamation *see* Land
    reclamation
Prakrits
  languages   491.3–.4
  see also other spec. subj.
Prawns *see* Shrimps
Prayer
  Christian religion
    gen. wks.   †248.3
    see also Family prayer
  gen. wks.   291.4
  see also other spec. rel.
Prayer meetings
  Christian liturgy   264
  see also other spec. rel.
Prayer of Manasses
  Apocrypha   229
  liturgy   264
Prayers
  Christian religion
    gen. wks.   264
    private   **†242**
  comparative religion
    gen. wks.   291.3
    private   291.4
  see also other spec. rel.
Praying
  mantises *see* Insects
Preachers *see* Clergy
Preaching *see* Homiletics
Precious
  metals *see* Metals

Public
  education
    government (continued)
      support   379
      see also Public schools
    entertainment
      gen. wks.   791
      see also spec. activities
    expenditure
      administration *see*
        Financial
        administration
      economics   336.3
    finance *see* Finance
    health
      engineering *see* Sanitation
        engineering
      govt. control
        gen. wks.   †350
        *see also spec. levels of
          govt.*
      med. sci.
        animals
          gen. wks.   636.089
          see also spec. animals
        man   614
    information
      services
        gen. wks. *see*
          Communication
          services
        mil. sci. *see* Special
          services
    land
      economics   333.1
      landscaping   712–719
      see also   *area* –14
    libraries
      gen. wks.   027.4
      see also spec. functions
    morals
      govt. control
        gen. wks.   †350
        *see also spec. levels of
          govt.*
      police services   363.4
    opinion
      practical pol.   329
      sociology   301.15

Public (continued)
  order
    govt. control
      gen. wks.   †350
      *see also spec. levels of
        govt.*
    police services   363.3
  parks *see* Recreational land
  relations
    advertising *see*
      Advertising
    business
      economics   338.4
      technology   659.2
    effects
      psychology   †155.9
      sociology   301.15
    religion
      Christian   254.4
      gen. wks.   291.6
      see also other spec. rel.
  schools
    gen. wks.   371
    see also spec. levels of ed.
  securities
    administration
      gen. wks.   †350
      *see also spec. levels of
        govt.*
    economics
      investments   332.63
      transactions   336.3
  servants
    economics
      labor   331.7
      production   338.1–.4
    management *see*
      Personnel
    see also Civil service
  spending *see* Public
    expenditure
  utilities
    departments *see* Executive
      departments
    govt. control
      gen. wks.   †350
      *see also spec. levels of
        govt.*
    services   †363.6

Punishments (continued)
  religion *see* Eschatology
  school discipline
    gen. wks.   †371.5
    see also spec. levels of ed.
  see also Judicial system
Punjab   *area* –54
Punjabi *see* Prakrits
Puppet
  plays *see* Miniature theater
Puppets *see* Toys
Purchasing operations
  gen. wks. *see* Procurement
  libraries *see* Order work
Pure
  democracy
    pol. sci.   321.4
    see also spec. areas
  sciences *see* Sciences
Purim *see* Holy days
Puritanism
  churches
    religion   285
    see also Church buildings
  history *see* Reformation
Purses *see* Luggage
Pursuit
  aviation forces *see* Air forces
  planes *see* Heavier-than-air
      aircraft
Pushball *see* Football
Puzzles
  entertainment   **793.7**
  folklore   398.6
  see also Literature
Pyrography *see* Wood carvings
Pyromania *see* Personality-
      disorders
Pyrotechnics *see* Fireworks

Q

Qatar   *area* –53
Qattara Depression
      Egypt   *area* –62
Qoran *see* Koran
Quackery
  govt. control
    gen. wks.   350
    see also spec. levels of
      govt.

Quackery (continued)
  medicine
    animals
      gen. wks.   636.089
      see also spec. animals
    man   615
    see also spec. diseases
  see also Defrauding
Quagga *see* Equidae
Quails
  conservation   †639
  culture   636.5
  food *see* Poultry
  see also Galliformes
Quakers *see* Society of Friends
Qualitative
  analysis
    chemistry
      gen. wks.   544
      organic   547
    sound
      gen. wks.   534
      subsonic *see* Subsonics
      ultrasonic *see*
        Ultrasonics
Quality
  control
    mathematics   519
    production *see*
      Operational
      management
    see also Statistical
      method
Quantitative
  analysis
    chemistry
      gen. wks.   545
      organic   547
    sound
      gen. wks.   534
      subsonic *see* Subsonics
      ultrasonic *see*
        Ultrasonics
  psychology
    animals   †156
    gen. wks.   †152.8
Quantity (metaphysical)
  gen. wks.   119
  see also spec. philosophers

R

Rasp
  carving *see* Wood carvings
Ratchets *see* Gears
Rationalism
  philosophy   149
  psychology
    gen. wks.   †150.19
    see also spec. aspects
  religion
    gen. wks.   211
    see also spec. rel.
Rationing *see* Restricted
        consumption
Rats *see* Myomorphs
Rattanwork *see* Braiding
Rayon *see* Cellulosics
Reaction-time
  studies *see* Quantitative
        psychology
Reactors
  engineering
    electrical   621.313
    nuclear   621.48
  physics
    electrical   537.6
    nuclear   **539.75–.76**
  see also spec. kinds
Reader
  advisory services
    libraries   †025.5
    see also other spec.
        institutions
Readers
  elementary ed.   372.4
  linguistics
    English   428.6
    see also other spec.
        languages
Reading
  gen. wks.   **028**
  linguistics
    English   428.4
    see also other spec.
        languages
  psychology   †153.7
  study & teaching
    elementary schools   372.4
    see also   *s.s.–07*
Real
  property
    gen. wks. *see* Real-estate
    law *see* Private law

Real-estate
  business
    economics   338.4
    management   658
  economics   333.3
  law *see* Private law
  taxes *see* Taxation
Realism
  arts   709.03
  literature   808.8
  philosophy   149
  religion
    gen. wks.   291
    see also spec. rel.
Realization
  accounting *see* Financial
        accounting
Realty
  law *see* Private law
Reasoning
  philosophy   **160**
  psychology
    animals   †156
    gen. wks.   †153.4
Rebellion *see* Civil war
Recent
  Christian sects
    religion   289.9
    see also Church buildings
Receptions *see* Hospitality
Recipes
  food *see* Cookery
  formulas   *s.s.–021*
Recitals
  gen. wks.   780.73
  see also spec. mediums
Reclamation
  land *see* Land reclamation
  soil *see* Soil conservation
  water *see* Water
        reclamation
Recollects *see* Religious
        congregations
Recording
  accounting *see* Bookkeeping
  printed matter *see*
        Cataloging
Recordings
  gen. wks. *see*
        Electroacoustical
        devices

Reemployment
  labor economics †331.1
  management 658.31
Reference
  libraries *see* Research
    libraries
  services
    libraries †025.5
    museums 069
    see also other spec.
     institutions
Reflection
  light *see* Light (radiation)
  radio waves *see* Hertzian
    waves
  sound waves 534
  thermal *see* Heat transfer
Reflex
  actions
    biology
      animals 591.1
      gen. wks. 574.1
      plants 581.1
      see also spec. organisms
    psychology
      animals †156
      gen. wks. †152.3
Reflexology *see* Reductionism
Reforestation *see* Forestation
Reform
  movements
    pol. status 322
    see also Group behavior
  schools *see* Reformatories
Reformation
  church history 270.6
  gen. history 940.2
Reformative
  measures
    criminology 364.6
    penology 365
Reformatories
  administration
    gen. wks. †350
    see also spec. levels of
     govt.
  criminology 364.7
Reformatory
  buildings *see* Prison
    buildings
  labor *see* Prison labor

Reformed
  churches
    religion
      American 285
      European 284
    see also Church buildings
Refractory
  materials
    manufacture
      economics 338.4
      technology 666
    metallurgical use 669.8
    see also other spec.
     applications
Refrigerators
  engineering
    economics 338.4
    technology
      gen. wks. 621.5
      see also spec. branches
  home economics 643
  see also spec. applications
Refuge
  programs *see* Wildlife
    reserves
Refugees *see* Displaced
  persons
Refuse
  disposal
    operations *see* Waste
     disposal
    structures *see* Sanitary
     engineering
    treatment *see* Garbage
     treatment
Regattas *see* Boating
Regencies *see* Executive
  departments
Regenerated
  cellulose *see* Cellulosics
Regeneration
  religion *see* Salvation
Regimentation *see* Group
  behavior
Regiments *see* Organizational
  units
Regional
  libraries *see* Public libraries
  planning *see* Planning

528

Retirement
  income
    insurance *see* Annuities
  problems *see* Aged people
  systems *see* Pension systems
Retreats
  mil. sci. *see* Battle tactics
  religion *see* Spiritual
    renewal
Retrievers *see* Gun dogs
Réunion Indian Ocean   *area* –69
Revelation
  N.T.
    gen. wks.   228
    pseudepigrapha   229
  religion
    Christian   231
    see also other spec. rel.
Revenants *see* Ghosts
Revenues
  administration
    gen. wks.   †350
    see also spec. levels of
      govt.
  economics   336.1–.2
Revivals *see* Spiritual renewal
Revolutionary
  groups
    pol. status   323.2
    sociology   †301.18
  movements
    sociology   301.15
    see also Revolutionary
      wars
  socialism *see* Communist
    states
  wars
    societies *see* Hereditary
      societies
    U.S. history   973.3
    see also other spec.
      countries
Revolvers *see* Small arms
Revues *see* Musical shows
Rhaeto-Romanic
  ethnic groups   *area* –174
  languages   459
  lingual groups   *area* –175
  see also other spec. subj.
Rheas
  conservation   †639

Rheas (continued)
  culture   636.6
  see also Palaeognathae
Rheiformes *see* Palaeognathae
Rhetoric
  gen. wks.   **808**
  study & teaching
    elementary ed.   †372.6
    see also   *s.s.*–07
Rhinoceroses
  conservation   †639
  culture   636.9
  hunting
    sports   799.27
  see also Rhinocerotidae
Rhinocerotidae
  paleozoology   569
  zoology   599.7
Rhode Island   *area* –745
Rhodes *see* Dodecanese
    Greece
Rhodesia   *area* –689
Rhodium *see* Metals
Rhopalocera *see* Lepidoptera
Rhymes
  folklore   398.8
  see also Poetry
Rhynchocephalia *see* Lepidosauria
Rhythm *see* Composition
Rhythmic
  arts
    religion
      Christian
        gen. wks.   246
        pub. worship   264
      gen. wks.   291.3
      see also other spec. rel.
      see also spec. elements
Rickettsiae *see* Ultramicrobes
Rickshaws *see* Wheeled
    supports
Riddles *see* Puzzles
Riding
  horses *see* Equestrian sports
Riemann
  geometry
    gen. wks.   513
    see also   *s.s.*–01
Rifles *see* Small arms
Rigveda *see* Vedas
Rimes *see* Rhymes

Roman
  Catholic Church
    religion   282
      see also Church buildings
  Catholics   *area* −176
  law
    gen. wks.   349.37
    mil. sci.
      gen. wks.   355.1
        see also spec. branches
  religion *see* Classical
    religions
Romance
  languages
    gen. wks.   479.1
      see also spec. languages
Romania   *area* −†498
Romanian
  ethnic groups   *area* −174
  language   459
  lingual groups   *area* −175
    see also other spec. subj.
Romans (N.T.) *see* Pauline
    epistles
Romansh *see* Rhaeto-Romanic
Romanticism
  art   709.03
  literature   808.8
  philosophy   141
Romany *see* Prakrits
Roof
  coverings *see* Roofing
          operations
  structures
    architecture   721
    construction   690
      see also spec. structures
Roofing
  operations
    economics   338.4
    technology   695
Roofs
  architecture   721
  construction
    economics   338.4
    technology   624
      see also spec. structures
Rooms
  decorative treatment
    art   747
    home economics   645

Rooms (continued)
  equipment   643
    see also Architectural
          construction
Roosters *see* Chickens
Ropes *see* Cordage
Roque *see* Mallet games
Rosh Hashanah *see* Holy days
Rosicrucian
  mysteries *see* Mystic
          traditions
Rosicrucians
  gen. wks.   366
    see also spec. doctrines
Ross & Cromarty
        Scotland   *area* −411
Rotogravure
  printing *see*
        Photomechanical
        printing
Roulette *see* Wheel games
Round
  Table *see* Mythology
Rowboats *see* Hand-propelled
        craft
Rowing *see* Boating
Roxburgh Scotland   *area* −414
Royalty
  class *see* Social classes
  education *see* Exceptional
        children
  gen. wks.   929.7
  heraldry   929.6
  pol. sci.   321.5−.6
    see also spec. areas
Ruanda-Urundi   *area* −67
Rubber
  crafts   745.57
    see also Elastomers
Rubbish
  treatment *see* Garbage
        treatment
Rubies
  mineralogy   549.5
  synthetic *see* Synthetic
        minerals
    see also Precious stones
Rugby *see* Football
Rugs
  crafts   746.7

534

Rugs (continued)
  interior decoration
    arts   747
    home economics   645
  manufacture
    economics   338.4
    technology   677
Rulers *see* Chief executives
Rumania *see* Romania
Rumanian *see* Romanian
Ruminantia
  paleozoology   569
  zoology   599.7
Ruminants
  hunting
    industries   †639
    sports   799.27
  husbandry   636.2–.3
  see also Ruminantia
Running *see* Track athletics
Runways
  engineering
    economics   338.4
    technology
      gen. wks.   629.136
      military   623.6
    see also Transportation
Rural
  areas *see* Agricultural areas
  communities *see*
          Communities
  electrification
    agriculture   631.3
    engineering
      economics   338.4
      technology   621.39
  living
    psychology   †155.9
    sociology   301.3
  parishes
    govt. & admin.   254.2
  see also spec. aspects
Russia   *area –47*
Russian
  ethnic groups   *area –174*
  language   491.71–.78
  lingual groups   *area –175*
  see also other spec. subj.
Ruth (O.T.) *see* Historical
          books (O.T.)
Ruthenian *see* Ukrainian

Rutland Eng.   *area –425*
Rwanda   *area –67*
Ryukyu Isls.   *area –528*

S

Saba West Indies   *area –729 7*
Sabah Malaysia   *area –911*
Sabbath *see* Holy days
Sabean *see* South Arabic
Sabellianism *see* Heresies
Sacramentals
  gen. wks.   264
  see also Grace
Sacraments
  gen. wks.   265
  grace   234
  public worship   264
Sacred
  books *see* Scriptures
  furniture
    art
      architecture   729
      decoration   747
    manufacture
      economics   338.4
      technology   684.1
    religion
      Christian   247
      gen. wks.   291.3
      see also other spec. rel.
    see also Furniture
  music
    gen. wks.   783
    see also spec. mediums
  places
    geography *see spec.*
          places
    religion
      Christian   246
      gen. wks.   291.3
      see also other spec. rel.
  times *see* Liturgical year
Sacrifice
  Christian religion
    gen. wks.   232
    see also Crucifixion
  see also Sacrificial offerings

Sanitation
  engineering (continued)
    technology
      gen. wks.   628
      military   623.7
      ships   623.85
    home economics   648
    pub. health   †614
    see also Plumbing
Sanskrit
  language   491.2
  see also other spec. subj.
Santali *see* Austroasian
São
  Tomé (isl.)   *area* –66
Saponifying
  oils *see* Fixed oils
Sapphires
  mineralogy   549.5
  synthetic *see* Synthetic
    minerals
  see also Precious stones
Saps
  forest products   634.9
  processing
    economics   338.4
    technology   668
Sarawak Malaysia   *area* –911
Sardinia
  ancient   *area* –37
  modern   *area* –459
Sarmatia   *area* –39
Saskatchewan
  (province)   *area* –712 4
Satan *see* Demonology
Satanism *see* Demonology
Satellite
  communication system *see*
    Telecommunication
  communities *see*
    Communities
  states *see* Dependent states
Satellites
  artificial *see* Artificial
    satellites
  astronomy
    descriptive   523.9
    theoretical   521
    see also   *s.s.*–01
Satire *see* Humor
Sauces *see* Auxiliary foods

Saudi Arabia   *area* –53
Sauropsida
  paleozoology   568
  zoology   **598**
Savings
  bus. accounting *see*
    Financial
    administration
  economics *see* Deferred
    consumption
  institutions *see* Financial
    institutions
Saviors *see* Messiahs
Sawflies
  agricultural pests   632
  culture   638
  see also Hymenoptera
Sawing-machinery *see* Tools
Sawmill
  products
    manufacture
      economics   338.4
      technology   674
    see also spec. applications
Saws *see* Tools
Saxhorns *see* Wind instruments
  (musical)
Saxophones *see* Wind
    instruments (musical)
Scale
  insects *see* Insects
Scales (biological) *see spec.*
    organisms
Scales (tonal) *see* Audiology
Scales (weight) *see*
    Metrology
Scaly
  anteaters *see* Edentates
Scandinavia   *area* –48
Scandinavian *see* Germanic
Scenario
  writing *see* Rhetoric
Schipperkes *see* Nonsporting
    dogs
Schismatic
  churches
    medieval *see spec.*
      churches
    modern
      religion   284
      see also Church
      buildings

Sculpture (continued)
  religion
    Christian   246
    gen. wks.   291.3
    see also other spec. rel.
  study & teaching
    elementary ed   372.5
    see also   *s.s.–07*
Scythia   *area* –39
Sea
  bears *see* Eared seals
  biology *see* Hydrographic
        biology
  cows
    culture   636.9
    hunting
      industries   †639
      sports   799.27
    see also Sirenia
  fishing *see* Salt-water fishing
  forces *see* Naval forces
  laws *see* Commercial law
  lions *see* Eared seals
  serpents *see* Imaginary
        animals
  warfare
    international law   341.3
    mil. sci.   **359**
    see also hist. of spec. wars
  waters *see* Marine waters
Seadromes *see* Airports
Seafaring
  life
    gen. wks.   910.4
    see also spec. aspects
Seafood
  cookery   641.6
  gen. wks.   641.3
  marketing   658.8
  preservation
    commercial   664
    home   641.4
Seals (animals)
  eared *see* Eared seals
  earless *see* Earless seals
Seals (heraldry) *see* Heraldic
        design
Seals (stamps)
  manufacture
    gen. wks.   671.8
    see also spec. metals

Seals (stamps) (continued)
    numismatics   †737
    see also spec. applications
Sealyhams *see* Terriers
Seamanship
  engineering   623.88
  services   387
Seaplanes *see* Heavier-than-air
        aircraft
Seaports *see* Harbors
Seas *see* Marine waters
Seasonal
  workers
    labor economics   331.6
    see also Social classes
Seasons
  astronomy   525
  meteorology   551.5–.6
Sea-water
  conversion
    economics   338.4
    technology
      gen. wks.   628
      naval   623.85
    see also spec. applications
Second
  coming of Jesus Christ *see*
        Advent
Secondary
  education
    gen. wks.   373
    govt. control
      gen. wks.   †350
      *see also spec. levels of
        govt.*
  industries
    economics   338.4
    govt. control
      gen. wks.   †350
      *see also spec. levels of
        govt.*
    management   658
    technology *see spec.
        industries*
  school
    libraries *see* School
        libraries
  schools
    gen. wks.   373.1–.2

540

Semiprecious
  stones (continued)
    industries
      extractive
        economics   338.2
        technology   622
      glyptics   736
Semiquantitative
  analysis *see* Qualitative
    analysis
Semiskilled
  occupations *see* Occupations
Semisovereign
  states *see* Dependent states
Semitic
  ethnic groups   *area* –174
  languages   **492**
  lingual groups   *area* –175
  see also other spec. subj.
Senates *see* Legislative bodies
Senegal   *area* –66
Senility *see* Gerontology
Senior
  citizens *see* Aged people
  colleges *see* Colleges
  high schools *see* Secondary
    schools
Sensation
  physiology *see* Physiology
  psychology *see* Perception
Sensationalism
  philosophy   145
  see also Perception
Sentiments
  psychology   †152.4
  see also Personality
Septic
  tanks *see* Unsewered
    structures
Serbia Yugoslavia   *area* –†497
Serbian *see* Serbo-Croatian
Serbo-Croatian
  ethnic groups   *area* –174
  language   491.8
  lingual groups   *area* –175
  see also other spec. subj.
Serenades
  customs   392
  music *see spec. mediums*
Serfs *see* Social classes

Serial
  advertising
    economics   338.4
    technology   659.13
  publications
    printing   655.1–.3
    publishing   655.5
  see also Serials
Serials
  general   **050**
  library treatment   025.17
  see also   *s.s.* –05
Series
  writings *see* Collected
    writings
Serigraphy *see* Silk-screen
    printing
Sermons
  Christian religion
    gen. wks.   †252
    pub. worship   264
    gen. wks.   291.3
    see also other spec. rel.
Serpentes
  paleozoology   568
  zoology   598.12
Serpents *see* Snakes
Service
  club
    songs *see* Fraternal songs
  occupations see Occupations
  stations (motor vehicles)
    management   658
  services
    gen. wks.   388.3
    repairs   629.28
Servomechanisms *see* Automatic
    control
Session
  laws *see* Statutes
Setters *see* Gun dogs
Setting-up
  exercises *see* Gymnastics
Seven
  Years' War
    gen. wks.   940.2
    see also spec. countries
Seventh-day
  observance *see* Holy days
  schools *see* Religious training

Sign
  language *see* Nonverbal
      language
  painting
    economics   338.4
    technology   698.1
Signaling *see* Communication
      systems
Signets *see* Seals (stamps)
Signs
  advertising   659.13
  folklore   398.3
  symbolic *see* Divination
Sikkim   *area* –†549
Silhouette
  photography *see* Trick
      photography
Silhouettes
  drawings   741.7
  see also other art forms
Silk *see* Textiles
Silk-screen
  printing
    arts
      gen. wks.   764
      textiles   746.6
    industry
      economics   338.4
      technology
        gen. wks.   †655.3
        textiles   667
Silkworms
  culture   638
  see also Lepidoptera
Silver
  alloys *see* Metals
  art metalwork *see*
      Silversmithing
  coinage
    finance   †332.4
    see also Coins
Silversmithing
  arts   739.2
  manufacturing
    economics   338.4
    technology   673
Silviculture *see* Forestry
Simple
  ball games
    customs   394
    gen. wks.   796.31
    see also Child play

Simple (continued)
  machines
    physics   531
    see also spec. applications
Sinai Peninsula
  ancient   *area* –39
  modern   *area* –53
Sindhi *see* Prakrits
Singing
  gen. wks. *see* Vocal
      expressions
  music *see* Songs
  pub. worship *see* Music
Singing-games *see* Child play
Single-reed
  instruments *see* Wind instru-
      ments (musical)
Single-wicket
  cricket *see* Bat games
Sinhalese *see* Prakrits
Sinop Turkey   *area* –563
Sins
  dogmatics
    Christian religion   233
    gen. wks.   291.2
    see also other spec. rel.
  morality *see* Evils
Siouan *see* Hokan-Siouan
Sioux (subject) *see* Hokan-
      Siouan
Siphonaptera
  paleozoology   565
  zoology   595.77
Sirach *see* Ecclesiasticus
Sirenia
  paleozoology   569
  zoology   599.5
Sirups (food) *see* Sugars
Sisterhoods *see* Religious
      congregations
Site
  planning
    art   711
    management   658.2
Sittidae *see* Passeriformes
Sivas Turkey   *area* –565
Skaraborg Sweden   *area* –486
Skates (footwear) *see*
      Footwear
Skating
  ice *see* Ice sports
  roller *see* Roller skating

Small	
arms	
art metalwork	739.7
manufacture	
economics	338.4
technology	
gen. wks.	683
military	623.4
mil. sci.	
gen. wks.	355.8
practice *see* Training	
maneuvers	
see also spec. mil.	
branches	
businesses	
economics	338.6
management	†658
craft	
engineering	623.82
see also Transportation	
services	
forge work	
economics	338.4
technology	682
Small-arms	
ammunition	
manufacture	
economics	338.4
technology	623.4
mil. sci.	
gen. wks.	355.8
see also spec. mil.	
branches	
see also spec. applications	
Small-boat	
installations *see* Docks	
Smog *see* Air pollution	
Smokers'	
supplies	
manufacture	
economics	338.4
technology	688
see also spec. applications	
Smoking	
tobacco	
customs	
private	392
public	394
habit *see* Addictions	
Smuggling *see* Offenses	
Smyrna Turkey *see* Izmir	

Snack	
bars *see* Public	
accommodations	
Snakes	
agricultural pests	632
culture	†639
see also Serpentes	
Snow	
formations	
climatology	†551.6
meteorology	†551.5
precipitation	
climatology	†551.6
meteorology	†551.5
removal	
highways *see* Highway	
maintenance	
runways *see* Runways	
streets	
economics	338.4
technology	628
sculpture	736
sports	
customs	394
gen. wks.	796.9
Snowfall *see* Snow precipitation	
Snowshoeing *see* Snow sports	
Snowshoes *see* Footwear	
Snuff *see* Tobacco products	
Soap	
sculpture	
arts	736
study & teaching	
elementary ed.	372.5
see also	s.s.–07
Soaps	
manufacture	
economics	338.4
technology	668
marketing	658.8
see also spec. applications	
Soaring	
engineering *see*	
Aerodynamics	
sports *see* Air sports	
Soccer *see* Football	
Social	
accounting *see* National	
accounting	
anthropology *see* Culture	

Speech	
arts	
rhetoric	**808.5**
study & teaching	
elementary ed.	†372.6
see also	*s.s.*–07
disorders	
med. sci.	
gen. wks.	616.85
pediatrics	618.92
psychology	
gen. wks.	†157
pedology	†155.45
see also Exceptional	
children	
see also Mental hygiene	
see also Vocal expressions	
Speeches	
literature	
collections	808.85
criticism	809.5
rhetoric	808.5
see also Collected writings	
Speedboats *see* Small craft	
Speleology *see* Caves	
Spelling	
English language	
phonology	421
usage	†428
gen. wks. *see* Phonology	
study & teaching	
elementary ed.	†372.6
see also	*s.s.*–07
see also other spec.	
languages	
Spelling games *see* Puzzles	
Spells *see* Magic arts	
Spelunking *see* Outdoor life	
Sperm	
whales *see* Odontocetes	
Spermatophyta	
botany	**582**
paleobotany	561
see also spec. plants	
Spermatophytes *see*	
Spermatophyta	
Sphenisciformes	
paleozoology	568
zoology	598.4

Spherical	
astronomy	
gen. wks.	522
geodesy	526
geometry *see* Solid geometry	
Spice Isls. *see* Moluccas	
Spiders	
agricultural pests	632
culture	†639
see also Araneida	
Spies *see* Espionage	
Spinets *see* Keyboard string	
instruments	
Spiny	
anteaters	
conservation	†639
culture	636.9
see also Monotremata	
Spires *see* Roof structures	
Spirit (The) *see* Soul	
Spiritism *see* Spiritualism	
Spirits (alcoholic)	
cookery	641.6
drinking *see* Drinking	
manufacture	
economics	338.4
technology	
commercial	663
domestic	†641.8
marketing	
technology	658.8
see also Liquor traffic	
Spirits (apparitions) *see*	
Ghosts	
Spiritual	
renewal	
Christian religion	269
gen. wks.	291.7
see also other spec. rel.	
Spiritualism	
occultism	133.9
philosophy	141
religion *see spec. rel.*	
Spiritualist	
Church *see* Recent	
Christian sects	
Spirituals *see* Ethnic songs	
Spitsbergen *see* Svalbard	
Spoonbills (birds)	
conservation	†639
culture	636.6
see also Ciconiiformes	

Storehouses
  gen. wks. *see* Storage
        buildings
  military *see* Military
        buildings
Stores *see* Commercial
        buildings
Storks
  conservation   †639
  culture   636.6
  see also Ciconiiformes
Storms
  climatology   †551.6
  history
    gen.wks.   †904
    see also spec. places
  meteorology   551.5
  see also Disasters
Storytelling
  library services   027.62
  rhetoric   808.54
  schools   †372.6
Strains (biological) *see*
        Genetics
Strains (mechanical)
  engineering
    materials   620.1
    structures   624
    see also spec. kinds
  mechanics
    solids   531
    see also spec. branches
Strategy
  mil. sci.
    gen. wks.   355.4
    see also spec. mil. branches
  see also hist. of spec. wars
Stratigraphy
  geology   551.7
  paleontology   560.17
Streams *see* Water bodies
Street
  cleaning
    engineering
      economics   338.4
      technology   628
      pub. health   614
  fighting *see* Battle tactics
  lighting *see* Illumination
  organs *see* Mechanical
        musical instruments
  songs *see* Folk songs

Streetcar
  advertising *see*
        Transportation
        advertising
Streets *see* Trafficways
Strength
  tests
    engineering
      materials   620.1
      structures   624
      see also spec. kinds
    physics   531
Stresses (mechanical) *see*
        Strains (mechanical)
Strikes (work stoppage)
  labor *see* Union-
        management
        disputes
  sociology *see* Group
        behavior
String
  bands *see* Orchestras
  basses *see* String instruments
  instruments
    manufacture
      economics   338.4
      technology   681
    music   787
Strings *see* Cordage
Structural
  analysis
    engineering
      gen. wks.   624
      see also spec. branches
  ships *see* Naval
        architecture
  clay products
    materials
      construction   691
      engineering   620.1
      see also spec. applications
  design *see* Structural analysis
  elements
    architecture   721
    area planning   711
    engineering *see* Structural
        analysis
  engineering
    gen. wks.   624
    see also spec. structures

Topology (continued)
  geometry
    gen. wks.   513
    see also   s.s.–01
Torah *see* Historical
    books (O.T.)
Tornadoes
  effects *see* Disasters
  meteorology *see* Storms
Tortoises *see* Turtles
Torts
  internal law   347.5
  international law   †341.5
Tosefta *see* Talmud
Totalitarian
  states
    economics
      Marxian   **335.4**
      nationalist   335.6
    pol. sci.   †321.9
    see also spec. areas
Totemism
  religion
    gen. wks.   291.2
    see also spec. rel.
  soc. customs   392
Totems *see* Totemism
Toucans
  culture   636.6
  see also Piciformes
Touracos *see* Plantain eaters
Touring
  travel   910.4
  see also Motoring
Tourist
  guides *see* Travels
  inns *see* Public
    accommodations
Tournaments
  soc. customs *see* Knightly
    customs
  sports *see spec. sports*
Tours *see* Travels
Towboats *see* Small craft
Towed
  craft
    construction
      economics   338.4
      technology   623.82
    see also Transportation
      services

Town
  governments *see* Local
    governments
  halls *see* Government
    buildings
  libraries *see* Public libraries
  meeting
    government *see* Pure
      democracy
Towns *see* Communities
Townships *see* Communities
Toy
  dogs *see* Miniature dogs
  theater *see* Miniature theater
Toys
  child play *see* Child play
  crafts   745.59
  manufacture
    economics   338.4
    technology   688.7
  marketing   658.8
Trabzon Turkey *see* Trebizond
Track
  athletics
    customs   394
    gen. wks.   796.4
  racing
    horses *see* Equestrian
      sports
Tracking
  game *see* Hunting (activity)
Traction
  systems *see* Electric traction
Tractors
  agriculture   631.3
  engineering
    economics   338.4
    technology
      gasoline   629.22
      steam   621.1
  see also spec. applications
Trade (activity)
  govt. control
    gen. wks.   †350
    see also spec. levels of
      govt.
  management   **†658.8**
  services
    gen. wks.   †380.1
    see also spec. kinds

Transits
  astronomy (continued)
    theoretical · 521
    see also · s.s.–01
Translating-machines *see*
        Language translators
Translation
  linguistics
    gen. wks. · †418
    see also spec. languages
  mechanics *see* Statics
Transmission
  devices
    motor vehicles *see* Motor
        vehicles
  of electricity
    economics · 338.4
    technology · 621.319
  of mechanical power *see*
        Power transmission
Transmitters
  communication *see*
        Telecommunication
Transmutations
  chemistry · 541
  engineering · 621.48
  physics · 539.75
  see also Alchemy
Transoxiana *see* Sogdiana
Transport
  commands *see* Air forces
  equipment *see spec. kinds*
  laws *see* Commercial law
  phenomena
    air pollution
      engineering · 628
      medicine · 614
    geology · 551.3
    physics *see spec. branches*
Transportation
  advertising
    economics · 338.4
    technology · 659.13
  area planning · 711
  buildings
    architecture · 725
    construction
      economics · 338.4
      technology · 690.5
    see also Transportation
        services

Transportation (continued)
  engineering *see spec.*
        elements
  equipment
    engineering *see spec.*
        elements
  govt. control
    gen. wks. · †350
    see also spec. levels of
        govt.
  insurance
    accident · 368.3
    liability · 368.5
    property loss · 368.2
    see also Financial
        institutions
  services
    civilian
      gen. wks. · †380.5
      spec. kinds · **385–388**
    management
      economics · 338.4
      technology · 658
    military
      gen. wks. · 358
      see also spec. kinds of
        warfare
Transposition (music) *see*
        Arrangement (music)
Transshipment *see* Trade
        (activity)
Transvestism *see* Sexual
        disorders
Trapeze
  work
    circus *see* Circuses
    gymnastics *see* Gymnastics
Trapping *see* Hunting
        (activity)
Trappists *see* Religious
        congregations
Trapshooting *see* Shooting
        (activities)
Trautoniums *see* Electronic
        musical instruments
Travelers
  checks *see* Credit
        instruments
Traveling
  shows
    management · 658
    performance · 791.1

Troop (continued)
  carriers *see* Heavier-than-air
    aircraft
  movements *see* Logistics
  ships *see* Government vessels
Troops *see* Organizational units
Tropic
  birds *see* Gannets
  photography *see* Hot-
    weather photography
Tropical
  plants
    botany   581.909
    floriculture   635.9
    see also spec. plants
Tropics
  climatology   †551.6
  geography   910.09
  history   909
  subj. treatment   *area* –13
  see also spec. areas
Troy (ancient city)   *area* –39
Trucial Oman   *area* –53
Trucks *see* Motor
  vehicles
Trumpets *see* Wind instruments
  (musical)
Trunks *see* Luggage
Trust Territory of the Pacific
  Isls.   *area* –96
Trust
  companies
    banks *see* Financial
      institutions
    industrial *see*
      Combinations
  services
    banks   †332.1
    courts   347.9
  territories *see* Dependent
    states
Truth
  metaphysics   111.8
  religion
    gen. wks.   210
    see also spec. rel.
Truthfulness
  ethics   177
  religion
    Christian   241.4
    see also other spec. rel.

Tsimshian *see* Macro-Penutian
Tuamotu Isls.   *area* –96
Tuareg *see* Berber
Tuataras *see* Lepidosauria
Tubas *see* Wind instruments
  (musical)
Tubes
  manufacture
    economics   338.4
    technology   671.8
  materials
    engineering
      gen. wks.   620.1
    see also spec.
      applications
  see also Materials-handling
Tubuai Isls.   *area* –96
Tugboats *see* Small craft
Tulu *see* Dravidian
Tumbling *see* Gymnastics
Tunceli Turkey   *area* –566
Tundra *see* Plains
Tungsten *see* Metals
Tungusic
  ethnic groups   *area* –174
  languages   494
  lingual groups   *area* –175
  see also other spec. subj.
Tunicata
  paleozoology   566
  zoology   596
Tunisia   *area* –61
Tunneling
  mining   622
  see also Tunnels
Tunnels
  architecture   725
  construction
    economics   338.4
    technology
      gen. wks.   624
      military   623.6
  govt. control
    gen. wks.   †350
    see also spec. levels of
      govt.
  transportation   388.1
  see also other spec.
    applications
Tupi *see* Amerindians

Ugro-Ostyak *see* Finno-Ugric
Uighur *see* Turkic
Ukraine   area –†477
Ukrainian
  ethnic groups   area –174
  language   491.79
  lingual groups   area –175
  see also other spec. subj.
Ukuleles *see* String instruments
Ulster Ireland   area –416
Ultramicrobes
  biology   576
  medicine
    animals
      gen. wks.   636.089
      see also spec. animals
    man   616.01
    see also spec. diseases
Ultrasonic
  vibrations *see* Ultrasonics
Ultrasonics
  engineering
    gen. wks.   †620.2
    see also spec. branches
  physics   534.5
  see also spec. applications
Ultraviolet *see* Paraphotic
    phenomena
Unarmed
  combat
    ethics   175
    gen. wks.   613.6
    mil. training *see* Training
      maneuvers
    sports
      management   658
      performance   796.8
Unconscious
  metaphysics   127
  psychology *see* Depth
    psychology
Unconventional
  warfare
    history *see hist. of spec.*
      countries
    services *see* Special
      services
Underconsumption
  economics
    gen. wks.   339.4
    see also spec. elements
  see also other spec. aspects

Undergraduate
  schools *see* Universities
Underground
  railways *see* Rapid transit
    railways
  waters *see* Ground waters
Underpasses *see* Bridges
Underprivileged
  classes *see* Social classes
Understanding *see* Perception
Undertaking
  customs *see* Funeral rites
  pub. health   614
Underwater
  operations
    engineering
      economics   338.4
      technology   627
    services   387.5
    see also Diving
  photography
    gen. wks.   778.7
    see also spec. applications
Underwear *see* Garments
Underweight
  people
    cookbooks   641.5
    hygiene   613.2
    see also Body contours
Unemployment
  insurance
    gen. wks.   368.4
    see also Financial
      institutions
  labor economics   331.1
  managerial aspects   †658.31
Unfunded
  debts *see* Public securities
Unguiculata
  paleozoology   569
  zoology   599.3
Ungulates *see* Hoofed
    mammals
Unicameral
  legislatures *see* Legislative
    bodies
Unicellular
  animals *see* Protozoa
  plants *see* Schizomycetes

Uniforms
  customs *see* Costume
  garments *see* Garments
  mil. sci.
    administration   355.6
    gen. wks.   355.8
    see also spec. mil.
      branches
Unincorporated
  companies
    economics   338.7
    management   †658
    see also   *s.s.–065*
Union
  Isls. *see* Tokelau
  of Soviet Socialist Republics
    see Soviet Union
Union
  catalogs
    books   017–019
    library functions   †021.6
    see also   *s.s.–021*
  rugby *see* Football
Union-management
  disputes
    conciliation practices   331.15
    gen. wks.   331.89
  relationships *see* Employer-
    employee
    relationships
Unions
  labor
    economics   **331.88**
    management   658
  see also Organizations
Unit
  method *see* Project method
  operations
    gen. wks.   660.28
    see also spec. products
  packaging
    production *see*
      Operational
      management
  processes *see* Synthesis
Unitarian
  Church *see* Unitarianism
  Universalist Association *see*
    Unitarianism

Unitarianism
  religion   288
  see also Church buildings
Unitary
  states
    pol. sci.   321
    see also spec. areas
United
  Arab Republic *see* Egypt
  Kingdom   *area –42*
  States of America   *area –73*
United
  Brethren
    in Christ *see* Recent
      Christian sects
    Moravian *see* Moravian
      Church
  charities *see* Community
    welfare
  Church of Canada *see*
    Methodist churches
  Church of Christ *see*
    Congregationalism
  Confederate Veterans *see*
    Military societies
  Daughters of the
    Confederacy *see*
    Hereditary societies
  Free Church *see* Moravian
    Church
  Nations
    gen. wks.   **341.13**
    see also spec. services
  Society of True Believers in
    Christ's Second
    Appearing *see*
    Shakers
Uniterms *see* Subject headings
Unitized
  cargo *see* Transportation
    services
Unity
  metaphysics   111.8
  rhetoric *see* Rhetoric
Unity School of Christianity
    see Recent Christian
    sects
Universal
  algebra
    gen. wks.   512
    see also   *s.s.–01*

Uruguay (country)   *area* –895
Usak Turkey   *area* –562
Usury *see* Interest rates
Utah (state)   *area* –792
Ute *see* Macro-Penutian
Utilitarianism
   economics *see* Economic
     systems
   philosophy
     ethics   171
     gen. wks.   144
Utility
   lines
     installation
       area planning   711
       engineering   625.7
     see also spec. kinds
Utopias *see* Ideal states
Uzbekistan USSR   *area* –58

V

Vacation
   Bible schools *see* Religious
     training
Vacuum
   cleaners *see* Household
     appliances
   production
     engineering
       economics   338.4
       technology
         gen. wks.   621.55
         see also spec.
           branches
     physics   533
Vagrancy *see* Offenses
Valleys
   geography
     gen. wks.   910.09
     physical   †910.02
   geology   551.4
   subj. treatment   *area* –14
   see also spec. areas
Value
   psychology   †153.4
   see also   *s.s.*–01
Values
   metaphysics   121
   see also other spec. aspects

Valves (electronic)
   engineering
     economics   338.4
     technology   621.381
     see also spec. branches
   physics   537.5
Valves (mechanical)
   engineering
     economics   338.4
     technology
       gen. wks.   621.8
       see also spec. branches
     see also spec. applications
Vampires *see* Demonology
Van Turkey   *area* –566
Vanadium *see* Metals
Vandalism *see* Offenses
Vanity *see* Evils
Vans *see* Motor vehicles
Vapor
   plating *see* Surface finishing
   pressure
     physics   536
     see also Physical
       transformations
Variations
   biology *see* Genetics
   calculus *see* Calculus
   music
     gen. wks.   781.5
     see also spec. mediums
Variety
   shows *see* Drama
   stores *see* Retail marketing
Varmland Sweden   *area* –487
Varnishes
   manufacture
     economics   338.4
     technology   667
   marketing   658.8
   see also spec. applications
Vascular
   cryptogams *see* Pteridophyta
Vases *see* Containers
Vassal
   states *see* Dependent states
Vasterbotten Sweden   *area* –488
Vasternorrland Sweden   *area* –488
Vastmanland Sweden   *area* –487
Vatican City   *area* –456
Vaudeville *see* Drama

Weather
  folklore
    hist. & criticism   398.3
    legends   398.2
  physical geology   †551.6
Weathering
  materials *see* Deterioration
  soils *see* Soil erosion
Weatherings
  installation   695
  manufacture *see spec.*
    materials
Weather-satellites *see*
    Artificial satellites
Weaver
  finches *see* Passeriformes
Weaverbirds *see* Passeriformes
Weaving
  crafts   746.1
  industry   677
  study & teaching
    elementary ed.   372.5
  see also   *s.s.*–07
Wedding
  music
    gen. wks.   783.2
    see also spec. mediums
  rites *see* Marriage rites
Wedges *see* Simple machines
Weed
  killers *see* Pesticides
Weeds
  agricultural pests   632
  botany
    gen. wks.   581.6
    see also spec. plants
Weeks (feast of) *see* Holy
    days
Weight
  gaining programs *see*
    Underweight people
  lifting *see* Gymnastics
  losing programs *see*
    Overweight people
Weights *see* Metrology
Weimaraners *see* Gun dogs
Weirs
  hydraulic eng.   627
  see also Hydrodynamics

Welding
  metals
    arts   739
    shipbuilding *see* Hull
      construction
    technology
      gen. wks.   671.5
      see also spec. metals
    see also spec. products
Welfare
  administration
    private   658
    public
      gen. wks.   †350
      see also spec. levels of
        govt.
    social
      gen. wks.   †350
      see also spec. levels of
        govt.
  buildings
    architecture   725
    construction
      economics   338.4
      technology   690.5
  departments *see* Executive
    departments
  services
    personnel management
      business   658.38
      government
        gen. wks.   †350
        see also spec. levels
          of govt.
    public   †363
    religion
      Christian   258–259
      gen. wks.   291.7
      see also other spec. rel.
    social   361–362
  work
    private   361.7
    public   361.6
  see also Community welfare
Welsh
  corgis *see* Working dogs
  language *see* Celtic
Wendish
  ethnic groups   *area* –174
  language   491.8
  lingual groups   *area* –175
  see also other spec. subj.

Young
  people (continued)
    organizations
      gen. wks.   369
      see also spec. activities
    psychology   †155.5
    sociology
      gen. wks.   301.43
      welfare services   362.7
    see also Children
  Women's
    Christian Associations
      gen. wks.   267
      see also spec. services
    Hebrew Associations
      gen. wks.   296.6
      see also spec. services
Youth *see* Young people
Yozgat Turkey   *area* −563
Yugoslav *see* Serbo-Croatian
Yugoslavia   *area* −497
Yukian *see* Hokan-Siouan
Yukon (ter.)   *area* −712
Yurak *see* Samoyedic

Z

Zacharias (O.T.) *see* Prophetic
  books
Zambia *see* Northern Rhodesia
Zanzibar   *area* −678
Zapotec *see* Macro-
  Otomanguean
Zebras
  husbandry   636.1
  see also Equidae
Zebrula
  husbandry   636.1
  see also Equidae
Zebrule *see* Zebrula
Zebus
  culture   636.2
  see also Bovoidea
Zechariah (O.T.) *see* Prophetic
  books
Zen *see* Buddhism
Zephaniah (O.T.) *see* Prophetic
  books
Zeppelins *see* Lighter-than-air
  aircraft
Zetland Scotland *see* Shetland
  Isls.

Zinc *see* Metals
Zincographs *see* Prints
Zincography *see* Planographic
  processes
Zircon
  glyptics   736
  mineralogy   549.6
Zithers *see* String instruments
Zodiac
  astrology   133.5
  astronomy   523.2
  folklore   398.3
Zodiacal
  light
    astronomy   523.5
    meteorology   551.5
  signs *see* Zodiac
Zonguldak Turkey   *area* −563
Zoning
  govt. control   352
  laws   †340
Zoo
  animals
    culture
      gen. wks.   636.08
      see also spec. animals
    zoology   591
Zoogeography *see* Biogeography
Zoological
  gardens
    gen. wks.   590.74
    see also Recreational land
  sciences
    agriculture   **636–638**
    paleozoology   562–569
    zoology   **591**
    see also   s.s. −01
Zoology *see* Zoological sciences
Zootechny *see* Livestock
Zoroastrianism
  culture groups
    geography   910.09
    history   909
    subj. treatment   *area* −176
  philosophy   181
  religion   295
Zulu *see* Niger-Congo
Zululand   *area* −68
Zwinglianism *see* Reformed
  churches